THE ART OF COLLECTIVITY

The ART of COLLECTIVITY

Social Circus and the Cultural Politics of a Post-Neoliberal Vision

EDITED BY JENNIFER BETH SPIEGEL
AND BENJAMIN ORTIZ CHOUKROUN

with contributions from Katherine M. Boydell, Arturo Campaña, Lynn Fels, Judith Marcuse, and Annalee Yassi

McGill-Queen's University Press
Montreal & Kingston | London | Chicago

ISBN 978-0-7735-5734-5 (cloth)
ISBN 978-0-7735-5735-2 (paper)
ISBN 978-0-7735-5836-6 (ePDF)
ISBN 978-0-7735-5837-3 (ePUB)

Legal deposit third quarter 2019
Bibliothèque nationale du Québec

Printed in Canada on acid-free paper

We acknowledge the support of the Canada Council for the Arts.

Nous remercions le Conseil des arts du Canada de son soutien.

Library and Archives Canada Cataloguing in Publication

Title: The art of collectivity : social circus and the cultural politics
    of a post-neoliberal vision / edited by Jennifer Beth Spiegel and
    Benjamin Ortiz Choukroun ; with contributions from Katherine
    M. Boydell, Arturo Campaña, Lynn Fels, Judith Marcuse, and
    Annalee Yassi.
Names: Spiegel, Jennifer Beth, editor. | Choukroun, Benjamin Ortiz,
    editor.
Description: Includes bibliographical references and index.
Identifiers: Canadiana (print) 20190098309 | Canadiana (ebook)
    20190098376 | ISBN 9780773557352 (softcover) |
    ISBN 9780773557345 (hardcover) | ISBN 9780773558366 (ePDF) |
    ISBN 9780773558373 (ePUB)
Subjects: LCSH: Community arts projects. | LCSH: Arts and society. |
    LCSH: Arts—Political aspects.
Classification: LCC NX180.A77 A78 2019 | DDC 700.1/03—dc23

Set in 10.5/13.5 Calluna with Calluna Sans and Gill Sans Nova Inline
Book design & typesetting by Garet Markvoort, zijn digital

CONTENTS

ACKNOWLEDGMENTS

We thank the Canadian Institutes of Health Research (CIHR) for funding the study upon which this book is based through the operating grant *Social Circus and Health Equity: An Interdisciplinary, Intercultural, International Collaboration (MOP-133595)*. We also thank the Art for Social Change Partnership – an integrated research program in teaching, evaluation, and capacity-building, funded by the Social Science and Humanities Research Council (SSHRC) of Canada – for its support.

The editors would like to sincerely thank Dr Annalee Yassi, the nominated principal investigator on the CIHR grant, for her skillful project leadership and mentorship, in addition to serving as a co-author on several of the chapters and assisting the editors throughout this process. We are also enormously grateful to Dr Yassi's team at the Global Health Research Program in the School of Population and Public Health at the University of British Columbia, including Stephanie Parent, Stephen Barker, Karen Lockhart, and José Antonio de Anda Romero, for their valuable assistance in coordinating the project, performing statistical analyses, preparing graphics, and providing translations, among numerous other invaluable tasks.

In addition, we would like to thank Dr Jaime Breilh, now rector of the Universidad Andina Simón Bolívar (UASB), for his overall guidance, insight, and support; we also are grateful to the UASB team of María José Breilh, María Cristina Breilh, Erika Arteaga, and Bayron Torres. We also thank Dr Patrick Leroux, along with Roy Gomez Cruz and Alison Funk from Concordia University, who contributed at different points in the research, and also Jeremy Rubenstein and Julia Martínez for their timely collaboration. Additionally, the valuable comments and insightful questions from, amongst others, Sam Spiegel, John Bryans, Thomas Lamarre, Norma Rantisi, Alanna Thain, members of the Montreal Circus Research group, as well as participants at the 2017 Arts for Changing the World conference, and the students and faculty of the School of Journalism and Communications at Carleton University were all greatly appreciated.

We wish to express our appreciation to the Ecuadorean leaders who were responsible for *Circo Social Ecuador*, including President Lenin Moreno; Julio Bueno, the right arm of the vice president in launching this project; Alexander Vega, who worked in the vice presidency in the *Sonríe Ecuador* team and subsequently was assistant secretary for Arts and Creativity in the Ministry of Culture; the current undersecretary Valentina Brevi; Alex Grijalva, in charge of *Circo Social Ecuador*; and Alex Pazmiño, specialist in performing arts. We also thank the directors of the *Círculo* foundation, Matías Belmar and Tanya Sánchez, and the artists who formed the groups of teachers, trainers, and resident artists of the early stages who also provided valuable information for this research, particularly the former pedagogical directors Álvaro Soto, Tommaso Negri, Soraya Sepúlveda, and Yacine Ortiz.

We are grateful to Gil Favreau, Emmanuel Bochud, Anik Couture, and David Simard of the *Cirque du Monde* and *Cirque du Soleil* corporate citizenship office for their enthusiastic support. We also acknowledge the foundations and institutions that opened their doors to us, including the *Casa Metropolitana de las Juventudes* program, the *Honrar la Vida* foundation, and the *Virgilo Guerrero* youth guidance centre. As well, we thank the leaders of the new initiatives *Circo Social Yachay* and the *Tejido de Circo Social*, who kindly contributed information for this research, and a host of interviewees who shared their expertise, including Clara Bucheli, Deborah Barndt, Jacques Rajotte, and Marc Bonomo.

Finally, we wish to recognize all those who participated in the interviews, the participatory action research, and discussion groups, in Ecuador, across Canada, and in Quebec. Only a few are quoted in this book; some have been cited in other publications we have produced and/or will be cited in our research products to come, but all contributed to the analysis. We also thank the people who helped with data collection, translations, and transcriptions, or reviewed literature and other documents. We especially thank the participants, volunteers, instructors, coordinators, and directors of the social circus programs in Cuenca, Quito, Loja, and Tena who openly shared their stories and perceptions, among them Christian Padilla, Alexander Gomez, Jorge Hidalgo, Pablo Muñoz, Karla Barbosa, Fernando Rodríguez, Jairo Galindo, Christian Nolivos, Juan Carlos Ortiz, Nury Carranza, Galo Quinche, Paula Riveros, Adrián Llumipanta, Gabriel Flores, Julia Portilla, Luciana Espinoza, Mario Sánchez, Stephan Mier, Nancy Jaramillo, Soledad Contreras, Álvaro Soto, Mayra Guzmán, Leonardo Rojas, Javier Figueroa, Henry Urdiales, Zoila Castillo, Daniel Gonzales, Josué Tapanca, Josué Valencia, Yadira Vélez, Camilo Garzón, Jorge Jiménez, Carlos Jiménez, Luis Cosíos, Gina Ordoñez, Lizbeth Moreno, Paola Pinza, Diego Apolo, Juan Jefferson Sánchez, Carolina Bustos, Alex Santafé, Arianna Paéz, Micaela Ruiz, Ana Morales, Mickael Enríquez, Richard Quintana, Juan Pizarro, Natalia Casillas, Estefanía Casillas, Cinthya Merizalde, Roberto Ramírez, Claudia Davila, Johnny Paguay, Diego Martillo, Paula Laverve, and the participants who preferred not to be named.

THE ART OF COLLECTIVITY

1 Creative Collectivity: An Introduction

JENNIFER BETH SPIEGEL

Since the beginning of the millennium, artistic practices have been increasingly used as a response to austerity measures and policies of social exclusion. While social movements are drawing upon creative protest techniques, community organizations are launching arts-based social programs to offer tools to youth for surviving the ubiquitous culture of alienation. Whereas policies within this late capitalist (neoliberal) era tend to promote individuality, many of those resisting market-driven governance advocate for collectivity – that is to say, for acting *together* to navigate the various challenges and possibilities encountered. Sometimes social movements and artistic social programs work in tandem toward a "post-neoliberal" vision. This book is about one such experiment. Focusing on a massive social arts initiative launched by the Ecuadorean government as part of a plan to realize its "Citizens' Revolution," we explore the intersection between global cultural politics, participatory arts, and social transformations. How, we ask, does this intersection shape the potential of creating collectivity in the present era?

As approaches to socially oriented and community-engaged arts around the world multiply and inform one another, the myriad ways in which programs are nuanced by the visions that drive them is becoming apparent. Goals, program structures, pedagogical models, target groups, as well as social, cultural, and political dynamics differ radically across community arts programs. How, to what extent, or even whether engagement with the arts can help catalyze the quest for an ever-elusive better world are questions that have occasioned debate for millennia. As local initiatives increasingly draw on international models, the interests and cultural sensibilities promoted by such interventions are further called into question (Kester 2017). Community arts initiatives constitute important sites of counter-hegemonic struggle around the world (Lane 2003; Purcell 2009). However, well-meaning organizations and artists are often inadvertently complicit in efforts that distract from fundamental inequities, and may even depoliticize and instrumentalize creative expression as a means to transform potentially dissident youth into productive and cooperative "citizens" (Duncombe 2007; Matarasso 2013; Plastow 2015; Spiegel and Parent 2017).

Latin America served as the world's "laboratory for neoliberal experiments" following brutal dictatorships in the 1960s and 1970s that abolished social rights (Sader 2008, 5), deeply entrenching policies in the 1980s and 1990s predicated on market-based solutions integrated in globalized economies. Within this climate, Latin America became a major recipient of international aid programs that oriented its social and cultural development. In the 2000s, however, opposition sprang up decisively in response to the resulting exacerbation of social inequalities. Latin America has thus attracted much attention for the social and cultural transformations that left-leaning governments, elected after decades of neoliberalism, strove to achieve. Amongst these initiatives, Ecuador enshrined in policy, and indeed in a new constitution, an ambitious vision for society. As part of Latin America's socialist "pink tide," the cultural policies of Ecuador were shaped out of the struggles that helped bring the government to power (Hammond 2003; Munck 2003; French and Fortes 2005; Sankey 2016). As such, Ecuador began to model a new kind of relationship between civil society and the state. The government elected in 2006 named the philosophy of *Buen Vivir* as the guiding principle of the new society it aimed to promote (Government of Ecuador 2008). A Spanish-language adaptation of the Kichwan *Sumak Kawsay*, this notion has been translated into English as "good living or living fully" (Dávalos 2014). This policy was explicitly framed as moving toward a post-neoliberal future. Highly politicized, it is a complex and holistic concept, subject now to much debate concerning its true interpretation, intent, and utility.

In Ecuador, as elsewhere in Latin America, the neoliberal economic model that dominated the country for decades led to high rates of poverty and reduced public services resulting in severe problems in health, education, and housing (Weisbrot et al. 2017). In this context, the artistic expression of street-involved youth caught the attention of Ecuador's then new vice president, Lenin Moreno (later elected president). During a trip to Montreal, Moreno learned of "social circus" – the use of circus arts as social intervention – and decided to employ this approach to actualize some of the key principles of the Citizens' Revolution his government was promoting. Building from grassroots circus and theatrical initiatives already underway in the country, *Circo Social Ecuador* materialized in April 2011 through an agreement between the vice-president and several municipalities in Ecuador. A month later, he signed an accord with the Montreal-based transnational circus company, *Cirque du Soleil* (Spiegel et al. 2015, 2018), to provide consultation and training for the new initiative.

Neoliberal governance is premised on the notion that individuals must assume responsibility for their own development and wellbeing (Rose 1999). Across Latin America, in response to the entrenchment of repressive regimes in the 1970s, civil society was called upon to fill the gaps left by the withdrawal of state social support. The private sector was also increasingly summoned to fund arts and community projects as part of their growing corporate social responsibility (CSR) agendas (Barnett 2007). Ecuador's providing of extensive state support for a national community arts pro-gram – and particularly for social circus – was thus remarkable for model-ling an explicit transformation in social and cultural logic.

While in many ways unique, the social circus program launched within the *Buen Vivir* plan embodies cultural and social aspirations, challenges, and contradictions that permeate the social arts world globally. Like many other programs, it strives toward creative collectivity in the service of positive transformation. Under the *Buen Vivir* Plan, social circus programs sought to cultivate a sense of togetherness that might balance goals at the personal (micro) and societal (macro) levels wherein a range of complex local, national, and international pressures collide. The extent to which the operationalization of *Buen Vivir* furthered the stated post-neoliberal vision has been hotly contested (Becker 2011; Farah and Vasapollo 2011; Yates and Bakker 2013; González and Vázquez 2015). Ecuador's social circus program thus became a microcosm wherein the various challenges of ac-tualizing post-neoliberal ideals in a neoliberal world play out.

These debates concerning the pursuit of a post-neoliberal vision have implications well beyond the borders of Ecuador. While social move-ments everywhere pressure policy-makers to respond to the needs of the populace, it has been far less common to see governments elected after campaigning on social movement mandates. The role of community arts within the implementation of an explicit social politic has been almost entirely overlooked in policy studies. How might "subjectivity" be altered by changing governmental visions? And what role are community arts playing within such processes? In highlighting these questions, this book seeks to offer much-needed tools of reflection as to the implications of practices and policies for generating "creative collectivity."

Neoliberal Subjectivity and the Global Politics of Collectivity

Since the late twentieth century, there has been a global trend toward scaling back the welfare state by cutting services such as healthcare, education, and cultural programs, as well as social services and supports. These economic policies have been accompanied by the fostering of what has often been called "neoliberal subjectivity," a way of thinking emphasizing responsibility for one's fate as an individual enterprise. As explained by Michel Foucault in his seminal lectures on *The Birth of Biopolitics* (Foucault et al. 2008, 12), the subjectivity that develops under neoliberalism not only views the world in terms of exchange (as was the case under "classic liberalism") but also in terms of competition. The logic of market competition extends to every domain of life. Human beings become "human capital," and each person "an entrepreneur of himself" (Foucault et al. 2008, 226). Citing the real power of neoliberalism as foreclosing the sense of what is possible, philosopher Jason Read concludes: "A political response to neoliberalism must meet it on its terrain, that of the production of subjectivity, freedom and possibility" (Read 2009, 36). The rise in theoretical and practical projects to explore collectivity occurs within this context.

It is important to appreciate that neoliberal "governmentality," as described by Foucault, is not merely a function of how the state itself exerts control but extends to the various ways in which subjectivity is formed under the current world order. As such, neoliberal governmentality has been radically uneven in its effects around the world. Gender, race, class, as well as geopolitical positioning have all oriented both effects *and* responses to this individualizing approach to global governance. The exploration of collectivity and transformation of subjectivities that occurs through creative practices necessarily engages with legacies of colonialism, imperialism, and postcolonial struggle. The development of post-neoliberal subjectivity through fostering what we are calling here "arts of collectivity" is a project that is, at its core, counter-hegemonic in the sense articulated by the great Marxist analyst, Antonio Gramsci. He argued that each individual "participates in a particular conception of the world, has a conscious line of moral conduct, and therefore contributes to sustain a conception of the world or to modify it" (Gramsci 1971, 138). However, given the ubiquitous nature of neoliberal governance in late capitalism, it is not merely a matter of conceiving the world but also living and navigating it from within. It is in this sense that performative practices have emerged to transform social and cultural identities, offering new conceptions of what is possible.

Social theorist Arturo Escobar wrote in 2010 that "Latin America is the only region in the world where some counter-hegemonic processes of importance might be taking place at the level of the State" (Escobar 2010, 1–2). Notions of post-neoliberalism and "post-developmentalism" have featured prominently in the policy discourses of Ecuador, Venezuela, and Bolivia, all countries whose governments were brought to power with the support of left social activists and Indigenous movements. Moreover, at least discursively, the celebration of notions of pluriculturalism and plurinationalism, including the embracing of Afro-Ecuadorean and Indigenous ontologies and practices, points to the idea of collectivity displacing the hegemony of the neoliberal subject. While the extoling of collectivity as a counter-hegemonic strategy in the face of austerity is embraced by social movements around the world (Hardt and Negri 2004; Virno 2004; Spiegel 2015a, 2015b), Latin America is relatively unusual in having elected governments whose discourse, policies, and even constitutions and procedural innovations embraced such a notion. This terrain of subjectivity – changing the ways that citizens think – was a stated goal of the Ecuadorean government's *Buen Vivir* policies of "transition to a post-neoliberal society."

Just as there has been questioning of the government's economic policies, the production of post-neoliberal subjectivity by the social and cultural development strategy of *Buen Vivir* has also been quite contentious. Several scholars have pointed out that, despite nods to local Indigenous movements, the development plan repeats much of the multicultural approach popularized by European countries (Walsh 2010; Radcliffe 2012). Indeed, some argue that such a project of state transformation away from neoliberal governmentality is itself inherently limited. As Escobar writes, "Mired in the production of 'modern citizens' – that is, individuals that produce, consume, and make decisions out of their own free will – the State seems unable to tackle any re-composition of the cultural production of persons and communities. One of the greatest achievements of neoliberalism was precisely the entrenchment of individualism and consumption as cultural norms" (Escobar 2010, 41).

As we will see, one of the main critiques of the process of transition in Ecuador was that government policies failed to actualize their stated purpose. On the contrary, most were widely seen as anchored in an ongoing project of "growth," albeit in various "strategic" ways. In the case of social circus, a flagship government program, the model used was imported by *Cirque du Soleil*'s CSR initiative. The government threw off many of the development constraints and policies that the International Monetary Fund (IMF) and World Bank had been imposing since the 1970s, and adopted an explicitly anti-American, anti-imperialist stance on the international scene (Escobar 2010). However, the ongoing relationship with international companies as a means of implementing its new vision has caused many scholars to question the extent to which the model manages to actualize a post-developmental, post-growth, and post-Western model (Escobar 2010; Walsh 2010; Radcliffe 2012; Gago 2017).

As practices circulate within global networks of "development programs" and their various nationalized and/or radicalized counterparts, the "beneficiaries" and indeed even the "practitioners" of such practices are caught in the nexus of institutional cultures. Indeed, ubiquitous terms such as "target population," "artist," and "community member," and the implicit assumptions concerning who belongs to which category, are fraught with colonial and class politics. As Homi Bhabha (2012) famously theorized, this practice of engaging with new images and visions can involve cultural submission, cultural resistance, or sometimes both simultaneously, particularly within the context of colonial practices and cultural hierarchies. In Latin America, in particular, Diana Taylor (2003) has argued that "transculturation" has become a *modus operandi* as well as a way of understanding the dynamic change at work in and through *mestizo* culture, wherein a foreign cultural process is encountered, a local cultural process is displaced, and a new hybrid cultural phenomenon is ultimately developed. Such a process of cultural fusion is increasingly the norm in the age of globalization. Nonetheless, colonial and neo-imperial dynamics, particularly with respect to development strategies, colour the cultural politics that emerge. These globalized approaches affect not only emergent cultural identity but also the manner in which social and cultural institutions operate, in turn orienting how subjectivity and collectivity are produced.

In the case of the post-neoliberal vision that emerged across Latin America, much of this process of transculturation involved engaging with what Verónica Gago has discussed as "neoliberalism from below." Under a neoliberal regional and world order, she writes, "a network of practices and skills operates, assuming calculation as its primordial subjective frame and functioning as the motor of a powerful popular economy that combines community skills of self-management and intimate know-how as a technology of mass self-entrepreneurship in the crisis" (Gago 2017, 5).

This "neoliberalism from below" has been supported by organizations that offer micro-financing to help small-scale business ventures as well as encourage the development of soft skills for surviving the increasing individualization of responsibility for one's fate (Rankin 2002; Maclean 2012; Kumar 2013). Similar initiatives are being launched around the world; modest government programs offer funds conditional on the development of entrepreneurial potential (Lazzarato 2012). Those engaged in these processes have not necessarily embraced the logic of neoliberalism, and often struggle against it, but must operate with a fundamental ambivalence in order to survive. In much of the world, including North America, where austerity measures increasingly chip away at social services, "neoliberalism from below" has become ubiquitous. The emerging networks and economies are, as Gago points out, "vitalist," in the sense that they are born out of conditions of necessity and draw on the ingenuity of collectives working together. To understand this phenomenon and how it plays out, this book explores promoting a post-neoliberal subjectivity via one set of cultural policies and programs: social circus.

Around the world, social circus is being adopted and adapted in ways that oscillate between the production of neoliberal and post-neoliberal subjectivity. As such, these programs tap into a particular set of tensions between globalization, anti-imperialism, and alter-globalization. With the rise of the "pink tide" in Latin America and *Buen Vivir* policies in particular in Ecuador, a new opportunity seemed to have arisen with government support for a post-neoliberal subjectivity moving, at least in principle, beyond the logic of self-management and entrepreneurship. However, as we shall see in this book, the attempted transition was far from smooth.

Corporeal Politics and the Rise of a Global Social Circus Movement

Within the global cultural imaginary, circus is known as an art of spectacular risk, an activity to delight families, and a place to which wistful, troubled, or dreamy youth run away. Not only has circus traditionally attracted marginalized peoples as performers, it has been historically situated as a "low" art – popular entertainment designed for the masses rather than for the cultured elite. Since the nineteenth century in the Americas,

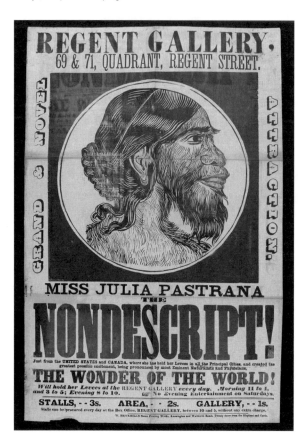

Photo 1.1
Advertisement for an exhibition of Julia Pastrana, a Mexican "bearded lady" born in the 1830s, held at London's Regent Gallery, where she appeared three times a day in 1857. Pastrana was one of the many famous disabled people, dwarves, giants, and other "freaks" toured in nineteenth-century circus shows.

circus has been embroiled in a colonial politic as employer and exploiter of Indigenous and African-American performers, as well as of non-normative bodies and gender presentations (the dwarf, the bearded lady, etc.; see Bogdan 1988, and photo 1.1). Thus, for most of its history, circus has occupied a culturally ambiguous space. It is a site of spectacle where "freaks" can be put on display for the monetary benefit of the circus owner and the delight of mainstream viewers who, through their encounter with the "other" (whether as representative of nature, animal, or someone from a different culture), have their worldview solidified. At the same time, circus creates a nomadic family and way of life for those with no place in society (Stoddart 2000; Sussman 2013).

The cultural and corporeal politics of circus have always been deeply fraught, contested, and in flux. They have reflected a conquest of the "other," a celebration of exceptional bodies, and, in more recent years, an attempt to demystify what bodies can do by casting the circus performer as an ordinary person doing extraordinary things. It was not until the 1970s that circus began to be accepted within the art world. With a rising appreciation of physical theatre forms and the growth of large circus companies, including notably *Cirque du Soleil*, circus is now gaining a place within global cultural industries (Leroux and Batson 2016). Cultural politics have, however, complicated this acceptance. *Cirque du Soleil*, for instance, continues to come under attack for cultural appropriation (Fricker 2016) as well as for labour practices that take especial advantage of the precarity of geographically displaced performers (Zhang 2016). Cultural policies in the Global North, in places like Canada, have also been criticized for the ways in which they continue to exacerbate the precarity of circus artists (Stephens 2015). Well into the twenty-first century, despite its increased visibility, circus remains on the fringes of the art world, still very much associated with popular culture and nomadic lifestyles.

In the late twentieth century, however, the use of circus for social outreach began to take off. The diversity of modalities – from clowning to trapeze, juggling, and acrobatics – the necessity of building trust to conduct superhuman feats, and the historic association with fringe culture, are all elements contributing to its suitability to reach the disenfranchised (Hurtubise et al. 2003; Spiegel 2016c; Bessone 2017).

Circus draws upon and exploits "kinaesthetic sociality" (Martin 2012) – a mode of creating collectively whereby multiple bodies and voices combine in acts of performance, transforming patterns of social interaction (Spiegel 2016c). By the 1990s, such initiatives became known around the world as "social circus." Because of its diverse beginnings, the movement can boast no singular origin story. Lavers and Burtt note that in the 1950s, a priest in Spain started a circus company as a fund-raising initiative for street-involved youth (Lavers and Burtt 2015). Psychoanalyst Felix Guattari used circus arts as part of his patient therapy in 1960s Paris (Spiegel 2016c). Both of these initiatives pre-date the work of Reg Bolton with rural and Indigenous communities in Australia in the 1970s (Bolton 2004). As the popularity of contemporary circus grew, so too did socially engaged circus initiatives. While extraordinary transformations have been attributed to social circus, both labour and cultural processes have coloured its reception and impact.

The South American history of social circus begins in the early 1990s in Brazil with *Se Essa Rua Fosse Minha*, one of the most important precursors of social circus worldwide (photo 1.2). The notion of social circus as the meeting of community outreach work and circus arts began to de-

Photo 1.2 *Si Essa Rua Fosse Minha* in 1998. One of the first social circus projects in Latin America, operating since the late 1980s in Rio de Janeiro, Brazil.

velop globally during that period. *Parada* arose in Romania shortly before 1996, the Dutch Creative-World Foundation initiated projects in Tanzania, Costa Rica, and Mexico as well as in the Netherlands (Dutch Creative World Foundation 2017), and has been working with IWE in Bangladesh (One World Experience 2017), Be More in Uganda (Be More 2018), and Out of Area in Bosnia (Out of Area 2017). The *Escuela Nacional Circo Para Todos* in Cali, Colombia, was the first circus school focusing on street children. Clowns Without Borders runs workshops worldwide (Clowns Without Borders 2017). There is a mobile circus program in Afghanistan (Afghan Mobile Mini Children's Circus 2017); in Australia, a strong social circus program exists for disadvantaged women (Women's Circus 2016); and the Zip Zap Circus School runs a social circus program in South Africa addressing youth with HIV (Zip Zap Circus School 2016), to name a few.

Social circus programs in different parts of the world often interact with each other. A social circus program, for example, exists in Indonesia (Rednose Foundation 2017); CircEsteem (Circesteem 2017) operates in Chicago; and in 2017, the participants from CircEsteem joined social circus enthusiasts from Indonesia.

CARAVAN (Caravan European Youth Circus and Education Network 2011), an international non-profit association that gathers twenty-eight

Photo 1.3 Participants in the Chicago-based program *CircEsteem*, which has worked with thousands of youth from disadvantaged neighbourhoods in Chicago since 2001, are shown performing in an Indonesian community whose main source of income is scavenging from Jakarta's main landfill, Bantar Gebang. The photo was taken during an exchange visit with counterparts from *Yayasan Hidung Merah* (Red Nose Foundation) in 2017.

youth and social circus schools from twenty-four countries across the globe, provides support and training through a worldwide network. They also work on developing links between social circus trainers and formal university programs (Caravan – European Youth and Social Circus Network 2016; Caravan – European Youth and Social Circus Network 2018) and implement an international social circus training-for-trainers program called *Circus Trans-Formation*.

While *Cirque du Soleil* started social programs in 1989, according to Gaétan Morency, vice president of *Cirque du Soleil* 1992–2012, *Cirque du Monde* was officially launched in 1995 as a large-scale institutional partnership between *Cirque du Soleil* and the non-governmental organization (NGO) *Jeunesses Musicales/Jeunesses du Monde,* in Quebec. Since then, for over twenty years, *Cirque du Monde* has partnered with local organizations

Photo 1.4 A social circus training session for social circus trainers organized in partnership between *Caravan-Le Plus Petit Cirque du Monde* and *Cirque du Monde* in 2009 in Bagneux, France, which contributed to Caravan's launch of Circus Trans-Formation.

Photo 1.5 This photo is from a parade at *Cirque du Soleil/Cirque du Monde* in Montreal, Canada, illustrating the diversity of participants in social circus.

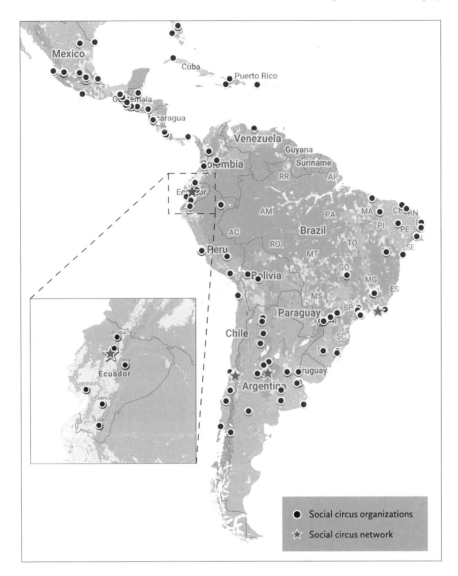

Figure 1.1 Map of Latin America showing social circus organizations and networks as reported by *Cirque du Monde*

Created from data obtained at http://apps.cirquedusoleil.com/social-circus-map/, accessed for updating 12 September 2018.

in more than eighty communities in twenty-six countries around the world and has always seen these relationships as core for the success and sustainability of their programs (photo 1.5). As explained in *Cirque du Soleil's Community Workers Guide* (2016), "the primary goal [of social circus] is not to

Photo 1.6 Volunteers from Ecuador's social circus projects are shown here with artists from China, Russia, Brazil, and Mexico at the end of an improvised show at the Calderón Park in Cuenca in 2013. It was organized by the vice presidency of Ecuador, with support from *Cirque du Monde* one day after the launch of the big tent in that city.

learn circus arts, but rather to assist with participants' personal and social development by nurturing their self-esteem and trust in others, as well as by helping them to acquire social skills, become active citizens, express their creativity and realize their potential.

The origins of *Cirque du Monde's* partnerships lie in Brazil, and in Quebec in the 1980s. Quebecois Paul Laporte worked with a Brazilian NGO in Sao Paolo serving street-involved youth. Paul Vachon, a circus professional, teacher, and another early pioneer of social circus, began working with street-involved youth in Montreal in the mid-1990s, partnering with local social service agencies. A particular focus was placed on Latin America with programs such as *Circo del Mundo Chile*. In Brazil, at the time of writing, there were more than thirty-eight projects offering social circus.

In recent years, *Cirque* has developed new approaches to partnerships and the philosophy that underpins them; *Cirque* still provides training ("training the trainers") at no cost, but now encourages more local involvement by helping partners leverage existing relationships or create new partnerships, offering networking advice, and introducing new connections by using their own extensive networks and experience to open doors (interviews conducted by various team members with Gil Favreau and Emmanuel Bochud, 2016). Indeed, *Cirque* often facilitates the bringing together of social circus participants from different parts of the world.

When *Cirque du Monde* conducted a survey in 2015 of over 350 social circus programs worldwide (see figure 1.2), social circus in Ecuador showed a marked difference of funding model compared to social circus elsewhere in Latin America and worldwide (see figure 1.3), attributable to the unprecedented government commitment as part of its *Buen Vivir* plan. At the time of the surveys (with responses from four social circus programs in Ecuador amidst the 205 worldwide respondents), Ecuadorean programs were reported to be 91% state funded, as compared to only 26% state funded for social circus programs elsewhere in Latin America and 31% worldwide. While *Circo Social Ecuador* partnered with private foundations and religious organizations as frequently as other social circus programs according to the data collected, they reported no partnering with private companies. The influence of *Cirque du Soleil* was apparently seen as too arms-length to be reported by the coordinators at the four individual Ecuadorean programs that responded to the survey as constituting a "partnership with their local programs"; while training and advisory services were provided by *Cirque du Soleil,* no operating funds were provided by the company.

There are vastly different visions of social circus. Some programs focus on artistic training for economically marginalized groups, with the professionalization of its participants – and especially labour and economic inclusion – constituting "success." Others conceptualize circus art modalities as tools to satisfy social needs, concentrating on the psychological and social transformation of the participants. The extent to which visions of social circus are being actualized, under what conditions, and with what challenges is only beginning to be explored. Most analyses examine the ways in which individuals are being supported to build skills and transform their lives, and, to a lesser extent, how individuals thus empowered are making a difference in their communities. Gains have been found in helping participants to "reconnect to their bodies" and increase their physical expression and mobility (Kelaher and Dunt 2009; Loiselle 2015; Spiegel

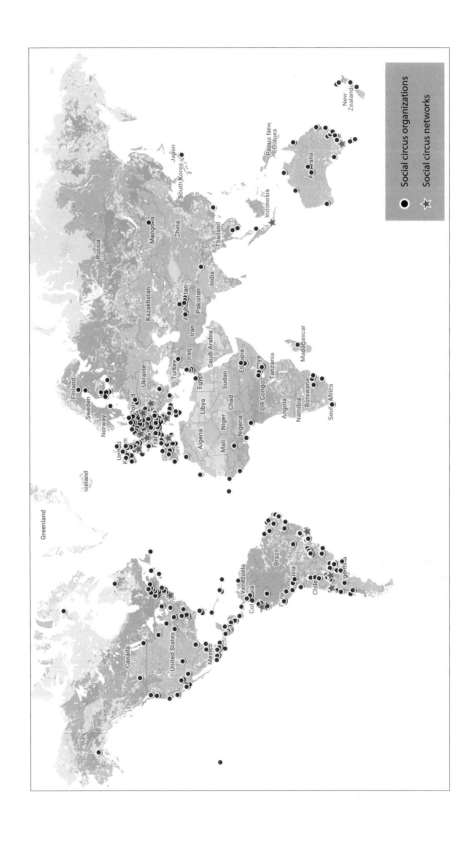

Social circus organizations

Social circus networks

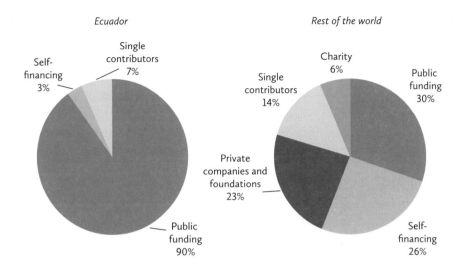

Figure 1.2 (*opposite*) Map of the world showing social circus organizations and networks as reported by *Cirque du Monde*

Created from data obtained at http://apps.cirquedusoleil.com/social-circus-map/, accessed for updating 12 September 2018.

Figure 1.3 (*above*) Financing of social circus programs, comparing Ecuador with the rest of the world

Note: Data obtained from survey conducted by David Simard of *Cirque du Monde* in 2015.

and Parent 2017), "feel empowered" or "self-confident" (Kelaher and Dunt 2009; McCaffery 2011; Trotman 2012; Archambault 2014; Loiselle 2015; Savolainen and Suoniemi 2015; Spiegel and Parent 2017), as well increase their general "sense of happiness," "wellbeing," or "fun" (Trotman 2012; Cadwell and Rooney 2013; Kinnunen et al. 2013). Potential improvement of social, interpersonal skills, and "social participation" or "engagement" are also increasingly being reported and analyzed (Kelaher and Dunt 2009; Trotman 2012; Kinnunen et al. 2013; Loiselle 2015; Savolainen and Suoniemi 2015; Spiegel 2016c; Spiegel and Parent 2017). In studying the role of the *Machincuepa* social circus in Las Aguilas, Mexico, a community struggling with the impact of poverty, including open drug use in the streets, McCauley (2011) found that social circus workshops provide safety for youth and thus help them combat alienation and share experiences and resources.

Kristy Seymour's research explores how circus can open up a new world to children diagnosed on the autistic spectrum, enabling them to take risks, physically and emotionally, and to stretch the capacities of their bodies in an environment that enriches their social development. Social circus, according to Seymour (2012), sets out to re-create the freedom and fun associated with a healthy childhood, building playful attitudes in an easy-going environment in which participants can feel safe while developing connections with each other. These findings resonate with those I have previously explored in Quebec (Spiegel and Parent 2017). Applying a critical mixed-method design, we analyzed how the physicality, humour, and creative expression of circus arts are leveraged as community development practices. As an art grounded in corporeal interaction and creative expression traditionally associated with migrant or nomadic labour, circus is notorious for recruiting "freaks." Notwithstanding this fundamental cultural ambivalence, by making a spectacle of what bodies can collectively do, we found circus an art well-poised to mitigate, if not combat, the alienation from oneself and others associated with late capitalist, neoliberal sociality.

Although *Cirque du Monde* has offered social circus through worldwide partnerships for over twenty years, researchers note the paucity of research concerning the impacts of these programs (Fournier et al. 2014). In a rare study of a *Cirque du Monde* program for Indigenous Inuit youth in Northern Canada (Schwan and Lightman 2013), in-depth interviews were conducted over two-and-a-half years with four circus trainers, the director of *Cirque du Monde*, and the director of the Nunavik Recreation Department. The trainers identify the main challenges to the program to be non-commitment from youth, inconsistent attendance, frequent quitting, and lack of adult volunteerism. The authors note that the trainers' narratives about these behaviours commonly focus on individual pathology, family problems, or substance abuse, and the solution in their view was disciplining and modeling a healthy community. However, when historic and contemporary colonial practices are taken into account (e.g. the oppressive residential school system, outlawing of spiritual and artistic practices, etc.), the research suggest that the behaviour of the young participants is better understood as micro-interactional efforts towards decolonization rather than socially deviant, unhealthy, or maladaptive. The analysis also indicates that the contrast between Western and Inuit conceptions of time, accountability, health, and community was not critically enough addressed in the program design, and therefore may not have met the youths' needs. This led to intensifying efforts to recruit more Inuit youth as trainers.

In my in-depth study of a *Cirque du Soleil*-partnered program in Montreal, *Cirque Hors Piste* (Spiegel 2016c), I also call attention to the cultural

Photo 1.7 Used to develop trust and team-building in social circus programs throughout the world, this exercise was being modeled at a workshop held at the "First Meeting of Circus and Pedagogy" in Loja, 2014.

politics that impact the collective well-being of street-involved youth in such programs, drawing attention to how differences in positionality and framing between the desires of youth and the policy goals that shaped their programs can create tensions. This study was part of the critical mixed-method study of four social circus programs in Quebec (Spiegel and Parent 2017) which served as a precursor for the research project that is the focus of this book.

As we will see throughout this book, the Ecuadorean vision of social circus aligns in many ways with the methodology of *Cirque du Monde* (photo 1.7), while simultaneously fostering a distinct set of principles, values, and challenges. According to Moreno, *Circo Social Ecuador* was designed to: 1) create a cultural alternative for empowering vulnerable communities; 2) support protection of children and adolescents at-risk; 3) bring together young people to promote social movements, and to advance and strengthen their sense of national cultural identity in a manner appropriate to each locality; 4) facilitate integrative activities with other national social projects as well as public and private initiatives; and 5) develop values of solidarity, participation, discipline, concentration, cooperation, self-esteem, personal and collective development, and a sense of belonging. Importantly, the goal was also explicitly to "achieve a multiplier effect throughout the country" (Programa Circo Social Ecuador 2012).

As social circus gains in popularity around the world, it is becoming a key means of propagating community-based arts integrated with social programs. However, the complex relationship between cultural politics, policy, program structures, participant experiences, and multi-level impacts of such programs are only beginning to be understood. Moreover, the reasons for the spike in popularity of social circus in recent years remains undertheorized. By exploring the relationships between the particularities of social circus, the cultural policies and program structures through which they emerge, as well as the pedagogical philosophy and practices and the geo-political and historical contexts that are propelling such programs, the present book offers much needed analysis of the cultural politics of social circus.

The Art of Collective Transformation

The development and aspirations of social circus are part of a larger story concerning the changing relationships between art, politics, and sociality, as well as problematizations of the very notion of "cultural development." Building largely on critical analyses advanced in the 1960s and 70s and extending into the twenty-first century, there has recently been increased attention to the social and political implications of cultural practices. In developing his "ethico-aesthetic paradigm" for understanding personal and social transformation, Guattari wrote that "art is not just the activities of established artists but of a whole subjective creativity which traverses the generations and oppressed peoples, ghettoes, minorities" (Guattari 1995, 91). From this perspective, community-based art allows experimentation with different social configurations, as well as different ways of working together and of imagining possible modes of both self and collective realization.

Much of community art operates in the spaces of dis/continuity between identity and its representation – between what individuals or groups perform in "real life" and what is made and presented as artifice on the stages, pages, and exhibition spaces. In Latin America, much understanding builds on the seminal works of Brazilians, such as Paolo Freire's *Pedagogy of the Oppressed* (1972) and Augusto Boal's *Theatre of the Oppressed* ([1985] 2008). In these works, principles of popular education in community arts

are particularly strong, inviting community members to utilize their own experience as the basis of the art they produce, while beckoning to analysis of broader social and cultural dynamics. For Boal, this meant exploring the structural dynamics governing the lives of those involved in community art – making both artistic creation and spectatorship an active process. Community members are explicitly called upon to explore aspects of their lives, impulses, or desires. Much of this work, explicitly or implicitly, is oriented toward transforming individual and collective identity as well as the affects generated. Boal maintained that every art form offers a different set of analytic tools and potentials. Circus has risen in popularity as a social mode of intervention today alongside the globalization of neoliberal policy and the growing aspirations of post-neoliberal societies. Throughout this book, we will explore the potentialities offered by social circus within this particular moment.

Socially engaged art often strives toward transformation in personal and collective spheres, generating grassroots opportunities to re-create cultural landscapes. Nevertheless, the field remains haunted by legacies of cultural power and privilege that pervade the very ways we think of both art and of transformation. Those anchored in non-Western traditions, as well as those coming to the arts via other forms of community engagement and organizing, continue to be alienated by the arts and culture industry. Drawing on the work of Victor Turner, performance theorist Richard Schechner (1993) characterized the role of art as falling somewhere in the "ritual-entertainment braid." Community-oriented works that seek to fulfill a social function tend to align with what has traditionally been viewed as "ritual" – whether rituals of maintaining social order or rituals of controlled transformation. In contrast, work that focuses on aesthetics tend to line up more closely with the "entertainment" function. The division, however, is fluid, and the functions tend to form tightly woven braids. Traditional storytelling techniques can perform both a ritual and an entertainment function, and also serve to pass down cultural values and lessons. Moreover, participatory and community-engaged works can be seen as challenging social hierarchies or, alternatively, bolstering and maintaining existing power dynamics within climates of social unrest and economic precarity. Such projects can generate a host of artists that may, within certain economies, serve as the exploitable, low culture "other" of recognized "high-brow" artists. Institutional and pedagogical processes, as well as social and creative visions, shape these dynamics, with far reaching implications for how artists, community workers, and participants are

recognized for their efforts. As we will see, some programs can be under-stood to be serving many aims simultaneously, creating rifts within a single program.

In recent years, policy imperatives for community arts programs to "show results" have led to increased interest in research on the part of practitioners. Several literature reviews have been conducted on arts pro-grams for street-involved youth (Kidd 2009; Conrad and Sinner 2015), the core "target population" of most youth-oriented social circus programs, in-cluding *Circo Social Ecuador*. However, with the exceptions cited through-out this book, very few studies on social circus have documented either the impacts of or challenges to these programs. As numerous theorists have argued, fostering a range of ways of seeing and engaging with the world can alter how people navigate the world more broadly (Flynn and Tinius 2015; Rancière 2004). Nevertheless, the trend toward emphasiz-ing transferable skills points to a concerning phenomenon, namely that community-engaged art is being looked at as an *"expedient"* (Yúdice 2003) to, as Max Haiven puts it, "generate social cohesion, improve civic engage-ment, stimulate economic growth and incubate 'innovation' [precisely] at the moment ameliorative social programs – for instance, for 'at risk' chil-dren in urban areas – are slashed" (Haiven 2017, 536). Nonetheless, while the use of the arts to pick up the slack left by neoliberal policies is increas-ingly seen around the world (Bishop 2012), many community-engaged and community-based artists are paying ever-more attention to the structural dynamics of their programs (Jackson 2011).

Much of community-engaged work is premised on partnerships (Cohen-Cruz 2015). Socially engaged art projects, and related North-South community-based partnership initiatives, have taken a multitude of forms, entailing collaborations amongst arts organizations, individual artists, NGOs, service organizations, community centres, private foundations, re-ligious organizations, social enterprises, schools, universities, government agencies, banks, international development agencies, small businesses, and larger corporations and/or individual sponsors. Each partnering or-ganization comes with its own mandate and its own vision for what it hopes to achieve; indeed, different individuals within the same organiz-ation may even have different objectives. Deborah Barndt (2011), a Can-adian scholar who has worked in many forms of North-South arts-infused collaborations, writes that "Community art is often implicitly a critique of the domination of Western mass media and popular consumer culture ...

a cauldron of diverse cultural practices ... (and) new cultural fusions are drawing on traditions that challenge the Eurocentric content and individualism of hegemonic white Western culture."

Building on years of grassroots organizing, the first Latin American arts and health forum took place in Peru in 2009. This led to a declaration on "arts as a bridge to health and social development" signed by the Latin American Network of Arts for Social Transformation and the Pan-American Health Organization (Pan-American Health Organization 2009). After this, arts for health initiatives grew rapidly. Notwithstanding the anti-oppressive pedagogy that typically undergirds the initial creation of such projects, UK-based arts and health scholars Clive Parkinson and Mike White point out the frequency with which art has, in the past, been "used as a vehicle for propaganda by oppressive ideologies (including neo-liberalism)" (Parkinson and White 2013, 184). They caution that art which is seen to be somehow working to the service of the state, and the inequalities it perpetuates, runs the risk of provoking cynicism. It would be easy to make the mistake of thinking that the arts and public health agenda is instrumentalism, necessarily reducing culture and the arts to being a subservient tool for social engineers, well-intentioned or otherwise.

This repurposing of social arts pedagogy for ends never intended is experienced worldwide. UK-based professor of African theatre, Jane Plastow (2015), for instance, notes how traditionally subversive forms of theatre in Africa are now being used to encourage subservience. The growth of transnational collaborations brings renewed concern about the instrumentalization of community arts programs (Kester 2011; Parkinson and White 2013). Global and local economic dynamics are becoming a major force directing such participatory projects despite the fact that, in most cases, the traditions adopted originate in the communities seeking to empower themselves (Cohen Cruz 1998; Goldbard and Adams 2001; Goldbard 2006; Kester 2011; Plastow 2015). Barndt speaks about "the ethical, interpersonal and logistical challenges when trying to equalize the implications and effects of cultural difference, economic disparity and histories of colonization." She notes that, in her experience, despite the efforts of each player to access financial resources, in all or most projects funding ultimately comes from the Northern partner and, as such, the dynamics of colonialism, even if unconscious, can become a specter in the room. She states that "when a Northern partner is seen more as a donor (Ms Moneybags), it can become a complicated negotiation to unpack both historical and current realities,

including often-unspoken perspectives that can colour and inhibit the development of trusting and equal relationships (interview with Deborah Barndt, 2016).

Calling upon Northern partners in various ways, social circus embodies a challenge to hegemonic culture, celebrating "marginalized" bodies and modes of expression, while remaining entangled in global development politics that critical artists have been navigating for years. Large international funding agencies such as the IMF and the World Bank include arts interventions as legitimate forms of development work, allowing up to 15% of project expenses to support "attitudinal change" (interviews with Jacques Rajotte, the former director of ONE Drop, a Montreal-based international NGO supported by *Cirque du Soleil*, and with Gil Favreau, former director of *Cirque du Soleil's* Corporate Citizenship Office). In the case of Ecuador, the program was launched as part of a broader social transformation and thus in tandem with other social programs. Nevertheless, contradictory tendencies and logics persist. This is partly due to the ways in which these tensions are deeply anchored in many of the models of community art that circulate globally. However, such tensions are particularly at play in Latin America, given the predominance of NGO- and World Bank-funded programs throughout the region. The social circus program in Ecuador was developed in the context of a broader regional movement to reject the development model of the IMF and World Bank in order to renationalize cultural and social policies. Nevertheless, the imperative to function within existing global networks, as well as the need to create a social and cultural initiative capable of carrying the country beyond its extractivist, resource-based economy, placed competing pressures on those involved in the program.

Global Collectivity as a Multifaceted Lens of Inquiry

Collectivity – and more specifically, ways of generating collectivity – are fundamental to the art of social transformation. Whether *intracultural* or *intercultural*, the politics of community arts colour the relevance of research design as well as the nature of collaboration. Collectivity is an operative element of *Buen Vivir* as a way out, however troubled or unrealized, of a colonial world order. Given the need to work with those affected in order to understand the key tensions and impacts of the phenomenon that is *Circo Social Ecuador*, it seemed fitting to produce our own "collectivity." In so doing, we hybridized epistemologies from the North and South,

from across our various disciplines and communities of practice and study and continue to navigate questions of power and positionality as they emerge.

The factors that shape successful North–South community-university partnerships have been the subject of considerable literature (Corbin and Mittelmark 2008; Yassi, Zungu et al. 2016; Canadian Coalition for Global Health Research 2017). One element that cuts across discourses of social engagement is an attempt to alter the balance of power amongst those engaged in the cultural life of the community. This endeavour, of course, moves beyond artistic techniques and social technologies to invoke questions about who is driving the processes and what resources they are able to access. As such, the question of what change one might like to see is an iterative one, inherently tied to who determines the objectives and what pressures and supports are orienting such agenda-setting. The kind of change pursued, as well as the context that animates the desired transformation, must orient the nature of the research conducted and the process of inquiry itself.

Current Ecuadorean society emerged from a long history of domination but also of struggles and resistance. As well documented by historians (Instituto de Investigaciones Económicas UCE 1975; Cueva 1979; Velasco 1981; Guerra Vilaboy 2006), the land that is now Ecuador was inhabited for well over 10,000 years by Indigenous groups. It was then controlled for a relatively short period (seventy years) by the Inca Empire until 1532 when nearly three centuries of exploitation by the Kingdom of Spain began. The territory later passed through the period of American Independence that carved the geographic boundaries of a nation soon to fall under the political, economic, and cultural power of local rulers, mainly landowners (the Catholic Church among them). Ecuador continued to be dominated by an oligarchy that, in its anti-feudal and secular zeal, would forge the capitalist development model that launched the neoliberal era. Throughout much of this history, Indigenous peoples and later also Afro-Ecuadorean communities became subjugated and relegated to an exploited workforce and/or forced to take refuge in wilderness habitats to sustain their ways of life.

In an attempt to break with this colonial inheritance, the new constitution of 2008 aimed to "articulate the struggle for social justice, equality, and the abolition of privileges with the construction of a society that respected diversity and nature" (Government of Ecuador 2008). Notwithstanding significant technical and political challenges, Ecuador's national development plan of 2009–13, *Plan Nacional Para el Buen Vivir*, posed a con-

ceptual break with more orthodox approaches to development, specifying five aspects of justice: social and economic justice; democratic and participatory justice; interpersonal and intergenerational justice; transnational justice; and justice as fairness (Secretaría Nacional de Planificación y Desarrollo 2013).

In framing the new constitution and the *Plan Nacional Para el Buen Vivir*, the national government led initiatives to meet a somewhat invisible dimension of well-being – one pertaining much more to the growth of consciousness and collective health than with standard international indicators based on rates of growth and individual productivity, or even conventional health outcomes. The measures implemented were widely reported to have improved quality of life, although geographic, ethnic, gender, age, and socio-economic inequities persisted especially among the most vulnerable (Carriel Mancilla 2012; Weisbrot et al. 2017). The redistribution of wealth and per-capita income that emerged from the new government's social and economic measures moved Ecuador from a low-income country to one of higher social standing, but with serious structural gaps. In this context much of the population, especially children and young people, remained vulnerable and the conditions for harmonious and healthy development, albeit materially improved, remained what some authorities (including mental health specialist, team member Arturo Campaña) considered to be "spiritually inadequate."

Commenting on the new vision of the Ecuadorean government, cultural theorist Catherine Walsh explains: "It is a project that entails, and demands, the creation of radically different conditions of existence and of knowledge, power, and life, conditions that could contribute to construct really intercultural societies, where the values of complementarity, relationality, reciprocity, and solidarity get to prevail. Are they willing to think and act with the historically subordinated and marginalized peoples; to unlearn their uninational, colonial, and monocultural learning; and to relearn to learn so as to be able to complement each other, and co-exist and co-live ethically?" (Walsh 2009, 212, 235). This vision – and the social, cultural, and epistemological politics and challenges toward which it points – form the context of the present inquiry. In light of the post-colonial ambitions that characterized the launching of *Circo Social Ecuador*, it became crucial for us to develop a lens of inquiry in keeping with the stated aims and constructed through dialogue concerning these goals. *Buen Vivir*, as such, became not simply one *object* of inquiry, the relevance of which will be unpacked in chapter 3, but also a *lens* of inquiry that draws together in unique, revelatory, and sometimes problematic ways, various disciplines

and facets of life. While originating from the Kichwan language and culture, and adapted as part of a political program in Bolivia and Ecuador with different manifestations in each national context, the conceptual rise to prominence of *Buen Vivir* owes much to the work of scholars deeply engaged in post-colonial thinking on the very nature of "wellbeing," "culture," "health," and even "community."

González and Vázquez (2016) refer to this as the "ontological turn" in the debate – focusing on the experiential nature of being, expressing concern that the academic focus on epistemologies – or how knowledges are constructed – is "foreclosing the possibility of engaging more pragmatic discussions." Early on, for instance, Acosta (2011), as well as González and Vázquez themselves (2015), had celebrated the non-Western roots and collectivist equity-oriented strategy that the discourse of *Buen Vivir* implies. The concern later expressed by these scholars, however, is that the focus on the discursive issues masks issues relating to strategies of actual implementation. Analyzing urban cultural development trends, Burgos-Vina (2017) expressed a similar concern that *Buen Vivir* had become more of a marketing strategy than a pervasive social policy, while Mezzandra (2012) argued that the rhetoric was clandestinely fostering industrialization and precarious workforces. Moreover, as Escobar pointed out, "the fact that while [President] Rafael Correa prizes the role of academic knowledge in illuminating social change and in cultivating a well-informed citizenship (many of his cabinet members belong to intellectual/academic circles rather than political circles), this means his government is seen by some as based on urban middle sectors and that it marginalizes non-academic knowledges, such as those of indigenous and Afro-Ecuadorian minorities" (Escobar 2010, 24).

By the time this study was completed Correa was no longer in office, having been succeeded by his former vice president, Lenín Moreno. Nonetheless, the marginalization of "non-academic knowledges" – and in particular knowledges whose lineages cannot be easily traced to European institutions – was neither unique to the Correa government nor to Latin American governance more broadly. It is, rather, a problematic that has traversed the globe, occasioning resistance within academic circles and well beyond (Meyerhoff and Noterman 2017). It is, in many ways, a problematic that is even more endemic in the Global North (see Simpson 2014) than the Global South, where organized resistance against epistemecide, and in particular against the eclipsing and colonization of epistemologies of the South, has reached a level of institutional recognition. Writing from Latin America, Santos warns that "in the global North of our time radical ideas are not translated into radical practices and vice versa" (Santos

2014, 3). In its small way, this book seeks to open avenues for a collaborative praxis that might begin to redress this gulf as it affects both the South and the North.

The critical framework we adopt reflects the multiplicity of our team of researchers – Canadian and Ecuadorean academics and practitioners from across the fields of health, social sciences, humanities, arts, and indeed the practice of social circus itself. It also reflects a multiplicity of ways of engaging with community at various levels, from program participants, to instructors and coordinators, to high-level government officials. In adopting *Buen Vivir* as part of our lens of inquiry, we place the philosophy and goals of Ecuador's social circus program into conversation with the various discourses and traditions with which it explicitly or implicitly engages, in order to better study the implications of the socio-cultural vision promoted. We engage with diverse interpretations of *Buen Vivir*: as an anti-colonial lens of equitable social transformation, as a global Marxism rebranded by intellectuals and government officials, and as a populist "productivist" paradigm still mired in extracting and exploiting the land and those living in situations of precarity – and analyze the policies, pedagogies, structures, and experiences of the individuals and communities concerning the social circus initiative in light of these interpretive debates. Ultimately, we unpack how the "post-neoliberal vision" orients the adaption of the program, the ways in which this shapes cultural transformation and collective wellbeing. We also analyze the significance of these visions and practices for collective creative practice globally. The questions broached throughout this book point to broader discussions concerning cultural politics and how visions for the creation of new societies through collective practice come about and transform. As we shall see, approaches to creative collective function are rife with tensions and beg the bringing together of multiple perspectives – without forcing a smooth synthesis.

Chapter 2 details the methodological processes we developed for working together as community-engaged researchers pursuing heterogeneous perspectives, but with extensive cross-referencing and thematic cross-resonance. This is presented using the various characteristics of the "rhizome" as listed by Deleuze and Guattari (1987). The chapter explains how and why we combined techniques from the arts, humanities, social sciences, and health sciences with the potentialities of community artists to analyze individual and collective transformations related to social circus. In so doing, it reflects on how our study can be characterized by 1) multiplicity, 2) connection and heterogeneity, 3) asignifying rupture, and 4) cartog-

raphy and delacalomia, in order to emphasize the importance of trans-disciplinarity and attentiveness to relations of power.

Chapter 3 positions *Circo Social Ecuador* as an explicit operationalizing of Ecuador's new constitution of 2008. The program is analyzed as a reflection – and indeed a microcosm – of a new social policy with its hopes, dreams, and promises of a new era but also subject to the constraints and disappointments characterizing its implementation. Situating this program within the government's *Buen Vivir* philosophy and placing it into dialogue with the international programs and policies that informed the development of the vision, the chapter explores how the historical, socio-economic, and political context influenced the design of the national program. It also explores the diverse manner in which the social circus program was put into practice in various municipalities. Here the focus of investigation becomes how policy reframes and redesigns social circus as an intervention for a post-neoliberal society, while adapting it from programs that spread as remedial interventions, largely by NGOs and CSR programs at the height of global neoliberal policy in the 1980s.

Chapter 4 focuses on the adaptation of the pedagogical model inspired by *Cirque du Monde*'s globalizing approach, for Ecuador's national vision and particular local realities. The chapter introduces the core pillars and philosophical principles of social circus, teasing out the uniqueness of social circus pedagogy as a community art while situating it within the particular traditions that have both influenced its development and to which it contributes. It further analyzes how this pedagogical model functioned and was transformed within the Ecuadorean context, exploring how a global train-the-trainer program combined with local values and traditions to result in a national social circus program with unique characteristics. The chapter highlights the philosophical underpinnings concerning how embodied knowledge and experience are harnessed to build trust and solidarity, as well as how pedagogical practices and conditions orient the ways in which these aspirations can be realized.

Chapter 5 explores the politics of arts facilitation, both within community arts programs and as an approach to conducting research. The chapter focuses on two workshops conducted by our research team: the first, a three-day arts-based research workshop with many participants, volunteers, instructors, and program administrators, as well as many of the authors of this book, utilizing embodied exercises to explore lived experience; the second a photovoice workshop. The chapter explores the logic of adapting techniques similar to the everyday practices of those involved in

social circus within community-based research. In so doing, it highlights the complex relationships between the cultural politics of creative social programming, of knowledge production, and ultimately of facilitated arts processes designed to mitigate the systemic inequities in which they are nonetheless entangled.

The large quantitative survey results presented in chapter 6 statistically compare indicators associated with mental and physical health before and after participation, as well as within and between different *Circo Social* municipal programs. The survey also compares participant experiences in social circus with those of youth attending other community arts and culture programs, including capoeira and parkour. Focusing on the relationships between personal growth, social inclusion, and social engagement, as well as the ways in which these intersect with factors such as nutrition, housing, substance use, and employment, the chapter offers a comparative analysis of how and for whom social circus sparks the greatest transformations. Differences between programs and program sites are put into dialogue in order to suggest what program attributes orient the kinds of impacts measured.

Chapter 7 analyzes the relationship between engagement in socially-oriented creative practices and conditions of precarity amongst those involved in social circus in Ecuador. In particular, it focuses on how political and institutional changes over the years alter the class, gender, and cultural dynamics of the program and thus how creativity is leveraged as a social force. Placing *Circo Social Ecuador* into conversation with programs elsewhere in the world, especially in Quebec where many of the consultants who helped launch Ecuador's national social circus initiative are based, the chapter further explores how differences in global cultural politics, including local artistic traditions and cultural policies, impact and are impacted by lived realities.

We end the book with an epilogue exploring recent developments in the ways in which social circus practices in Ecuador and beyond are navigating neoliberal and post-neoliberal policies and organizational strategies.

In analyzing how collectivity is being cultivated through one bold program – from the actualization of a social policy and the adaptation of a pedagogical model to the evolving structure, experiences, and impacts of the various program sites – this book seeks to contribute a valuable resource to understanding the "art of collectivity," with all its messiness, tension, and success.

The Art of Transdisciplinary Community-based Research: A Rhizomatic Approach

KATHERINE M. BOYDELL, JENNIFER BETH SPIEGEL, AND ANNALEE YASSI

Any point of a rhizome can be connected to any other, and must be ... A rhizome ceaselessly establishes connections between semiotic chains, organizations of power, and circumstances relative to the arts, social sciences, and social struggles.

Deleuze and Guattari 1987, 7

The arts have been employed in community development initiatives for decades (Belfiore 2002), and the value of creativity in promoting healthy communities has long been recognized by practitioners and scholars alike (Hancock 1983; Guetzko 2002; Clift 2012). It has been argued that the arts are of great value to building social capital (Newman et al. 2003), improving the health and well-being of individuals and communities (Cameron et al. 2013), enhancing cohesive social bonds, and creating a shared identity (Lowe 2000). However, despite growing interest in the impact of programs using the arts, there remains considerable controversy regarding how such initiatives should be studied.

Research related to circus arts is particularly limited, especially with respect to a key constituency for the social circus movement, namely marginalized youth. To date, social circus in diverse settings has been studied using a variety of methods. One study analyzed personal stories as well as reviewed questionnaires comparing responses before and after the annual circus performance of 103 Australians who

had experienced sexual assault and enrolled in social circus (Kelaher and Dunt 2009). In Finland, 164 surveys were collected and 100 interviews conducted with circus participants comprised of young people with special needs, as well as their families, teachers, instructors, nurses, and specialists who worked with them (Kinnunen et al. 2013). Archambault (2014) studied the *Espace de Transition*, a program in Montreal that uses circus arts with adolescents and young adults with recently stabilized psychiatric disorders, conducting participatory observation before, during, and after the program, interviewing all twenty-four participants as well as eleven others who worked with them. Semi-structured interviews with participants in social circus workshops as well as their parents and program instructors were also conducted in a study of a program in Mexico (McCauley 2011). An ethnographic study conducted in Montreal, Quebec, examining issues of cultural politics that impact the well-being of street-involved youth (Spiegel 2016c), became part of a critical mixed method study of four social circus programs in Quebec (Spiegel and Parent 2017).

Theoretical frameworks for studying social circus also vary, and include the use of Hannah Arendt's valorization of "work" over "labour" (Rivard et al. 2010), Felix Guattari's theorization of aesthetics as a medium for shifting ethical frameworks (Spiegel 2016c), and Wilson's theorization of intercultural practice (Bessone 2013a). Increasingly, however, there is a recognition that a multiplicity of mutually informing lenses may be needed to understand community-based phenomena. Health researchers as well as social scientists have been stressing the importance of embracing different paradigms in studying health-related issues (Birn 2009; Krieger et al. 2010). Arguing against dominant foundational assumptions (traditional reductionist research objectives, methodologies, and ways of sharing research knowledge), calls have been surfacing for "integrating systematic inquiry approaches from a variety of disciplines" in researching community-based health promotion initiatives (Hawe and Potvin 2009). Meanwhile, performance studies researchers (Alvarez and Graham 2011) have been inviting greater "flow through the health/performance boundary," echoing our own experience in Ecuador (Spiegel and Yassi 2007). Following these calls, our project deploys a variety of methodologies and critical epistemologies in studying *Circo Social Ecuador*.

To take up the challenge, we draw on the work of French philosophers Gilles Deleuze and Felix Guattari, specifically their metaphor of the rhizome. *A Thousand Plateaus*, volume two of *Capitalism and Schizophrenia*, uses the term "rhizomatic" to describe research that allows for multiple,

non-hierarchical entry and exit points in data representation and interpretation (Deleuze and Guattari 1987). The principles of rhizomatic analysis, embracing ideas such as rupture, ambiguity, angst, and uncertainty
(Biehl and Locke 2010), provide a useful framework to explain how we conducted our study of *Circo Social Ecuador*.

The team assembled for this project includes people from community
arts backgrounds as well as from the humanities, social studies, and health
science, from both the Global North and the Global South. Understanding
our approach is a deep sensitivity to questions of cultural hegemony that
pervade hierarchical binaries such as research/practice, North/South, and
art/science, and we seek to navigate the complex histories that have shaped
the epistemologies associated with these.

The approach we adopt draws on theories concerning the "social *determination* of health," which contrasts with the more traditional "social *determinants* of health" analytical framing (Marmot et al. 2008; Spiegel et al.
2015, 2018). In this conceptualization, we focus not merely on the discrete
social conditions that impact health and wellbeing (e.g. nutrition, housing,
education, income, etc.), but also on the structural processes at the societal
level that lead to these social inequities, recognizing the dynamic social
processes that determine the "ways of living" of particular groups (Breilh
2008). This often occurs through social inclusion/exclusion, understood
as "the means, material or otherwise, to participate in social, economic,
political and cultural life" (Huxley et al. 2012). Whereas community-based
health interventions are often assessed in terms of impact on defined
health/disease "outcomes," we examine the program mainly with respect
to how it provides opportunities for changes in ways of living conditioned
by larger socioeconomic processes. As such, we were interested in personal
growth and providing the opportunity for social inclusion and ultimately
social transformation. From this framing, an overall research objective
driving this study of social circus was to better understand how social policies, as well as their associated interventions employing pedagogy in the
arts, intercede in constructing ways of being at both the individual and the
collective level.

Recognizing the importance of visual, performative, and literary modes
of communication, researchers are increasingly including arts-based inquiry in participatory research. In her book *Why Theatre Matters: Urban
Youth, Engagement and the Pedagogy of the Real*, Kathleen Gallagher shows
theatre as a rehearsal site for the social engagement of youth, highlighting
how "understanding the embodied languages of theatre enlivens research"

for both researchers and research participants" (Gallagher 2014, 17). We, too, embrace arts-based methods in researching social circus, including the analysis of theatrical circus performances in Ecuador and beyond.

It was clear to us that our study had to have a strong ethos of participatory action research (PAR). Embracing a PAR approach ensured that participants in our study are not viewed as passive subjects but instead as active agents of change. Some scholars (Kindon et al. 2008) have noted that PAR "offers a politically engaged means of exploring materialities, emotionalities, and aspects of nonrepresentational experience to inform progressive change." The factors that shape successful PAR in the context of North-South community-university partnerships have been the subject of considerable literature (Corbin and Mittelmark 2008; Yassi, Zungu, et al. 2016), and are rife with historically laden tensions.

The metaphor of the rhizome (Deleuze and Guattari 1987) facilitates discussion of how our study of social circus merged our epistemologies and methodologies in order to understand the tensions and disjunctures that arose. It also helps in our attempts to create an "ethical space" (Ermine et al. 2004, 21) from initial dialogue and solidification of our partnership to research dissemination. The rhizome represents an underground network of proliferating roots; these roots are acentric and non-hierarchical, and branch out to all sides in an unpredictable manner (Sermijn et al. 2008; de Freitas 2012). Dissimilar from the branches of a tree, they grow and expand, leading to new plants. They have no beginning or ending, only points in the middle that continuously connect to other points with multiple points of entry (Henriksen and Miller 2012). The rhizome as a model of thought, with its horizontal network and roots, characterizes the reflective interactions that occurred between and among community-based team members and those from academia.

The quotation from Deleuze and Guattari that opens this chapter draws attention to power relationships, the arts, social sciences, and social struggles. This characterizes our countless informal team discussions throughout the research process, some in person, others by Skype, and a three-hour session in Quito specifically devoted to epistemological, ethical, and methodological challenges. Additionally, the lead author of this chapter, who had interacted less with other team members, conducted semi-structured thirty- to sixty-minute Skype conversations with each of the seven other members from both North and South locales. Recordings and notes were listened to, read, and reread, in order to identify repeated patterns of meaning and develop a sense of the ways in which team members experienced their roles.

We apply the six rhizomatic principles to our study of social circus – principles meant to function together rather than being conceptualized as separate: connection and heterogeneity; multiplicity; assigning rupture; cartography and decalcomania. While the text follows a linear mode of explication to illuminate these characteristics, most, if not all, the examples in each section could equally have been described with respect to others of the six principles. Indeed, in true Deleuzian spirit, we begin with "multiplicity," deviating from the classic order Deleuze and Guattarí (1987) used when discussing these principles, beginning with "connection" and "heterogeneity."

Multiplicity: Gaining Insights from Qualitative, Quantitative, and Arts-based Methods

Recognizing the principle of "multiplicity," we see that our understanding "changes its nature as the number of its dimensions increase" (Deleuze and Guattari 1987, 9). Our study formally began in May 2013, following a trip to Quito scheduled to coincide with a visit by Cirque du Soleil/Cirque du Monde to work with personnel from the vice presidency, in keeping with the agreements signed (as noted in chapter 1 and discussed further in chapter 3). This led to a mutual decision to embrace a mixed methods approach (Spiegel et al. 2015), which came to include qualitative methods (including participant observation, interviews, focus group discussions, document analysis, and close readings of performances), quantitative methods (especially a longitudinal survey with comparison groups), as well as arts-based strategies (including theatre-based facilitation, performative inquiry, photovoice, and videography), each of which is discussed briefly below.

The study, funded by the Canadian Institutes of Health Research, built on a longstanding collaboration between Ecuadorean and Canadian health researchers (Spiegel et al. 2011), and tapped the expertise of researchers from the social science, the humanities, and arts education Conducted over an almost five-year period, this study built on social circus research in Quebec (Spiegel et al. 2014; Spiegel and Parent 2016, 2017), and the expertise of community artists, including co-editor Benjamin Ortiz Choukroun. Ortiz had trained instructors in Circo Social Tena (one of the the municipal programs of Circo Social Ecuador) in 2012 and had been the pedagogical director of Circo Social Ecuador for five months in 2013, as well as a trainer with Cirque du Monde (ongoing).

Our qualitative data-gathering methods centred on participant observation, attending social circus training, taking observational field notes,

Photo 2.1 Dr J. Spiegel and collaborator Julia Rodríguez discussing social circus with Quito social circus volunteer Adrián Llumipanta, during a workshop at the venue of *Circo Social Quito*, February 2015.

Photo 2.2 (*opposite, above*) Participatory observation during the planning of the research. Instructor Freddy Cercado shows a spinning exercise to Dr J. Spiegel and the group of instructors and volunteers. *Circo Social Tena*, 2013.

Photo 2.3 (*opposite, below*) Researcher Dr Arturo Campaña sharing the methods and preliminary results of the study with social circus instructors from across Ecuador gathered in the cultural centre La Voladora, Urcuquí, February 2017.

and participating in workshops and informal discussions with participants and instructors to understand their experiences – their concerns, their joys, and the challenges they faced. Confidential interviews were also held with volunteers and participants, as well as with current and former social workers, instructors, and coordinators, to supplement the group discussions that involved over 100 participants in various sessions. Some of these occurred spontaneously as part of other activities (see photo 2.1); some were scheduled as one-on-one interviews with participants. The programs in Tena were visited by international and Ecuadorean team members who participated in the training of volunteers (photo 2.2). The programs in Cuenca, Loja, and Quito were also visited by some of the international as well as Ecuadorean team members. Discussions were held with personnel from *Cirque du Soleil*, Ecuador's vice presidency and Ministry of Culture, as

Photo 2.4 Paula Riveros (left) and Cinthya Merizalde (right) explain the situation at *Circo Social Loja* to the research team and social circus instructors from across Ecuador at a workshop in La Voladora, Urcuquí, 2017, convened by the research team to share and discuss preliminary results.

well as municipal program directors, social workers, coordinators, and in-structors. In keeping with ethical obligations in community development and global health research (Yassi et al. 2013), and in community-artist-university partnerships more broadly (Yassi, Lockhart, et al. 2016), num-erous knowledge-sharing and debriefing meetings were held with social circus instructors, coordinators, and trainers throughout the project from the early sessions onward. The intention was not only to exchange ideas relevant to the project but also to mutually build skills in the vari-ous research techniques. One particularly important activity consisted of a three-hour session held in Yachay in 2017 in which research observations were shared with social circus volunteers and instructors (photo 2.3), and valuable feedback was received (photo 2.4). Art practitioners involved in other international arts-infused change intervention projects were also interviewed to help situate our observations and broaden the implications of this study.

Circo Social Ecuador and the municipalities hosting social circus programs were generous in sharing their documents, training materials, program plans, and information that helped us assess the extent to which the programs were meeting their goals. Government documents, including the constitution, the national development plans for 2009–13 and 2013–17, government program descriptions, the regular reports submitted to *Circo Social Ecuador* from the municipal programs, and data derived from registration records were all analyzed, along with training materials and data from instructor training and surveys provided by *Cirque du Monde* (Cirque du Monde 2013, 2014). The considerable expertise of co-editor Ortiz regarding the history of the program, its pedagogy, and the challenges it faced, greatly enriched our understanding of the nuances of each situation. We adopted a high degree of reflexivity (Rice and Ezzy 1999), well aware that research perspectives are always bound up not only with academic biographies but also with the "interpersonal, political and institutional contexts in which researchers are embedded" (Mauthner and Doucet 2003).

The quantitative component of the study consisted of a large longitudinal survey comparing results from 254 youth or young adults who were participating – or had participated – in social circus across the country, and 167 youths who were enrolled in various other community art activities in the Quito area. Questions focused on the impact of community-based creative practice on the emotional and physical wellbeing of participants, exploring constructs of personal growth (Robitschek 1998) and social inclusion (Huxley et al. 2012), as well as probing social engagement and health-related outcomes (nutrition, fitness, substance use, housing, income, etc.). We included an index of social class that had been developed by the Ecuadorean team leader (Breilh 2007; Breilh et al. 2009, 2012).

We also employed arts-based methods for studying community-based health interventions (Boydell, Gladstone, et al. 2012). Specifically, we used video, a three-day performative inquiry workshop, and a "photovoice" exercise (Wang, Cash, and Powers 2000) in which participants took photos to narrate their feelings and priorities. Indeed, following the initial feasibility work conducted in 2013 (Spiegel et al. 2015) and another set of meetings that occurred in November 2014 in Quito and Loja, the formal data-gathering phase of our work was launched via an arts-infused workshop in February 2015, which proved to be instrumental in developing a sense of collectivity as a team. For this, we adapted exercises advanced by theatre activist Augusto Boal (Boal [1985] 2008) in order to share insights with social circus participants, instructors, and other members of the social

Photo 2.5 Social circus artists and volunteers Alexander Gomez and Jorge Hidalgo experimenting with the disposable digital cameras given to them for the photovoice exercise in October 2015.

circus community in Ecuador. The photovoice exercise, conducted in October 2015, in which participants presented images that spoke to their experience and perspectives, served as a catalyst for dialogue with the group about their community, their lives, and *Circo Social*. Both workshops engaged social circus coordinators, instructors, volunteers, and participants. In keeping with the rhizomatic analogy, our process was non-linear. Methods were applied concurrently allowing the various research techniques to inform each other at multiple points through constant interaction among the researchers. No one methodology was prioritized over the others. Additionally, not only did our team members come from multiple educational backgrounds – including psychiatry, public health, drama education, sociology, dance, clowning, social theory, and art education, among others – but we conversed in three languages (English, French, and Spanish), creating a multiplicity that itself added richness to the insights developed.

Deleuze and Guattari (1987) claim that *arborescent* thinking results in false multiplicities, as all variations are branches from a single trunk and fundamentally are not different. True multiplicities are *rhizomatic* – with no points or positions but only lines that allow for proliferations in all directions to form an assemblage. There is no clear hierarchical structure or order (Sermijn et al. 2008), no centre. The survey, the ethnographic study, the pedagogical examination, the arts-based inquiry, the discourse analysis of social circus in its historical and political context – all informed the whole. Each technique ceased to exist as a singular method and instead came together with other techniques to form something new. We view this research as an assemblage that increased in dimensions of multiplicity and changed its nature as it expanded connections.

Connection and Heterogeneity: Knowing the Elephant

A group of blind men heard that a strange animal, called an elephant, had been brought to the town, but none of them were aware of its shape and form. Out of curiosity, they said: "We must inspect and know it by touch, of which we are capable." So, they sought it out, and when they found it they groped about it. The first person, whose hand landed on the trunk, said "This being is like a thick snake." For another one whose hand reached its ear, it seemed like a kind of fan. Another person, whose hand was upon its leg, said, the elephant is a pillar like a tree-trunk. The blind man who placed his hand upon its side said, "elephant is a wall." Yet another, who felt its tail, described it as a rope. The last felt its tusk, stating the elephant is that which is hard, smooth and like a spear.

Parable found in Buddhist text Udana 6.4,
dated to mid first millennium BCE

According to the parable of the blind men and the elephant (see figure 2.1), people have a tendency to project their partial experiences as the whole truth, ignoring other people's partial experiences (Goldstein 2010). In the rhizome, each point can and does connect to all others, regardless of how divergent these points may seem, which is why Deleuze and Guattari link these two characteristics most directly. The principles of connection and heterogeneity stress awareness of different disciplines and positionalities with their underlying ideological, ontological, epistemological, and methodological underpinnings – their values, their experiences, their knowledge systems, and their research techniques. These characteristics are apparent in this book; the chapters intersect with all other chapters in numerous

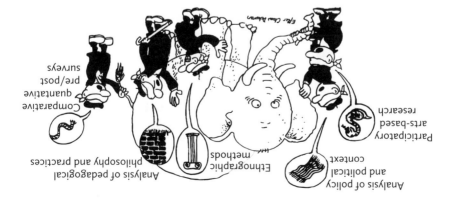

Figure 2.1 The parable of the elephant and the blind men

different ways, while also contributing new material and perspectives to the whole.

Our research team was acutely aware that we were operating under conditions often portrayed in the literature as dualistic – along the lines of the following binaries – academia/community, qualitative experiential/quantitative-data-based, North/South, theory/practice, privileged/marginalized (Christensen and Dahl 1997). Disconnectedness also characterizes the way many mainstream health researchers examine the social determinants of health, approaching "individual risk factors" as if they are independent of each other. The rhizome connects all these dualisms and disconnections to reveal their similar roots (Fornssler et al. 2014). Applying this metaphor to our work, we note that our Ecuadorean co-editor, a circus artist himself (a clown, to be more precise) works not only as a social circus instructor, trainer, and pedagogical director, but is also head of the network of social circus groups in Ecuador. His role as a co-editor along with lead editor, a Canadian critical theorist who also has experience as a circus artist as well as social circus researcher and instructor, epitomizes the blending of community-university and North-South perspectives. Through the process of working together, the two editors found their common vision for this book and for a Spanish-language companion resource (Spiegel et al., forthcoming). Similarly, an Ecuadorean psychiatrist and expert in community mental health, trained in quantitative research methods, co-authored the survey component of this study along with a Canadian population health researcher. The two also played a major role in presenting Ecuador's historical and social policy context, combining the

literature from Latin America with that from the English-speaking world. By crossing the North-South divide, and also disciplinary divides, a unified way forward was shaped.

These connections were particularly valuable in allowing our heterogeneous methods to inform each other. For example, at the opening exercise in our three-day arts-based workshop, participants were asked to offer a single word that described social circus for them. Responses included: "team," "emotion," "heart," "body," "effort," "sovereignty," "work," "effort," "structure," "movement," "family," "emotion," "hug," "solidarity," "touch," and "love" (as described in chapter 5). This embodied exercise from the arts world connected directly with one of the questions on the quantitative health survey (described in chapter 6), in which participants were asked to identify single words. In the same way, we were able to merge observations about the importance of Indigenous heritage that we gleaned from reviewing government documents and interviewing ministry personnel with the insights provided by participants in the photovoice exercise. And questionnaire results were interpreted very much in conjunction with what was learned from interviews and pedagogical analysis.

In the formal interviews conducted explicitly for this chapter, several individuals stated that they witnessed unexpected connections through the heterogeneity that characterized this project. One team member noted that through this process, he acquired a profound understanding that there are diverse ways in which health and wellbeing can be conceptualized – just as there are diverse interpretations of *Buen Vivir*. Conversely, some of the insights derived from social circus pedagogy and practice have now been embraced in community-based projects by team members previously unfamiliar with these concepts. And certainly, the sophisticated social theory on health conveyed by Ecuadorean teammates have strengthened the research and teaching surrounding population health in the Global North. The dialectical processes characterizing our interdisciplinary, community-university, and North-South interactions go hand in hand with appreciating the link between connection and heterogeneity.

Asignifying Rupture: Negotiating the Tensions to Move Forward

Each team member came to the project equipped with their own distinct world view, ways of knowing, and beliefs about "best practice" in research methodology, as well as methods of expressing these. As one team member stated, "We are using different language to talk about the same thing and

the same language to talk about different things." Just as the rhizome may become broken or disrupted at any given place, as it regrows on one of its own lines or on new lines, so did our research. Divergent beliefs at times caused ruptures in our collectivity, which were then repaired and eventually, after much dialogue and sharing of viewpoints, grew into new avenues. A poignant example of asignifying rupture occurred when our Canadian epidemiologist suggested conducting a "cross-over cluster randomized controlled trial" wherein municipalities and foundations would randomly allocate half of the target population who came forward to enroll in *Circo Social Ecuador* now and some would start late. The expectation was that randomizing would eliminate some of the biases that may arise in comparative studies when people self-select to join a specific program. While such randomization is considered the "gold standard" of health evaluation research (Barton 2000), the concern was raised that if the research team ran a social circus program as an intervention trial, it would no longer be *Circo Social Ecuador* but we were studying a social circus program designed and funded by researchers from the Global North. Further concerns were identified regarding imposing a program designed as a study funded from the Global North, as well as the research team's ability to ensure quality instruction, install secure equipment, and be responsible for the safe environment that is essential in social circus (see chapter 4 for a discussion of the pedagogical complexities). Finally, there were concerns about the sustainability of programs launched as part of a research project – and the ethics of doing so (Yassi et al. 2013). While there is certainly a role for *intervention studies* related to social circus – as was demonstrated by Loiselle (2015) in conducting a trial social circus project with children with disabilities in Montreal – the applicability of this design depends entirely on the research question being posed.

This debate over study design revealed different conceptions of the objective of the study: Was it to explore how a community art program could catalyze social transformation? Was it how "social circus" could be used as a pedagogical tool? Was it whether social circus has superior impact compared to other arts-based activities? Or was it to study *Circo Social Ecuador* in its historical and political setting? Harkening back to the realization that ongoing health promotion interventions should be examined in their social context (Poland et al. 2008), the team concluded that the main focus of the study ought to be *Circo Social Ecuador*, not an idealized acontextual intervention. We came to agree that a well-theorized mixed methods approach was a better alternative to a controlled intervention study (Grossman and Mackenzie 2005).

The identification of cracks and fissures in our process, the need to begin with the lived experience respecting and enlarging "the space of opportunity" and appreciating the "unexpected connections" was stressed by one team member. Another team member insisted that "mixed methods can indeed be used, with the caveat that the epistemologies have to be in conversation with each other." Reminding us that while we cannot take numbers at face value, that does not mean that we cannot use numbers, she stressed that "we need to use all the data but approach the interpretation critically and realize that things are more nuanced." The need to become "a professional rebel" was identified in order to "break those boundaries" with respect to what is often considered "legitimate research," particularly within the field of health research, where randomized controlled trials are too frequently placed at the top of the research hierarchy, with arts-based methods at the bottom (Boydell et al. 2016). Echoing other researchers (Matarasso 1997; Matarasso 2003; Newman et al. 2003; Goldenberg 2006; Stein and Faigin 2015), we note that prioritizing quantitative data risks reducing the import- ance of culture and contexts, albeit we acknowledge, as have other critical scholars (Galloway 2009), that community-based initiatives also benefit from "outcome measures" that have credibility with funders and decision- makers. Thus, while we reject the positivism associated with measuring predefined indicators, we strove to find a way to respond to the allure that statistical analyses bring.

The theme of "finding solutions whenever difficulties arose"– asigni- fying rupture – was also applied to the linguistic difficulties encountered, beckoning critical scrutiny to an aspect of hegemony of particular interest to Gramsci: the hegemony of language (Ives 2004). Language politics fig- ured prominently as an ongoing challenge, with several layers of difficul- ties. The first language of several team members is Spanish; for others it is English; and, for five of the seven main researchers, French is a second lan- guage. Some members conversed across two or all three of the languages, while others did not. Knowing that literal translation often fails to pick up nuances, some team members were concerned that the right words were not available in the translations they were receiving, and feared that this might result in miscommunication.

We noted that rather than a linguistics problem, the disconnect was often a cultural one. Individuals thought they were speaking the same lan- guage; however, different cultures sometimes made team members feel that there were communication barriers. An Ecuadorean team member further remarked on the diversity within Ecuador itself – that "there is a great deal of ethnic diversity ... even people who live here cannot know the

country." Similarly, incorporating visual ways of knowing where, as a researcher reflected, "[language] was not an issue all that much, because what we did was through the body," became an incisive way of crossing geo-cultural divides.

Cartography and Decalcomania: Charting New Paths as New Insight Arose

Hierarchical thinking traces a pattern onto reality, overpowering points to fit the tracing and discarding or criticizing points that fail to fit the pattern. In contrast, *rhizomatic* thinking allows the structure and pattern of reality to emerge through interaction and testing of reality, accepting all points as part of the pattern. Deleuze and Guattari group cartography and decalcomania together because both characteristics relate to structure or a network of pathways through the rhizome. Hamon (2010) explains Deleuze-Guattarian cartography as "the method of mapping for orientation from any point of entry" and decalcomania as "a method of forming through continuous negotiation with its context, constantly adapting by experimentation, thus performing a non-symmetrical active resistance against rigid organization and restriction." Decalcomania allows for new patterns in our thinking and actions precisely because a rhizome is a "map and not a tracing" (Daskalaki and Mould 2013).

In our research, this was reflected in having to decide where to conduct various activities, and having to adapt when the geographical plans were not working out as originally anticipated. We initially intended to hold the photovoice workshop in Loja, in accordance with the interests of the local social circus coordinator and the volunteers in that city (many of whom were university students), as well as the support of an associate of the co-ordinator at the University of Loja. However, the situation changed: the colleague left her university post, and the coordinator left the Loja program. We therefore decided to conduct the photovoice exercise in Quito instead. This turned out to have the advantage of enlisting participants and volunteers whose socioeconomic background was closer to that of the majority of social circus youth. More of the Quito workshop participants were street-involved youth than would have been the case had we conducted the exercise with staff and volunteers from the Loja program.

These two principles of cartography and decalcomania address the practical problem of placing ourselves within a rhizomatic structure and negotiating opportunities from wherever we happen to enter. Indeed, we added

the photovoice approach to our study methods only after ascertaining that social circus participants wanted to pursue the technique. These principles allow for the following of leads that emerge from the data – not only with respect to snowball sampling as an approach to interviews but also with respect to clarifying data by circling back to seek more information when needed. When the analysis of the quantitative data revealed that two of the comparison group activities – parkour and capoeira – showed results that resembled the outcomes in the strongest social circus program (see chapter 6), two members of the team re-interviewed the director of the youth programs to seek possible explanations. These principles mean being open to go where the data leads, sometimes quite literally.

Along with most others interviewed, Ecuadorean social art expert Clara Buchel spoke emphatically about the need for Northern researchers to consult with, and depend on, local expertise. Buchel argued that "de-spite best intentions, there is insufficient knowledge about how processes in the South work, and this can lead to less local motivation [on the part of Southern researchers] to participate." Northern team members were always acutely aware of the need for ongoing consultation with Southern counterparts. But, we note, the key issue here goes far beyond understand-ing the local realities. Conventional thinking often fails to be critical in its application of theoretical and epistemological framings that dominate in Northern settings. This inadequacy often results in devaluing the rich critical understandings that have emerged in the Global South (Spiegel et al. 2015). Ecuadorean team director Breilh noted: "In this case, in the project that we are working on together, we have been quite respectful in our objectives. Different perspectives have strengthened the project rather than weakened it and this does not always happen, you know. The North often wants to impose things."

The construction of non-academic (including ancestral) knowledge is typically not well understood in academia and this may lead to (mis)read-ings of a situation. The Ecuadoreans on the team noted that due to histor-ical inequities, it is very difficult for people in the South to establish trust in the North, "especially with academics." We were able to move forward only by recognizing that our endeavour was not to seek some universalizing truth about *Circo Social Ecuador*, but rather to chart new ways of thinking and doing that may encourage possibilities for social transformation.

The diverse ways of approaching time frames by various participants was another issue that required rhizomatic thinking. From one perspec-tive, academic research often seems rushed, seemingly oblivious to the

time needed for social processes to transpire. From another perspective – or a different point in the rhizome – the lengthy delay in releasing research products is problematic for those hoping to apply the study results in their own decision-making.

Towards "Collective Becoming"

Rhizoanalysis dissolves dualisms in favour of multiplicity (Masny 2016). Because it is conceptualized as relational, it allows creativity, connection, experimentation, and multiplicity in thinking to flourish (Fornssler et al. 2014). Rhizomatic analysis allowed us to view the positions and relations of researchers and participants not as *beings* but as *becomings* and assemblages, in movement and in constant flux rather than fixed. This allows us to give attention to what Deleuze and Guattari refer to as "lines of flight," connoting opportunities to foster alternative ways of thinking, and seeing unexpected potential to lead to new assemblages. The metaphor of a rhizome offers a framework for studying how the social circus movement in Ecuador promotes health and social transformation. And, we contend, it is applicable to gaining insights on the potential health and social justice benefits associated with community-based arts programs more generally. We further argue that this framing could be particularly useful for inter-disciplinary teams merging epistemologies and ontologies across disci-plines and cultures. Applying a rhizoanalysis, as we have done, allows us to attend to the intertwining features of knowledge, culture, attitudes, and values (Tillmanns et al. 2014, 6). As Tanja Tillmanns and colleagues note: "the rhizomatic perception of reality offered by Deleuze and Guattari is ... a viable alternative to more traditional, arborescent modes of conceiving and understanding our world" (6).

As discussed above, we sought to apply the principles of PAR, and indeed of all community-based participatory research (CBPR) in our methodological approach: co-learning characterized our research process as researchers interacted with social circus participants, instructors, coordinators, muni-cipal officials, national policy-makers, and international funders (including *Cirque du Soleil*). Several workshops served as sites of encounter, provid-ing a space for sharing and problematizing research techniques, modes of study, and ways of developing and experiencing praxis. While these efforts contributed to our quest for collectivity, the institutional hierarchies of knowledge, the ways they continue to stratify social and professional par-ticipation, and the complexity of overcoming colonial dynamics was, how-

ever, omnipresent. Those from *Circo Social Ecuador* noted that they felt "honoured" that a mainstream health-research funder in North America would view the Global South as important enough to study. We see this sentiment as at once gesturing toward a historical – and ongoing – global power dynamic, as well as a hope that transformations in this dynamic are underway. The desire of participants to receive certification for the learning acquired during the arts-based workshops highlighted this hier-archy. The research team, of course, happily provided such a certificate, with university logos from both the Ecuadorean and Canadian universities involved in the study. Nevertheless, we are cognizant of the colonial leg-acies that sanction some holders of knowledge as positioned to certify the learning of others (Meyerhoff and Noterman 2017). And we appreciate the irony of one group certifying another in situations where multi-directional learning is in fact taking place. We also reflect on the *Buen Vivir* paradox, noting that in its attempt to move the Ecuadorean economy from a re-source extraction-base, the Ecuadorean government has been formalizing sectors, including knowledge production, such that certification and aca-demic credentials are increasingly encouraged if not required.

Our study heeds the warning: "When art activities are framed in terms of their capacity to 'fix' the 'problems' of people identified by the dominant culture as 'deficient' or 'at risk', there is the danger that the arts simply be-come an instrument for perpetuating oppression and the status quo" (Stein and Faigin 2015, 72). This caution applies to *designing* community art pro-grams as well as to the research approach in *studying* the impact of these collective creative endeavours. While various epistemological and meth-odological approaches contribute to a fuller understanding, this is not to say that all are compatible. With our different cultures and disciplinary backgrounds, what was essential for successful collaboration was 1) a will-ingness to identify underlying principles and respect the different ways in which our research combined to elucidate the cultural, social, and political stakes of community-based practice, as well as 2) a shared commitment to adopt an "emancipatory" and inclusive approach to understanding impacts and processes at the individual and collective levels.

Some are reticent to characterize our approach as a methodology, but rather, in keeping with the nature of Cultural Studies, "a voyage of discovery,' a journey which itself produces the terrain it maps" (O'Sullivan 2002). Deleuze (1990; 1995), in writing about what his students took from his courses, explains that "nobody took in everything, but everyone took what they needed or wanted, what they could use" (139). We hope that this

chapter has generated new insight regarding how to navigate the complexities of working interculturally, transdisciplinarily, and globally when considering the power of community arts to promote social transformation. In addition to providing readers with the rich details of how we conducted this case study of *Circo Social Ecuador*, and in drawing lessons applicable to "arts for social change" more generally, we trust that we have also contributed a critical rhizomatic multi-methods approach that others can apply when undertaking community-driven-solidarity-engaged research.

We therefore conclude by asking you, the readers, to consider avoiding the quest for a singular meaning from this book. While the multiplicity and connectiveness of the chapters suggest the desirability of reading the book from beginning to end, in the spirit of Deleuze and Guattari, feel free to skip around – read some chapters and not others, go back and read some more deeply, and take from this book that which you find useful. Ask yourselves: What new perceptions does it open up? And what new possibilities for social transformation does this book catalyze?

3

Cultural Policy and the *Buen Vivir* Debate: Politics of Transition and the Development of *Circo Social Ecuador*

JENNIFER BETH SPIEGEL, BENJAMIN ORTIZ
CHOUKROUN, ARTURO CAMPAÑA, AND
ANNALEE YASSI

The word "transition" implies progressive movement. Transition implies temporary movement towards something, but is not a goal in itself. Any social, economic or cultural transformation requires a transition. Otherwise, it would be necessary to destroy everything and start from scratch. Without a transition, a transformation is very costly and too painful. To achieve the Socialism of Good Living – especially in a society with a neoliberal past – preliminary steps must be taken to start the transition. This is not just a question of changing production relationships, but mainly to change the ways that citizens think.

Constitución de la República del Ecuador 2008, 18

The first decade of the twenty-first century was dubbed a new dawn for Latin America (Yates and Bakker 2013). Raphael Correa, like Evo Morales in Bolivia, was elected in the wake of anti-neoliberal sentiment that emerged from the structural adjustment monetary policies of the 1990s. Correa, like Morales, pledged a form of "communitarian socialism." Escobar (2010), resonating with many other commentators, wrote that this was the "end of the long neoliberal night" and, as noted by Yates and Bakker, many scholars (Hammond 2003; Munck 2003; French and Fortes 2005) – echoing alter-globalization activists from the early days of this post-neoliberal trend – raved that this new "pink tide" demonstrated that "another world is possible."

Amidst this fervour, Ecuador's national social circus program – *Circo Social Ecuador* [1] – was launched as one branch of a multifaceted plan to implement a new vision, grounded in social, cultural, and economic trans-formation. It was an ambitious plan based on bringing together youth living in precarious conditions and heightening a set of skills already present amongst those earning cash juggling at streetlights. Through an intricate multi-staged program, these youth were to be offered a socially oriented training leading to greater social engagement, a strengthening of national identity, and even a bolstering of social movements as such. To be realized, however, multiple partners would have to participate in the "transition." *How* to transition, *who* should lead it, and *what*, ultimately, to transition *toward*, left much room for equivocation.

The use of arts to "*start the transition ... to change the ways that citizens think*" – as it was put in the constitution – is certainly not new. Around the world, cultural policy has shifted in response to changes in government and political climates (Ahearne 2006; Kiwan 2007; Zorba 2009; Chaney 2015). Even the use of circus arts for political purposes has its precedents. When the Chinese Communist Party founded the People's Republic of China in late 1949, it used circus "to promote socialist values and morals" (Zhang 2016). Zhang notes that between 1950 and 1966 acrobats in China became "revolutionary cultural workers ... dressing as peasants, workers, athletes, soldiers ... incorporating into their acts plain-looking bowls, plates, chairs, bicycles, and other objects that working-class people use in their daily lives ... producing shows such as the acrobatic musical *Long Live! The Cultural Revolution of the Proletariat.*"

In his article "New Models of Cultural Policy in Latin America: A Com-parative Analysis (2000–2014)," Cecchi noted that, in the first decade of the twenty-first century, the cultural field received more government attention in Latin American countries that had "reconstructed" themselves by rec-ognizing their multiethnic and pluricultural identities. He notes that in a context of marked political and economic change, political decisions about how cultural policies are implemented can open possibilities "for social in-clusion and mutual recognition, and finally also extending the margins of citizenship" (15). Ecuador, like Venezuela and Bolivia, saw culture elevated to a constitutional right, with correspondingly large increases in govern-ment spending.

Much of this transformation in policy involved participatory practices that would alter the landscape of who participates in cultural production. Ecuador appeared to be following in the footsteps of European govern-ments such as Finland that were generously funding social circus, includ-

ing the integration of new immigrant youth, people with physical disabilities, and other marginalized communities (Purovaara and Lakso 2015; CircusInfo Finland 2017). Nevertheless, the level of investment in social circus by the Republic of Ecuador was well beyond what had been seen anywhere in the world, particular for a country of comparable gross domestic product (GDP).

Cultural policies that focus on "participatory" arts have occasioned much political debate in recent years. Notably, as pointed out by Scotland-based scholar Jonathan Price, echoing others (Jancovich 2011; Hewison 2014; Matarasso 2015), participatory arts policy in the United Kingdom between 1997–2010 provided a "positive ethical charge as an essential component of cultural democracy" employed "in ever more diverse contexts in pursuit of social, economic, educational or therapeutic benefits" (Price 2015, 7). However, this policy remained neo-liberal, ultimately focusing on economic goals despite its strong participatory and social engagement agenda (Hesmondhalgh et al. 2015). Indeed, after several decades of international programming, many now argue that "participation" has become a "neoliberal buzzword" (Leol 2007). Theorists have noted that participatory community arts programming is being used as an expedience to generate social cohesion and encourage social inclusion precisely to avoid having to tackle deep structural issues concerning equitable modes of production (Bishop 2012; Haiven 2017). Debates about the political instrumentalization and indeed "commodification" of community arts (Gray 2007), the meaning of cultural democracy, and the response of artists and activists worldwide are longstanding.

In light of these arguments, this chapter asks: How did Ecuador's national social circus program reflect the politics and policies that had been adopted in the wake of the election and, in particular, how did its declared "politics of transition" away from neoliberalism play out in the evolution of the program? To address this question, we begin by discussing the goals and context of the *Buen Vivir* policy itself. We then proceed to detail the context, implementation, and evolution of the social circus program.

Buen Vivir and Its Relationship to *Circo Social Ecuador*

In the absence of deep cultural and anthropological changes in relation
to the articulations of desire and belief, the transition to *any* alternative
politics will remain an ideal. After all, socialism is not all about changing
the relations of production, but primarily the citizenship's mentality.

SENPLADES (*Secretaria Nacional de Planificación y Desarrollo*) *2013*,
11, as translated and cited by Gonzáles and Vázquez 2015

In history we were conquered, we also had bad governments that
suppressed communities ... By revitalizing the interior, spiritual part
of a person, as with social circus, we can start to work from the inside,
improve self-esteem ... have an Ecuadorean point of view not from
a submissive stance but from a position of being able and capable of
creating and proposing new ideas and change.

Official from the Ministry of Culture and Heritage, November 2014

The government elected in 2006 in Ecuador brought in a new constitution that aimed to "articulate the struggle for social justice, equality, and
the abolition of privileges with the construction of a society that respected
diversity and nature" (Government of Ecuador 2008). In what it called a
"Citizens' Revolution," the new constitution proposed *Buen Vivir* – which
has been translated in English as "good living or living fully" (Dávalos 2014),
or "better living" (Walsh 2010) – as the guiding principle of the new society.
Brought in as part of its *Buen Vivir* plan, *Circo Social Ecuador* was a program
designed to catalyze the desired "change in mentality" so as to actualize
this philosophy of the revolution. As Walsh explained, "the incorporation
of *Buen Vivir* ... responds to the urgency of a radically different social contract that presents alternatives to capitalism and the culture of death of its
neoliberal and development project" (Walsh 2010).

The concept of *Buen Vivir* has, however, attracted considerable debate
among researchers and social activists both within and far beyond the
Andean region. Some scholars have characterized *Buen Vivir* as an original
concept of development built on fundamentally different values (Gudynas
and Acosta 2011; Falconí 2013). Others, including Walsh (2010), noted that
beneath the radical discourse, in its *realization* it bears much resemblance
to other concepts of development that emerged since the 1990s. Walsh
describes a European model of what she calls "functional interculturalism and development" as "a way to replace the multicultural hegemony
of US neo-liberal development policy." Referring to an alliance among the
European Union, the Economic Commission of Latin America, and various international financial institutions, she argues that the real agenda of
positing "integral sustainable human development as a regional, national,
and even 'revolutionary' alternative" is actually the re-colonization of
lands, territories and their natural resources by means of new programs
of education and development.

Harkening to Eduardo Galeano's famous allusion to the importance
of a horizon to inspire Latin Americans to "keep on walking" (Galeano
1973), Ecuador's *2013–2017 National Development Plan* stated: "*Buen Vivir*

is our horizon" (Secretaria Nacional de Planificación y Desarrollo 2013, 22). This horizon, however, was vast, and left much room for interpretation. "As a mobilizing utopia, *Buen Vivir* provides social cohesion and a collective identity, for it uses an inclusive language with which (almost) everyone can identify. Though it cannot be attributed to a single social class or ethnic group, it certainly reflects the aspiration of various groups, a fact that played a fundamental role in the constituent process and the re-founding of the state" (Caria and Dominguez 2016). The historical context and the complementary movements that converged to create the social policy from which *Circo Social Ecuador* emerged included the worldwide urban academic thinking that brought renewed ideas of change, of rights, of the role of the state in social management, and of a different paradigm on healthy ways of living (Hancock and Duhl 1986; Braveman and Gruskin 2003; Krieger 2005; Birn 2009; Guzmán 2009; Navarro 2009; Krieger et al. 2010; ALAMES 2011; Breilh 2011, 2012). However, it also was very much linked with the emergence of the Ecuadorean Indigenous movement that, since the 1980s, increasingly staged popular uprisings, albeit mostly on a regional basis until 1986 when the *Confederation de las Nacionalidades de Indigenas del Ecuador* (Confederation of Indigenous Nationalities of Ecuador, also known as CONAIE) was created to bring together regional groups to push for Indigenous rights at the national level.[2] At the height of the movement in 1995, Indigenous activists formed the *Movimiento Unidad Plurinacional Pachakutik* (commonly referred to as *Pachakutik*) to actively participate in the electoral process. Although highly successful in the 1996 elections, a series of less successful subsequent outcomes and controversial decisions that splintered the *Pachakutik* party led the movement to focus instead on bringing Rafael Correa's *Alianza Pais* party to power in 2006.[3]

The rallying of Indigenous peoples in Ecuador around the *Pachakutik* since the beginning of the 1990s constituted an unprecedented movement to incorporate ancestral Indigenous perspectives in national politics. *Pachakutik* is translated as "return of the good times," implying a symbolic call not so much to return to the past but to recover the notion of *Sumak Kawsay* (loosely *Buen Vivir* in Spanish, or "Good Living" in English) – the ethical principle that guided the behaviour of the ancestors (Freidenberg and Alcantara Saez 2001).

While, as Freeman (2016) has pointed out, Indigenous cultures and histories in the region are vastly diverse, CONAIE emphasizes the importance of recognizing commonalities. *Abya Yala*, a Kuna term for the American continent stretching from the North American arctic to Patagonia, was employed to cultivate a sense of unity between tribes and reclaim the continent as Indigenous.[4] Commonly cited core values in this context include a reverence for the natural world, respect for past generations, strong sense of community, a nonlinear concept of time, and the value of harmony and balance (Brysk 2000, 56–7).

In understanding the importance of the values that underpinned the *Buen Vivir* discourse, the history of colonization figured prominently. For thousands of years these communities were nomadic, and the concept of private property was alien to them. As the population grew and family units formed tribes, skirmishes did occur, but communal work and cooperation continued to create spiritual life and culture – language, knowledge, customs, traditions, etc. – based on common interests. The invasion of the Incas that began in 1457 secured their conquest of local tribes largely by appealing to strategies of *Nunay* (trust and mutual love), *Yachay* (sharing knowledge and learning), and *Ruray* (working together). Rather than widespread dispossession and devastation, the Inca Empire was characterized more as cultural and economic amalgamation and adherence to the rules of community life and cooperation. This sharply contrasted with the 290 years of Spanish conquest that began in 1532, which they characterize as: appropriation of land, natural resources, and products of the pre-Colombian culture; religious persecution, imposition of Catholic beliefs, denial of ancestral culture and destruction of community life forms; and slavish exploitation of human labour (Instituto de Investigaciones Económicas UCE 1975; Cueva 1979; Velasco 1981; CONAIE 1990; Guerra Vilaboy 2006).

The recognition of Indigenous peoples as nations, the multicultural nature of the state, and the incorporation of "collective rights" in the 2008 constitution were important achievements built on years of Indigenous activism (see photo 3.1). While CONAIE's proposed wording was not adopted in its entirety, as discussed by Freeman (2016), the constitutional assembly did incorporate the term "plurinational," characterizing the state as "social, democratic, sovereign, independent, unitary, intercultural, plurinational and secular" (Government of Ecuador 2008). After Correa's 2009 re-election, Becker (2012) explains, Indigenous groups criticized Correa for his "petro populism," according to which he allowed oil extraction and mining in Indigenous territories in order to fund new social programs.

In the wake of disappointment with government policies, the Indigenous movement in Ecuador emphasized community development over political participation, in some cases even advocating "refusal to participate" in state sponsored initiatives.[5] From this perspective, the main question

Photo 3.1 Protest led by Marlon Santi, president of Ecuador's Indigenous National Confederation (CONAIE) on 21 June 2010 in Quito, to celebrate twenty years since the Indigenous uprising demanding attention to the plurinational character of the country.

becomes the extent to which government policies support, divert, or function completely separately from community projects, both within and beyond Indigenous communities.

Meanwhile, the development of export trade in agricultural produce had led to considerable labour migration from the sierra to the tropical plantations and port cities of the coast. Rapid growth fostered urban settlements, often with markedly unhealthy conditions and deficient public services, poverty, social exclusion, and marginalization, particularly in youth and children. Indeed, there is little disagreement that the neoliberal free market model brought about a deep economic crisis (Carriel Mancilla 2012).[6] Shortfalls in food, housing, education, and basic social services, coupled with unemployment, labour exploitation, and racial segregation, accompanied the cultural denial that hindered development (SIISE 2000; Instituto Nacional de Estadística y Censos 2001).

Since the 1970s the Ecuadorean state, as part of a worldwide trend in global capitalism, promoted integration with production chains driven by transnational capital. During the oil boom of the 1970s, growing foreign debt accompanied transnationalization until by 1982, Ecuador could no longer meet its repayment schedule. A new debt plan had to be negotiated which was subject to the dictates of international financial institutions such as the World Bank (Latorre et al. 2015). New products such as cut flowers and shrimp were also introduced for export, bringing an additional influx of transnational agribusiness whose financing was often accompanied by conditions imposed by international financial institutions and aid agencies (Robinson 2008).

As discussed by Latorre et al. (2015), Ecuador's neoliberal agenda led to great social unrest and political volatility, with the presidency changing hands ten times in twenty-four years – three times directly because of mobilizations led by the Indigenous movement. Finally in 2006, after more than a decade of intense political and economic instability, economic crisis, and massive emigration to Europe and the United States (United Nations Population Fund 2008), the election of Rafael Correa as President of the Republic launched a period of relative stability that continued with the election in 2017 of Lenin Moreno. There was, however, fierce criticism of Correa's government, particularly its justification of extractivism on the basis of generating funds for social investment, which critics refer to as a populist neo-productivist model antithetical to *Buen Vivir* (Acosta 2011; Alberto 2016; Breilh 2017). The term for this practice – (neo)extractivism – was coined by Gudynas (2009) to refer to post-neoliberal policies of progressive governments to control the extraction of resources through renegotiating contracts, increasing taxes and export duties, and even nationalizing companies, so as to generate surplus revenue to reduce poverty, diversify local economies, enhance social inclusion, and maintain political stability. Indeed the government's economic policies, and its ability to draw from the high revenue that Ecuador was receiving from its oil exports, allowed the state to make considerable investment in infrastructure as well as social services, health, and education (Instituto Nacional de Estadísticas y Censos 2012; Becker 2013). As noted by Becker:

> Correa's successes in overcoming political instability, inequality, and a weak economy led economist Jayati Ghosh (2012) to describe Ecuador as 'the most radical and exciting place on Earth' ... In the lead-up to the February 2013 presidential elections, he [Correa] raised taxes on bank profits in order to increase bonds designed to benefit the poorest sectors of society. In addition to tripling spending on education and health care, he increased subsidies for single mothers and

small farmers. Supporters applauded the subordination of private property to the public good, and the president's social policies played very well with Ecuador's impoverished majority. (Becker 2014)

The measures implemented had obvious effects on improving quality of life, although geographic, ethnic, gender, age, and socio-economic inequities persisted, especially among the most vulnerable (Carriel Mancilla 2012). However, the extent to which these policies reflected Indigenous values was repeatedly called into question. Luis Macas, former president of CONAIE, clarifies that *Sumak Kawsay* comes from two concepts in Kichua: *Sumak* and *Kawsay*. *Sumak* means fullness or greatness; and *Kawsay* is life that is permanent yet dynamic and ever-changing, understood from a holistic perspective. In other words, according to Macas, *Sumak Kawsay* is life in its fullness, the result of interaction of all human beings and all of nature; it manifests harmony, balance internally and externally from the community – not only human, but also with nature. He argues that *Sumak Kawsay* is much more than "good living," or that which could be inferred to imply economic prosperity and comfort (Macas 2010).

Critics argue that these ancient concepts – derived from the people of *Abya Yala* and influenced as well from the descents of the African diaspora – were distorted by the Ecuadorean government's Western interpretation. Contestations related to the conceptualization and implementation of *Buen Vivir* by the state range from accusations of "manipulation of traditions" to nothing more than an idealization of the Andean cosmovision in order to appeal to the Indigenous movement (Walsh 2010). Others characterize the policies and actions of Ecuador's government with respect to *Buen Vivir* as stemming from a rather more pragmatic political orientation (Caria and Dominguez 2016), aiming to redistribute resources without antagonizing the Ecuadoran exporters, or embracing "the humaneness of socialism while pursuing the efficiency of capitalism" (Becker 2014, 132). In light of such concerns, some have advocated for an expansion of the concept of extractivism "beyond its sectorialization in raw materials" to the very notion of "development" itself (Gago and Mezzandra 205; Gago 2017), offering it as a lens through which to critique certain visions of social transformation.

As explained by Gudynas (2014), *Buen Vivir* has multiple interpretations. He notes that this term can be used in a generic sense merely to characterize alternative social projects without a fundamental challenge to the existing socioeconomic system; this could include, for example, green pedestrian zones in cities, social support policies (or, for that matter, programs such as social circus). The second way the term *Buen Vivir* can be used, he stresses, is more restrictive, consisting of a complex criticism of contemporary capitalism; without necessarily questioning the values of capitalism or the goal of economic growth, it does reflect a more equitable allocation of resources by the state. In contrast, the third and more substantive use of the term *Buen Vivir* implies a radical criticism of development and the promotion of a post-capitalist and post-socialist society. These alternatives draw not only from Indigenous knowledge but also from a fluid intercultural set of ideas that reject the notion that wellbeing depends only upon material consumption. To quote Gudynas: "It is a notion of wellbeing, or a fulfilled life, which can only be achieved by deep relationships within a community" (Gudynas 2014, 201–2).

Debates of interpretation notwithstanding, *Buen Vivir* formed the ideological basis of *Circo Social Ecuador,* where the well-being of individuals was meant to be understood as inextricably linked to collective wellbeing. Within its new social policy, the national government, at least ostensibly, sought to establish programs promoting social inclusion, solidarity, and collective values, along with perseverance and discipline – attributes that the government saw as essential for forging a new society.

The Focus on Youth in the Ecuadorean State's New Approach

Arguably the group that suffered most from the impact of the economic crisis in Ecuador had been children and youth, the vast majority of whom did not have their basic needs met (United Nations Population Fund 2008). The impacts of poverty on the mental health of children and youth were exacerbated in the decades preceding the election of the new government because of what some experts characterize as forced family disintegration (United Nations Population Fund 2008). The economic crisis led not only to massive unemployment, underemployment, income reduction, and overall deterioration of quality of life, but also an unprecedented process of emigration (Acosta 2011). Between 1999 and 2007 indeed almost one million people – 7% of the population and 14% of the workforce – left Ecuador (United Nations Population Fund 2008). Forced migration of parents in search of work devastated the social and cultural development of young people as well as their economic wellbeing.

Child labour also impacted the physical and mental development of children. According to a national survey, the percentage of boys, girls, and adolescents working in 2007 was 12.5% (Agencia publicia de noticias del Ecuador y Suramerica 2013). Several authors also pointed to worrying rates of suicide especially among female adolescents and murder among young males (Betancourt 1992; Carrión 1994; Palomeque Vallejo 2000; Barreto 2007). The fact that suicide was the second leading cause of death among youth aged 12–17 for the years 2006–10 nationally, and in half of the Ecuadorean provinces (González-Andrade et al. 2011), illustrates the gravity of the problem of depression in this age group (Campaña 2014). Also revealing is the high rate of violence between and against young people (Campaña 2014). Additionally, there was substantial use among youth of drugs and substances such as alcohol and cigarettes – also a troubling indicator with respect to the physical and mental wellbeing of youth (Inter-American Drug Abuse Control Commission 2015).

As such, rights for children and youth in Ecuador took on much more prominence with the new government, including within the constitution itself.[7] The *Plan Nacional Para el Buen Vivir* 2009–13 thus included policies focusing on social and intercultural inclusion, aiming to eradicate violence against children and adolescents and ensure their access to education. Importantly, the 2013–17 development plan also emphasized new conceptualizations that encourage citizens to constitute "a critical, entrepreneurial, creative and supportive society." As noted above with respect not only to Ecuador but also to Bolivia and Venezuela, cultural industries became fundamental in the formulation of these "pink tide" governments; the development plan explicitly promoted values "in keeping with social inclusion, self-esteem and profound collective confidence in the country" (Secretaria Nacional de Planificación y Desarrollo 2013). The bridging of social and economic objectives of cultural initiatives was thus evident. A collective ethos that, from the beginning, coupled cultural development with economic growth, rather than a radical contestation of the logic of growth itself, raised questions of what kind of "mentality" was being cultivated in the name of transition. Within this context, the implications of these policies for cultural development require careful scrutiny.

Ecuador's Radical Art and the Development of Post-Colonial, Post-Neoliberal Culture

Before the Spanish colonization, many of the Indigenous peoples of Ecuador had reached a high level of cultural development and artistic expression: music, song, dance, performance, poetry, and storytelling, as well as spirituality, were integrated into the work of sowing and harvesting, family life, ceremonial practices, and relationship with nature. Indigenous culture, in broad terms, was marked by strong community vision and collective practice in contrast to the more individualistic values brought by the colonizers.

The eradication of collective lifestyles and exalting of individualism within capitalist modes of production not only reduced the time available for spiritual and artistic cultivation but cast aside spiritually and collective creativity as irrelevant. During the colonial period, art was used as an instrument of cultural alienation by supporting the predominance of Hispanic Christian culture (Godoy 1968; Sacco 2017). It privileged the pictorial arts, creating schools that mainly focused on religious subjects and adopted Western techniques. As a result, Ecuadorean society exalted Eurocentric art and relegated Indigenous art, as well as more contemporary and counter-cultural art, to a secondary place at best. Indeed, according to Stephanie Ávalos (2012), the cultural situation of Ecuadorean society until late in the twentieth century can be characterized as a moralistic and traditionalist society that denies its roots, embodying a contradiction between the values of its Indigenous past and those left by the conquest and its religious domination. The negation of the philosophical and social principles guiding its original peoples, however, began to change dramatically with the Indigenous movements of the 1990s.

It is important to note that *Circo Social Ecuador* was not just a product of the social and Indigenous movements influencing a newly elected national government; the desire to use the arts for social benefit had been growing over the previous decades. Rising appreciation of the cosmovision of Ecuador's ancestral inhabitants combined with the quest for an escape from what was increasingly viewed as a brutally capitalist and individualist society. Aboriginal spirituality, art, and culture was in revival with contemporary painters such as those from Tigua, an Andean town in Cotopaxi. Meanwhile, the murals of Ecuadorean artists such as Jaime Andrade and Oswaldo Guayasamín, influenced by radical Mexican muralists (Acevedo 2011),[8] critically reflected upon the ruthless legacy of colonialism: the military dictatorships and the social injustice that ensued. Artistic expression viscerally spoke to this desire for social transformation (see photo 3.2), and street theatre was commonly performed in Ecuador to express political dissent (photo 3.3), as it was elsewhere in the world (Cohen-Cruz 2010, 2013; Filewood 2011; Spiegel 2016a).

Performative tactics have been widely used for protest worldwide, especially since the new social movements of the 1970s. However, as Diana

Photo 3.2 Graffiti scrawled on the wall on a street in Quito in 2013, which roughly translates as "I don't have a fucking idea of what art is for if not for provocation."

Coryat, a communications scholar at the University of the Americas in Quito notes, social movements in Ecuador still used traditional marches, road blockades, and occupations of institutions, until feminist and eco-logical movements introduced more performative elements into protests in the 1990s, especially when urban youth were mobilized (Coryat 2015, 2017). In August 2013, when Correa announced that the government would allow oil extraction in Yasum National Park, diverse movement practices extensively integrated artistic and cultural modalities. As described by Coryat (2017), the weekly *zapateadas*,[9] the concerts, art exhibits, carnivals, flash mobs, theatre, and street performances were employed to heighten popular support and the visibility of the movement.

The second half of the 1990s and beginning of the 2000s spawned an increase in socially oriented theatrical initiatives in Ecuador, including some using circus arts. While not directly employing circus techniques

Photo 3.3 Political street theatre in the historical area of Quito just prior to the election of the Correa government in 2006, illustrating artistic expression protesting government corruption.

as occurred in the student movements in Colombia (King 2013), and in Quebec (Spiegel 2015a, 2016a, 2016b), these shows embraced themes related to ecological and social justice, with workshops often held in unconventional spaces – parks, plazas, beaches, and the streets of towns and cities – to attract heterogeneous populations.[10] In 2003, *Circóticos*, a group committed to social and counter-hegemonic ideals providing free shows and workshops throughout Ecuador since the late 1990s, began a project entitled *"Subamos al Sur"* (roughly translated as "Let's elevate the South" but also "Let's go up to the South" reversing the idea that the South is "lower" than the North, the classic Northern depiction). Having learned to apply a pedagogy acquired from *Circo Trunchini*, an Argentinian circus group that came to Ecuador in the early 1990s, *Circóticos* worked with street-involved children and other young people in marginalized social situations, beginning in parks in Baños and Quito on a tour that reached Argentina in 2005 (interview with Yacine Ortiz, February 2017).

While the election of a new government was key to the support that bolstered social circus, it is important to recognize that circus was already being employed for empowerment and social justice. From 1999 to 2009,

Photo 3.4 Free circus workshop on the beach, conducted by *Circoticos* in 2004 during a circus sociocultural tour in Canoas, Ecuador.

UNICEF and *INNFA* (*Instituto Nacional de la Niñez y la Familia* – the national institute for children and families) sponsored free tours of theatrical circus works for marginalized populations, with shows conveying a social message tailored to the specific needs of each population. From 2006 to 2014, the collective, *Arte Social*, that executed these *Minga del Arte por la Vida* events, conducted a tour of *Circo por los Derechos* (Circus for Rights) with themes adapted to local contexts (interview in 2017 with Eli Benson, founder and director of Arte Social). These efforts helped popularize the notion of circus as a social tool. Meanwhile, a docu-reality program *El Circo del Semáforo* (The Circus of the Traffic Lights) was being shown on television, somewhat unfortunately, as the reality-TV aesthetic highlighted artistic competition and ambitions and downplayed the potential social value of circus art.

In 2008 and again in 2009, the *Sonrie Ecuador* (Smile Ecuador) program established by the recently elected vice president Lenin Moreno launched *Circo de la Alegria* (The Caravans of Joy) which toured to marginalized populations. In that same year, the vice presidency funded the *El Triángulo* foundation to bring together a hundred artists – all of them children, young people, and adults with disabilities[11] – to produce a show serving as a powerful vehicle of expression and enhancing wellbeing while generating respect for the capabilities of each participant. Meanwhile more initiatives were taking form and gaining strength. From 2008 to 2011, and continuing on, the collective *La Murga Papagallada* presented workshops and theatrical circus shows for marginalized populations. And *Circomunidad*, a project of the *Círculo* foundation which began in 2008 until it merged into *Primera Escuela de Circo del Ecuador* (The First Circus School of Ecuador) in 2009, offered workshops within the youth centres of Quito (the *Casa Metro* system). There it applied a pedagogy with social objectives while promoting quality technical skills and an artistic process. Like social circus, this program targeted young people from marginal urban areas, emphasized a sense of belonging to a group and the community, and used circus activities to promote collective social values (interview with Matias Belmar and official webpage: www.circulo-artescenicas.com). Thus *Circo Social Ecuador* emerged not only as an initiative by the national government but from a growing yearning for creative practice and new creative spaces for socially progressive art.

Cirque du Soleil, Corporate Citizenship, and the Role of International Partnership

The discourse of social circus, as it was framed by the government's policy, appeared to be in keeping with *Buen Vivir*. But how was the vision of social circus operationalized in Ecuador? Many of the critiques of the way in which the Ecuadorean government interpreted the *Buen Vivir* philosophy (Alonso González and Vázquez 2015; Latorre et al. 2015), can be seen to apply to the operationalization of the social circus plan.

   While the artistic expression of street-involved youth certainly seeded the program that would develop, it was the learning about *Cirque du Soleil*'s social circus program, *Cirque du Monde,* during a trip to Montreal, that led Moreno to decide to include social circus as a flagship in his cultural program, *Sonríe Ecuador*. Ecuador's national social circus program, *Circo Social Ecuador*, materialized in 2011 through an agreement between the vice president and several municipalities, followed by an accord with *Cirque du Soleil*. Moreno's words clearly summarized the purpose: "Soon, young people from the most humble neighborhoods will creatively occupy their free time, developing themselves in the circus arts, and will bring excellence to the quality of life of the community" (Ecuador Vice President 2011). Ecuador thus began a unique, publicly supported social circus program. While other programs around the world received government funding, the extent of state funding in Ecuador exceeded anything seen elsewhere (see figure 1.3). It would also constitute the Canadian-based *Cirque du Soleil's* first partnership with a national government. Given the post-neoliberal, post-colonial ambitions of the policy, the choice by the Ecuadorean government to partner with a large multinational corporation was a curious one. It was not, however, out of keeping with the overall approach of the Ecuadorean government. Walsh (2010) has pointed out the extent to which the *Buen Vivir* strategy drew on European notions of development – in particular, the fostering of social cohesion and social inclusion for the sake of individual betterment – as a means of "humanizing capitalism."

Within this process, partnerships with Northern-based corporations were plentiful. *Cirque du Soleil* was only one of many Canadian multinationals to partner with the Ecuadorean government – the others being largely from the extractive sector (Grinspun and Mills 2015). Canadian mining companies were framed by proponents of this policy as helping to provide much-needed revenue to fund social programs. The extent to which the vision of development modeled by a Canadian corporate social responsibility program could help actualize a project to transition out of colonial capitalist dynamics was hardly straightforward. Nevertheless, as the foremost funder and diffuser of social circus in the world, and given its high-profile entertainment brand, *Cirque du Soleil* had broad popular appeal. It was a choice embraced as much by the Canadian Embassy in Ecuador[12] as by the Ecuadorean media, at least at first ("Cirque Du Soleil Arrives in Ecuador" 2011). The partnership included a promise that *Cirque de Soleil* would donate consultation services for setting up Ecuador's program as well as provide training to instructors twice a year, while the Ecuadorean government was to furnish the funds for running the programs, including materials such as circus tents, instructor salaries, and costs associated with training. The corporate social responsibility model of an internationally renowned company coloured the way the program would be built, received, and ultimately unfold.

The diversity of circus arts was seen as having strong potential to "catalyze the transition" described in Ecuador's National Development Plan, by building on the qualities flagged by *Cirque du Soleil* as the target of its own social circus community development strategy – learning to juggle, clown, balance, perform acrobatics and aerials amongst other circus arts, so as to promote working together (for example to create pyramids), taking care to protect others from physical harm, and collectively telling stories through physical expression (Spiegel 2014b). In their analysis of the youth development strategy underpinning the *Cirque du Monde* programs in Mexico and Quebec, Rivard and colleagues (2010) note that social circus works may be understood by applying Hannah Arendt's thesis (Arendt 1958) that three fundamental human activities – *hard physical work* carried out in a disciplined way, *creativity* that generates pride, and *full engagement* – are needed to give rise to the transformation of individuals and the collectivity. Social circus presents the opportunity for all three. Rivard (2007) also notes the ways in which this development strategy goes beyond a representation of at-risk youth as victims who need to be protected or "saved," as well as the notion of street-involved youth as themselves constituting a risk to the stability of communities through, for instance, their alleged propensity to engage in criminal behaviour. Rather, the approach was one in keeping with an "empowerment" paradigm, whereby the talents and visions of youth could be put to work for the betterment of all.

The *Cirque du Monde* model has been used around the world, including with Indigenous youth in Canada's northern regions. Cirqlniq in Nunavik was established in 2009 to help address youth suicide, substance abuse, and domestic violence, which were significant social problems (Lavers and Burtt 2015). A study by Schwan and Lightman (2013), however, indicates that although much positive change was reported, the contrast between Western and Inuit conceptions of time, accountability, health, and community was not addressed critically enough in program design. The solution adopted was to recruit more Inuit youth as trainers; the study did not address the extent to which the model itself was an appropriate vehicle for strengthening youth in the wake of colonial institutions that had led to the devastation of Inuit culture.

As will be further discussed in chapter 4, the pedagogy used by *Cirque du Monde/Cirque du Soleil*, and subsequently by *Circo Social Ecuador*, draws from Freire's *Pedagogy of the Oppressed* and Boal's *Theatre of the Oppressed*. It focuses on using the risk-taking, trust building, and boundary-exceeding characteristics of circus to discuss broader aspects of personal and social development in the lives of participants. However, while this approach emerged as a response to oppressive structures under a right-wing dictatorship in Brazil that ultimately required both Freire and Boal to flee the country, its adoption by arts organizations internationally, particularly NGOs, has led to depoliticization. Boal himself adopted the model when he began touring in North America and Europe, shifting this approach from an examination of overt structural violence to an examination of internalized oppressive dynamics. These techniques have since been re-adapted to serve as a role-play model for police trainings (Colborn-Roxworthy 2004), as well as for sex education and sexual assault (Rodríguez et al. 2006; Belknap et al. 2013), and other social programming goals (Spiegel and Yassi 2007), with varying levels of attention played to the broader societal visions that impact the dynamics experienced, dramatized, and discussed via the art. Whereas social arts pedagogies and practices by Boal and some of his followers have served as a "rehearsal for revolution," and Indigenous song and storytelling traditions were seen as forms of radical cultural resistance in Ecuador as across the Americas (Simpson 2011), the *Cirque du Monde* pedagogy follows a softer vision of transformation in keeping with use of arts in institutionalized international development (Prendergast et al. 2009; Kester 2011; Plastow 2014, 2015). As such, the pedagogy and the principles it promotes support the individual through the collective in a manner that coexists smoothly with liberal notions of care and neoliberal notions of building survival skills, regardless of the ultimate – often dissident – vision of society that participants and instructors themselves advocate (Spiegel 2016c).

The Ecuadorean government, consistent with the approach of *Cirque du Monde*, aimed to adapt the art in keeping with the culture of each locality. However, rather than marking a fundamental change in the logic of artistic production, the implementation merely signaled an integration of local customs – songs, dance forms, etc. – into an international model. Indeed, it paralleled here the "global" aesthetic of *Cirque de Soleil* itself, famous for appropriating acts and aesthetics from around the world into a contemporary circus aesthetic (Leroux 2016). This tendency has caused the entertainment company to come under attack by Indigenous communities amongst others – most notably during its productions of *Totem* and *Toruk* (no author 2013; McAllister 2014), where placing Indigenous songs on stage was seen as reminiscent of American circus traditions of displaying Native culture as spectacle, removing cultural expression from its own logic of production.

Concerns for the ways in which international organizations, and especially corporate social responsibility programs, have interacted with social movements go far beyond arts pedagogy. Numerous scholars have critiqued the ways in which the rise of "the NGO industrial complex" has undercut radical legacies through funding social programs or campaigns that offer targeted strategies for addressing individual or community hardship while maintaining the social and production logic – and theories of change – of neoliberal society (INCITE! Women of Color Against Violence 2007).

Artists working with corporate sponsorship have often sought strategies to resist the corporate values and branding that typically accompanies the funds offered (Moll 2011). Functioning at arms-length from the sales department of *Cirque du Soleil*, those in the citizenship office of *Cirque du Soleil* maintain that their interest in aiding the development strategies – typically of global NGOs, but in this case, of the government of Ecuador – has less to do with corporate profits than with exemplifying their goal of being good corporate citizens. Ecuador, they point out, is hardly an enormous market as compared to Las Vegas, the heart of *Cirque* sales (Casadesus-Masanell and Aucoin 2009).

Indeed, *Cirque du Monde* is actually one of two not-for-profit organizations subsidized by *Cirque du Soleil*, the other being One Drop, which, according to Jacques Rajotte, former director of One Drop in Montreal, provides clean water as well as arts-based sensitization around water sanitation and conservations to over a million people in Central America, India, and Africa (interview in 2016). One Drop's operations have, however, come under scrutiny for the social dynamics governing their use of funds. A concern was expressed, for example, that its operations had only limited benefits for local populations and were instead designed to brand *Cirque du Soleil*, and its founder and former CEO, Guy Laliberté, as Northern altruists (Leroux 2012).

Though following from their traditional modus operandi of working with NGOs – originally with *Jeunesse du Monde*, and more recently, local NGOs in various countries – *Cirque du Monde* operates within a global corporate structure. *Cirque du Soleil*'s vision relies on funding from their multi-billion-dollar entertainment company. As such, despite deep pedagogical influences from the theatre and pedagogy of the oppressed traditions (further discussed in chapter 4) political principles that could contradict those of growth-oriented capitalism are de-emphasized the pedagogy they promote. Moreover, despite the stated intention of the *Cirque du Monde/Cirque du Soleil* staff to highlight social circus over professional circus ambitions, the aesthetic symbolized by *Cirque du Soleil* has become a horizon toward which young aspiring performers, and the various municipal sponsors that fund them, orient their sights.

British-based cultural theorist Clive Gray (2007), discussing tendencies in arts and cultural policies to serve as part of wider political, social, and economic objectives, argues that this "commodification of public policy" creates "the ideological conditions within which exchange-value becomes increasingly favoured over use-value." He further contends that this "serves to re-focus the attention of policy makers away from the internal detail of policy itself and towards ... commodified forms of exchange relationships and social behaviours." Was social circus veritably in contradiction to the horizon of *Buen Vivir*? Or was this simply the implicit result of a strategy that drew on international models of development while attempting to fold in various cultural – including revolutionary – discourses, values, and ideals?

All involved in realizing the vision were ostensibly committed to reconciling these tensions; the social circus project was, after all, seen as part of the new government's "cultural revolution" and presented as an integral part of the "Citizens' Revolution." Concerns raised about the appropriateness of an international model for such a postcolonial strategy were set aside with confidence that the model would be re-localized by instructors and participants. In keeping with articulation of *Cirque du Monde* goals, and bolstered by legacies of effective outreach work with youth around the world, *Circo Social Ecuador* was established specifically to create a cultural alternative for "empowering vulnerable communities; protect children and adolescents at-risk; promote social movements and a sense of cultural identity; integrate with other social projects; and develop solidarity, participation, discipline, concentration, cooperation, self-esteem, collective development and a sense of belonging, with the intent that these values will be spread throughout the country" (Programa Circo Social Ecuador 2012).

Julio Bueno, manager of the *Sonrie Ecuador*, a musician by background and the key driver of social circus, as well as Alexander Vega, member of Bueno's team in the vice presidency and later in charge of art and creativity in the *Ministerio de Cultura y Patrimonio*, stress that, from the beginning, social circus was part of Objective 1 of the 2009–13 *National Plan for Good Living* to "Sponsor equality, cohesion and social integration." Both Bueno and Vega mention that social circus was also related to Objective 2: "To improve the capacities and potentialities of citizenship," and Objective 3: "Improving the quality of life of the population." In addition, they both noted that Objective 7: "Build and strengthen public, intercultural and common meeting spaces" and Objective 8: "Affirm and strengthen national identity, the different identities, plurinationality and interculturality" (Secretaria Nacional de Planificación y Desarrollo 2009) also guide *Circo Social Ecuador* (interviews 2015).

Arturo Escobar, writing about the rise in left Latin American governments in close connection with social movements, named the evolving relationship "a state-social movement nexus" (Escobar 2010, 46). Here

Escobar highlights the importance of the ways in which the state and social movements continue to interact in orienting the direction of policy implementation. In this case, and indeed across Latin America, corporate partnerships, even corporate citizenship and NGO development strategies, further function as part of this nexus.

In keeping with *Cirque du Monde's* own mandate, the vice president considers circus arts as "an intervention for social development of people in situations of vulnerability and risk," a tool that seeks to promote participants' "self-esteem, trust in others, social skills, the spirit of citizenship, and the expression of creativity and potential" (Programa Circo Social Ecuador 2012). Additionally, the documents state that participants, by "taking up their role as citizens in the community and enriching the community by their personality, social circus acts as a powerful lever of social transformation" (Programa Circo Social Ecuador 2012). Ecuador's program aimed to: "Promote the reconstitution of a culture of respect, kindness, joy and solidarity in society through communication and development of those principles and values." It was pointed out to the research team that this aim was also consistent with Objective 5.7 of the plan, namely to "Promote interculturality and cultural policy transversely in all sectors" and Objective 5.2, to "Reverse the trend in the participation of citizens in cultural, social, sporting and community activities" (Secretaria Nacional de Planificación y Desarrollo 2009).

Circo Social Ecuador thus does not focus its attention on inclusion in the labour force or economic outcomes directly but instead emphasizes its relationship to the principles of *Buen Vivir* in its more "restrictive" if not in the transformative "substantive" sense described by Gudynas. This contrasts to other social circus programs elsewhere. For example, the partnership of *La Tarumba*, *Circo del Mundo Chile*, and *Circo Social del Sur* with the Multilateral Investment Fund of the Inter-American Development Bank and *Cirque du Soleil*, describes its program as *"an alternative to improve the employability ...* training of entrepreneurship and the development of a regional model to help lower the rate of youth unemployment in the region" (Moreno 2013). Julio Bueno emphasized in his interviews with our team in 2016 that, while the goal of *Circo Social Ecuador* includes employability, its social objectives were primary: "It also has to do with employability, but it had more to do with the social integration, social development of children and young people at risk. Our case had to do with vulnerable groups [...] Our model was designed from the vice presidency through Program 20 (Management of Smiles Ecuador); in each of the cities each team that took charge, gave it a different connotation."

To ensure the program's proper adaptation to the realities and goals of a "transitioning" Ecuadorean society, the main responsibility to get the social circus project going was given to *Fundación Circulo*, whose pedagogical director, Matías Belmar, had trained at *Circo du Mondo Chile*. Working with the vice president's office and *Cirque du Monde*, *Circulo's* training plan comprised three main components. The first consisted of national and international social circus trainers travelling to various cities in Ecuador to offer training, generally consisting of five full days. The second component, designed to follow these training sessions, rested in the hands of resident artists (a position later referred to as "pedagogical directors"). These were coordinated by *Círculo* at first, and then by the national pedagogical director hired by the vice-presidency in 2013 to replace *Circulo*. The third component was the training conducted under the auspices of each of the municipalities.

These three stages of training were carried out more or less following this plan. The organization of the program itself, however, differed markedly from the proposal advanced by *Circulo*. The vice presidency and *Cirque du Soleil* proposed that each project be led by local government through a local coordinator who would consult with a resident artist responsible to *Sonrie Ecuador* but would report directly to the municipality and ultimately to the mayor of each city. Matias Belmar made a point of stressing that decentralizing the administration of the program was not part of *Circulo's* original plan but was how the government and *Cirque du Soleil* adapted his proposal.

Notwithstanding differences with respect to local versus national governance, the plan included four main activities: *training* for instructors and volunteers; social circus workshops called *"replicas"* (signifying that these were processes of replication of the teachings acquired by instructors and volunteers); end-of-process *demonstrations*; and *open circuses*. Instructors – mostly artists with experience in pedagogy and professionals with college degrees in different areas of social work or psychology – were selected from among those who responded to the calls from the municipalities. Volunteers – mostly young people with some experience in circus arts – were also recruited; they were not paid, but were offered free training each morning in exchange for providing assistance in *replicas* in the afternoon (see photo 3.5), or at open circus events (see photo 3.6)

The cornerstone of Ecuador's social circus program – the *replicas* – includes all age groups, although the focus in most locations is on young people in situations of vulnerability, often partnering with social assistance institutions, detention centres, and/or specialized education centres.

Photo 3.5 Practicing aerial acrobatics during a *replica* at *Circo Social Loja*.

Photo 3.6 Youth volunteers working with children in an open circus event organized by *Circo Social Quito* in REMAR, a social support foundation, 2013.

The *replicas* are generally conducted at venues within these institutions or other areas suitable for training. A session consists of workshops of two-hour duration at least twice per week for three to four months.

The idea is that the *replicas* would culminate in a small presentation for family and friends, respecting the needs and the level of participants. Emphasis is therefore initially placed on group work with limited solo and duos. Gradually, though, as skill and comfort levels advanced, the demonstrations become more public, until eventually these demonstrations are open to the entire community.

In what are usually two- to four-hour events, a social circus team also offers short "open circus" workshops introducing different circus disciplines to populations of all ages, but mainly children and adolescents, in diverse venues. The participants rotate in order to sample each circus practice; generally, the events end with small artistic presentations by instructors and volunteers. Open circus sessions have diverse objectives but often are held to announce and generate interest in the classes, or to stimulate community interaction.

The balance among various activities has been a source of constant tension, reflecting the different priorities associated with different political perspectives and social groups. As will be discussed in the next chapter, in social circus it is the process that participants experience during workshops that matters most, regardless of whether they ultimately put on a show. A public "presentation" – a word preferred over "show" if it occurs at all – is performed because the resident artist, instructors, and coordinator consider it useful for the participants, after carefully considering their physical and emotional security. However, we discovered that this vision differed from what many officials (particularly at the municipal level) wanted, namely impressive spectacles mounted quickly to persuade the public that social circus would stop children and young drug addicts from begging for money in the streets and help them "integrate" into mainstream society. Given the difficult and lengthy process of achieving a proficiency in circus arts, and more importantly, given that intention of social circus to place the "social" above the "circus," this difference in expectations caused confusion as well as substantial tension.

Despite the impressive numbers of people who participated in social circus, the program came under intensive attack from media heavily controlled by right-wing interests opposed to the *Alianza País* government. In July 2016, an explosive broadcast appeared on national television and circulated on social media during the presidential election campaign of

Lenin Moreo, denouncing *Circo Social Ecuador* as symbolizing excessive government expenditure (Vision 360 2016). Notwithstanding the accuracy – or lack thereof – of some of the allegations, the media failed to clarify the intent of social circus, its scope, methodology, or vision, and instead castigated *Circo Social Ecuador* as having never materialized (Vision 360 2016). On 10 October 2017, media coverage of a report from the country's comptroller's office (covering the period from 1 January 2011 until 31 July 2016), echoed the phraseology of the TV broadcast fifteen months earlier, claiming that "the emblematic project of Lenin Moreno in the Vice Presidency of the Republic never took off." It went on to erroneously refer to the program as "creating, with state money, a series of circuses where young Ecuadorians, who juggled in the streets of the main cities of our country, would get a decent job." It stated that "more than four million dollars were allocated to project expenses. In four cities of the country one of these circuses was going to be installed: Quito, Guayaquil, Cuenca and Tena." And it wrongly claimed that that "At least twenty youngsters were going to be converted from informal street vendors to stars of international level ... with the help of one of the most prestigious circuses in the world, Cirque du Soleil (Vision 360 2016)." This mischaracterizing of *Circo Social Ecuador* as aiming to create "stars" may have been a politically motivated mockery of a flagship initiative of the new president when he was vice president. Nonetheless, it also reflected a profound misunderstanding of the vision of the sociocultural intervention and its quest to foster a different way for people to relate to each other and to the world around them.

Municipal Politics, Inter-governmental Relations, and the Politics of Changing Cultural Development Visions

Our idea from a central government perspective is not to lose the essence of social circus ... Depending on who is in charge of the [municipal] social circus [program] it can just be a local spectacle and the essence of social change could be completely lost. We must look after preventing that.

Official from the Ecuadorean Ministry of
Culture and Heritage, November 2014

In examining the social context of a program, the national policy driving its concept and design matters. However, as Poland and colleagues stress (2008), so too do the local politics and social realities that shape the actual implementation. Milz (2010) argues that insufficient critical attention is paid in the scholarly literature to subnational dimensions of cultural policy development and implementation. Within the Canadian context, out of which *Cirque du Soleil* was born and evolved, the divergent articulations of cultural policy in Quebec and Ontario are explained by reference to their different historical and linguistic traditions, infrastructural contexts, and socio-political dynamics (Gattinger and Saint-Pierre 2010). Similarly, cultural spending priorities in the Canadian provinces of Manitoba and Saskatchewan have also been attributed to their "unique demographic, historical, political, and social contexts" and to the legacy of social democracy in these provinces (Jeannotte 2010). In the same vein, the long-standing commitment to a business or entrepreneurial approach to cultural development that predated neoliberal ideology is called upon to explain cultural policy in the provinces of Nova Scotia and British Columbia (Marontate and Murray 2010).

Cirque du Soleil itself finds its roots not only in a tradition of street performance in Quebec but also in the Quebec government's promotion of cultural activities in the wake of the 1960s Quiet Revolution in that province (Leslie and Rantisi 2010). While in the early days the street aesthetic bore something of a revolutionary moment that saw a transformation in cultural policy in Quebec, by the late 1980s the vision had become mainstreamed, bolstered as much by international capitalist logic as by its early roots as radical physical street theatre (Leroux 2016). The duality within *Cirque du Soleil* – a socially minded corporate social responsibility plan alongside the for-profit art vision – foreshadowed the rifts that would reverberate across Ecuador's national-municipal social circus partnerships.

With the signing of the respective agreements of inter-institutional cooperation on 28 April 2011 *Circo Social Cuenca, Circo Social Quito, Circo Social Guayaquil,* and *Circo Social Tena* were all launched. From the beginning each local project, while taking guidance from the national government, adopted a slightly different slant, except in the case of Guayaquil, which, since mid-2012, opted to operate in a completely independent manner, disconnected (at least until 2017) from the others and rejecting the common vision. Nonetheless, in 2012, social circus projects were active in all four cities – Quito, Cuenca, Tena, and Guayaquil (Spiegel et al. 2015); Loja joined shortly thereafter. There was a steady increase in participants in the *replicas* and regular volunteer and instructor training sessions, with well over 5,200 young people having had these intensive three to four-month sessions by the end of 2016. Open Circus attendees also increased dramatically after 2012, with an estimated over 100,000 having participated in *Circo Social Ecuador* since its inception.[13]

Regardless of the large number of Ecuadoreans participating in social circus, the ongoing attacks on the program revealed a deep political divide mirroring the lack of municipal government buy-in to its socially transformative objectives. At the end of the mandate of Lenin Moreno as vice president of the Republic in 2012, *Circo Social Ecuador*, like other projects in the *Sonríe Ecuador* program, had been moved out of the purview of the vice presidency. Without the national oversight previously provided, local social circus projects became almost completely autonomous. The position of national pedagogical director ceased to exist. Initially it was thought that the municipalities would employ new pedagogical leaders, but this did not happen. Instead, the coordinators were tasked with all the functions previously assumed by pedagogical directors, diminishing oversight on social circus pedagogy. Policies also differed regarding financial compensation to instructors and/or volunteers for public performances requested by the municipalities (Spiegel et al. 2015). On 31 December 2013, the term of the agreements between the national government and the municipalities officially ended and the municipalities began to *completely* manage their own projects. Table 3.1 outlines the numbers of people who attended each of the various activities over the years.

In Quito, there were at least five different groups using the facilities, some of which perform circus shows independently of *Circo Social Quito*. It was explained to us that *Circo Social Quito* does not close its doors to these young people even if they do not consider themselves to be part of *Circo Social Quito*. Interviewees noted that the groups sometimes perform together, as they have different skills that complement each other – for example one may focus on juggling, another on aerial acrobatics. The program leaders confirmed that there is a high demand for circus presentations, so the municipality adopted this position to serve the multiple needs. At the time of writing, *Circo Social Quito* consisted of a coordinator and three circus art instructors seeking to respond to the needs, and dreams, of approximately 200 youth in the city of Quito.

In Cuenca, the original focus was on street-involved youth, but this was changed amidst conflicts regarding working conditions for youth "volunteers," some of whom felt exploited when pressured to perform or instruct without remuneration, as discussed in chapter 7. Perhaps, too, this shift may have been at least partly attributable to the fact that the strategy of "harm reduction" for marginalized youth did not sit well with the conservative values of municipal leaders. In any case, *Circo Social Cuenca*'s decision to specialize in programs for children meant that youth volunteers had to leave the program.

Table 3.1 Number of individuals involved in the different circus projects

Group and Project[1]	2011	2012	2013	2014	2015	2016	Total
Workshop participants (replicas and intensive multi-day sessions during vacation periods)							
Cuenca	40	110	200	387	396	331	1,464
Guayaquil	n.a.	18	n.a.	n.a.	n.a.	n.a.	18
Loja			400	1,807[2]	464	634	3,305
Quito	n.a.	500	540	200	264	293	1,797
Tena	40	97	128	200			465
Yachay				300	400	400	1,100
Total participants	80	725	1,268	2,894	1,524	1,658	8,194[3]
Open circus attendees							
Cuenca	332	3,225	2,000	2,094	3,288	1,404	12,343
Guayaquil	n.a.	0	n.a.	n.a.	n.a.	n.a.	0
Loja			500	230	1,000	720	2,380
Quito	n.a.	2,850	1,750	12,000	15,279	14,362	46,241
Tena	0	300	1,000	100			1,400
Yachay				100	200	200	500
Total participants	332	6,375	5,250	14,524	19,767	16,686	62,934
Audience attending demonstrations							
Cuenca	100	1,800	630	800	1,900	600	5,830
Guayaquil	n.a.	300	n.a.	n.a.	n.a.	n.a.	300
Loja			23,340	19,600	13,890	14,230	71,060
Quito	n.a.	7,700[4]	500	900	2,000	3,600	14,700
Tena	0	120	400	100			620
Yachay				400	1,000	1,200	2,600
Total participants	100	9,920	24,870	21,800	18,790	19,630	95,110

/continued

In Tena, the social circus program was going strong at the time this study began (Spiegel et al. 2015), targeting not only youth, but also people with disabilities. In addition to the training in Tena, whose population is mostly Indigenous, social circus *replicas* were conducted in more remote communities in the Amazonian jungle such as in Campococha, which hosted a continuous program for almost a year. However, outsiders – from other parts of Ecuador and Latin America – formed the instructor team, with limited participation of local (especially Indigenous) young adults to serve as volunteers. As alluded to earlier in this chapter, the political debate within the Indigenous community, in which some Indigenous leaders advocated non-participation in national multicultural programs (Freeman 2016), may

Table 3.1/continued

Group and Project[1]	2011	2012	2013	2014	2015	2016	Total
Volunteers							
Cuenca	16	16	19	0	0	8	59
Guayaquil	n.a.	0	n.a.	n.a.	n.a.	n.a.	0
Loja			13	10	5	4	32
Quito	20	20	20	10	10	8	88
Tena	0	4	4	4			8
Yachay				n.a.	n.a.	n.a.	0
Total participants	36	40	56	24	15	20	191[1]
Grand total							
Cuenca	484	5,151	2,849	3,281	5,584	2,343	19,696
Guayaquil	n.a.	318	n.a.	n.a.	n.a.	n.a.	318
Loja			24,253	21,647	15,359	15,588	76,847
Quito	n.a.	11,070	2,810	13,110	17,553	18,263	62,806
Tena	40	521	1,532	404			2,457
Yachay				800	1,600	1,800	4,200
Grand total	528	17,060	31,444	39,242	40,096	37,994	166,324

1   The data were compiled from a variety of sources, including reports submitted by municipal programs to the Ministry of Culture and interviews conducted with coordinators and instructors.

2   Loja conducted more vacation workshops and 1–2 month-long sessions than the other cities. The number of participants who participated in regular longer-term training is estimated to be 120–200 this year.

3   Many participants may have participated in multiple years, such that the total number of participants (and volunteers) may constitute an over-estimate. However, given the extensive amount of missing data, the overall totals are still likely to be large underestimates.

4   In 2012, *Circo Social Quito* performed at the largest venue in the city, with three performances, each of ~800 people, contributing to this very large number attending demonstrations.

have dampened enthusiasm for this program. Instructors also noted that Indigenous communities may not have felt comfortable welcoming urban youth to train Indigenous children. In any case, when responsibility for this program was transferred from the national government to the municipalities, this program failed to meet the logistical challenge of sending instructors deep into the jungle to reach communities. In 2014, after the election of a right-wing mayor who was focused on economic development in the region and saw little value in supporting a program associated with the more left-wing *Alianza País* (see photo 3.7), the program closed, albeit not without some resistance from social circus instructors, volunteers, and participants.

Photo 3.7 Then vice president of the Republic of Ecuador (now president) Lenin Moreno visiting youth of *Circo Social Tena,* March 2013.

In Guayaquil, the source of major opposition to Correa's *Alianza País* government, where there have been right-wing municipal governments since 1992, the program followed a distinctly different path from other social circus projects in Ecuador. From what we were able to learn,[14] the training consisted of acting classes for television, modeling courses, and performance production. Once a performance ended its run, preparation for the next show began, emphasizing product over process. The social circus volunteers and instructors who were involved at the beginning left early in the history of this program, many having since found jobs as social circus instructors in other cities.

The Loja program launched later than the others, benefitting from their experience and starting with an explicit commitment to the goals articulated by the national program. *Circo Social Loja* had the largest team of instructors despite being the smallest city with a social circus project. The team quickly began offering *replicas*, as well as renovating their municipal space for training instructors and volunteers. The fact that the instructors were artists, able to perform at various events, strengthened the program's

Photo 3.8 Three volunteers with costumes reminiscent of *Cirque du Soleil* merged with local themes and colours in a joint initiative between social circus and the clothing design department at the university in Cuenca.

visibility in the city. However, preparing and conducting these perform-ances encroached on the time instructors had for their main objective: to provide social circus workshops. A mayor was elected in 2014 who was skeptical about providing programs for marginalized youth, and by the end of 2016, a misunderstanding about a performance request from the mayor led to dismissal of the majority of instructors.

In this context of vastly divergent municipal programs, the *Ministerio de Cultura y Patrimonio,* having taken charge of social circus in Ecuador in 2014, joined with *Cirque du Monde* to create autonomous social circus training initiatives to complement the training provided by *Cirque du Monde.* The relationship between the central vision and the role of the municipalities was articulated in our meetings with ministry personnel in November 2014 as follows:

> We need to understand one thing, the social circus in Ecuador is a government project and because of the politics in Ecuador, we have a lot of changes happening ... [T]he social circus [program] starts in the [national] government, then moves to the local governments – municipalities – and they play the role of managers for their social circus projects ... Each social circus project adopts different methods in Ecuador ...What is success? To be very proud of themselves – this is the basic objective of the government, to have an identity for the community – to have really good citizens. We could have a goal of having very good artists – but we already have very good artists; if that is what we wanted, we would have had to focus on a different type of school, a national circus school or something like that.

Perhaps misunderstandings occurred because of the images of *Cirque du Soleil* seen across the country, compounded by the focus on big tents with the lavish launch (photo 3.8). Perhaps, as well, confusion about social objectives was driven by an ideology exalting individual technical excellence above the development of collective values. As one official put it, "The best thing in Ecuador is that the social circus project is still going on, with different ideologies or little budget" (interview 2015).

A New Experimental Site: Social Circus and the Corporate-State-Social Movement-Nexus

In 2014, in the spirit of corporate social responsibility, the Yachay Public Company, established as a bold – albeit much criticized (Macías Vázquez and Alonso Gonzalez 2016; Wilson and Bayón 2017) – initiative of the *Alianza Pais* government to diversify its economy, created a cultural centre called "La Voladora" in the nearby community of Urcuquí. By the end of 2016, La Voladora had offered music, dance, capoeira, and social circus to more than 500 people, mainly from the surrounding rural areas. Although the centre is publicly funded through the Yachay Corporation, it is operated independently of the Ministry of Culture and Heritage and not considered part of *Circo Social Ecuador*.

"Yachay," from the Kichwan word for knowledge, is a planned city for technological innovation and knowledge intensive businesses, which, in the words of the Correa government, was designed to "create the world-wide scientific applications necessary to achieve *Buen Vivir.*" Just as social circus is considered the flagship project of the cultural revolution proposed by the *Buen Vivir* plan, Yachay, in February 2012 was declared the "Emblematic Project of the Citizen's Revolution." However, just as concern arose that social circus is prioritizing individual achievement over collective values, critics argue that the Yachay project is leading to a new pattern of economic accumulation (Macías Vázquez and Alonso Gonzalez 2016). They contend that to reduce Ecuador's social inequalities, what is needed instead is "a model based on local knowledge and delinked from extractivist and financial economies."

Moreover, drawing on the post-developmentalism articulated by other Latin American theorists (Escobar 2005), these scholars have been calling for creating "networks" involving interaction between rural and urban, global and local sectors, arguing against the logic of building the abilities of elite actors. They insist that "knowledge production is not constrained by the logic of scarcity, but rather by all the social barriers limiting the social ability to share and exchange" (56). Indeed, in an interview in February 2017, the project leader of Yachay's social circus programs, Jairo Galindo, echoed these concerns by stressing the need to strengthen relations with the other social Ecuadorean circus projects.

The Yachay project stands as an experiment in production, away from an imperial neoliberal model toward a still evolving, much contested cultural, social, and economic development model. As such it exemplifies an experimental "corporate-state-social movement" nexus. The ways in which these three polls will interact is still very much in transition and negotiation.

National Social Circus as a Catalyst for Social Transformation?

The *Buen Vivir* policy vision is what motivated the national government to support *Circo Social Ecuador*, promoting the notion that the wellbeing of individuals is inextricably linked to group solidarity and collective wellbeing. The desire to offer participants the opportunity for professionalization and decent work was not discarded, but the focus was on personal and social development as a form of social transformation. This practical approach – socially transformative in rhetoric, but pragmatic and unchallenging in its operation – very much reflected the approach of the government overall. According to Acosta "over the grandiose speeches and offerings of radical changes, remains the ... desire not to affect the concentration of wealth. There is no transformation of the productive matrix, much less the mode of accumulation" (Acosta 2011).

While the rush to see members of marginalized communities turn into circus performers may have displayed a misunderstanding of the vision of social circus, it also reflects the tension underlying the implementation of *Buen Vivir* itself. Nonetheless, cultural production in Ecuador, as everywhere on the globe, while often bolstered or redirected by government policy, has never operated entirely within its purview. In Canada, "amateur or/and cottage-industry grass-roots activities in many ways continue to operate autonomously of cultural policy decisions – neoliberal or not – and remain important to the cultural landscapes in all of Canada's provinces" (Miltz 2010, 277). Similarly, in Ecuador, street arts and indeed social circus pedagogy continued outside the bounds of the national and municipal programs with varying levels of contact. Indeed, in 2017, there were at least five social circus programs in various parts of Ecuador that did not depend on state financing and operated autonomously from the *Circo Social Ecuador* network.

Meanwhile, instructors involved in the government program began to germinate their own visions and a network emerged. Through discussions amongst workers belonging to different projects and independent social circus professionals, the idea of creating an independent association gradually matured, nurtured by encouragement from trainers with *Cirque du Monde*. In 2015, a process was launched to work together towards the creation of what would be called – the *Tejido de Circo Social* – loosely translated as the "fabric" of social circus, with the objective of "promoting and developing social circus in Ecuador, conducting training, workshops, meetings, research and methodological documentation, to benefit, encourage, promote, disseminate and develop their practice both in the country and the region as in the rest of the world, aiming to improve society and lead to the construction of a just and creative world through horizontal work with individuals and the community."

This new stage in the development of social circus in Ecuador provided a space for meeting and dialogue, and for generating actions to encourage this creative tool of social change. The social impacts that these various programs have had in seeding social transformation will be discussed later in his book. What is certain is that the complexity of international partnerships, combined with divergences between national and municipal visions, amongst civil society, grassroots arts initiatives, and visions introduced by both the international and national corporate sector, all converged on the program. The extent toward which these programs can help effectuate a transition away from colonial and imperialist neoliberal governance remains to be seen.

NOTES

1 *Circo Social Ecuador* refers strictly to projects that were born from the initiative of the vice presidency; there have been, and currently are, other social circus projects in Ecuador unaffiliated with government initiatives.

2 While the percentage of Indigenous people in Ecuador is highly contested, it was close to 40% by CONAIE's estimate at the time of the formation of CONAIE, with Indigenous populations divided between the Pacific coastal lowlands, the Sierra highlands, and the upper east Amazon basin. The majority of Indigenous people live the highlands, grouped as "Kichwa," the largest ethno-linguistic Quechua group.

3 In its first election in 1996, Pachakutik won 20.6% of the presidential vote, with Luis Macas, the president of CONAIE at the time, becoming a national deputy in the National Assembly. Following the 2003 election, however, in which Pachakutik joined a coalition to help elect Lucio Gutierrez as president, the party began to badly splinter as Gutierrez's commitment to Indigenous needs faltered. In the 2006 election, Pachakutik gained only 2.2% of the votes, and instead brought Rafael Correa's *Alianza Pais* party to power.

4 See http://www.e-ir.info/2014/05/20/self-determination-a-perspective-from-abya-yala/. The term "Abya Yala" emerged toward the end of the 1970s. It comes from the Kuna language and means "land in its full maturity." After the Kuna won a lawsuit to stop construction of a shopping mall in Dulenega, they told a group of reporters that Abya Yala refers to the Western Hemisphere – or the Americas – in its totality. The Bolivian Aymara leader, Takir Mamani, suggested that indigenous peoples and indigenous organizations use the term "Abya Yala" in their official declarations to refer to the American continent. Since the 1980s, many indigenous activists, writers, and organizations have embraced Mamani's suggestion.

5 While some scholars and Indigenous leaders argue that protecting Indigenous rights actually necessitates "refusing to participate" in the existing political structure (Simpson 2014), and the Indigenous movement in Ecuador emphasizes community development over political participation (Freeman 2016), the Pachaktukik movement opened space for a new paradigm for the transformation of society, which was substantially incorporated into Ecuador's constitution that came into force in 2008.

6 Health spending prior to 2005 did not reach 1% as a percentage of gross domestic product (GDP) and was barely 4% as a percentage of the overall

budget; state health spending came to just $35 USD per capita annually (Carriel Mancilla 2012).

7 Article 44 of the constitution is explicit that the state, family, and society as a whole all have responsibility to ensure the growth, maturation, and deployment of the capabilities, potential, and aspirations of children and youth. It refers to the "affective-emotional and cultural needs" noting that these should be supported by both "national and local policies." Article 45 provides that children and adolescents have the right to physical and mental well-being as well as education and culture, sport and recreation, amongst other guarantees. Article 46 also provides for the special protection that the state shall guarantee to children and adolescents from situations of economic or sexual exploitation, abuse, violence, disability, use of narcotics or psychotropic drugs, alcohol, or harmful substances.

8 The Manifesto from the radical Mexican muralists – more specifically of the *Sindicato de Obreros Técnicos Pintores y Escultores* (*SOTPE*) [Technical Workers, Painters, and Sculptors Union], published in 1924 – was "as an attempt to warn the proletariat and the indigenous populations of the imminent military coup," expressed a bond with the Indigenous heritage of its society, and explicitly aimed to advance "the fundamental aesthetic objective of the times to socialize artistic expression, encouraging the total extinction of pro-middle class individualism" according to Esther Acevedo (2011). https://icaadocs.mfah.org/icaadocs/THEARCHIVE/FullRecord/tabid/88/doc/751080/language/en-US/Default.aspx.

9 *Zapateadas* refers to joyous protest events in which people bring instruments and dance in a circular motion as is the custom in Andean dance. Another meaning of the *zapateadas*, according to Coryat (2014), is the process of helping participants push through difficulties and gather strength for the struggles ahead.

10 This information was derived from interviews with individuals involved, including Matías Belmar, *Fundación Círculo*, interviewed February and June 2016; Yacine Ortiz, director of *Circóticos*, interviewed June 2016 and January 2017; Elí Benson, founder and director of *Arte Social*, interviewed March 2017; Santiago Mendiet, a member of *Circóticos* and *Arte Social*, interviewed in January 2017; and Marco Bustos, ex artistic director of the *Triángulo* foundation, also interviewed in January 2017.

11 Lenin Moreno is one of the few heads of state to use a wheelchair, having lost the use of his legs after he was shot during a robbery; his attention to the needs of disabled people has been highly acclaimed.

12 Our research team kept ongoing contact with the Canadian Embassy staff, who were enthusiastic about *Cirque du Soleil's* presence in Ecuador. Various conversations at the embassy as well as at the ambassador's residence confirmed that showcasing this Canadian import to Ecuador was a welcome

counterbalance in the face of community disquiet about the extractive sector. For more about protests against Canadian mining in Ecuador, see Velásquez TA (2011).

13 Annual numbers of instructors, volunteers, participants in *replicas* and open circus sessions, as well as demonstrations are provided and discussed in detail in *"Circo Social Ecuador: Un studio del impact sociocultural"* / *"Circo Social Ecuador: A Study of the Sociocultural Impact,"* J.B. Spiegel et al., forthcoming. More detail is also available in J.B. Spiegel et al., 2018.

14 Our investigation did not obtain the same degree of permission from the municipality of Guayaquil as we did from other municipal programs. However, we obtained information on the project's history through interviews, public documents, retrieved documents, and brief exchanges between the research team and project managers. We know that in 2016, *Circo Social Guayaquil* was interrupted with the intention of restructuring both the organization and its objectives. We also understand that the intent is for *Circo Social Guayaquil* to interact again with Ecuador's other social circus programs.

Pedagogy of *Circo Social Ecuador*: Launching the Ball

BENJAMIN ORTIZ CHOUKROUN AND LYNN FELS

Creating a human pyramid – as each one of us seeks a footing, a hand up, shifting one's balance in relation to the group – the lesson lies not in the building of the pyramid, but rather in the metaphorical implications of how individuals need to cooperate and listen to create something together. Each individual has an equally valuable role and place in the pyramid. An acrobatic exercise becomes a pedagogical opportunity for participants to work collaboratively, to learn the importance of trusting others, to experience the benefits of solidarity and the importance of communication.

Social circus – from juggling and acrobatic skills to swinging on the trapeze or seeking balance on the equilibrium wire – teaches us, through creativity, emotion, and reflection, the thousand ways that we have of achieving success on the stage and throughout our lives. Balancing on objects – a ball, a wire, a balance board – or juggling with a partner creates a relational bridge to emotional balance, calmness, and patience, while simultaneously providing a metaphor regarding the required skills of negotiation, navigation, and offering and receiving within relational and communal encounters. Thus, circus lessons are transformed into life lessons.

Welcome to the Tatami

The pedagogy and practices of social circus are as organic and flexible as the origins of social circus itself, arriving on street corners, town squares, community halls, school gyms, temporary tents, and abandoned buildings, travelling from Brazil, Romania, and Canada into Ecuador. Social circus pedagogy and practices have proven to be adaptable to different contexts and situations, and, as illustrated in the previous chapter, are often shaped by political ideologies and community expectations.

This chapter explores the philosophy, pedagogy, and practices of *Circo Social Ecuador* as understood through interviews with key people involved with Ecuador's national and local programs, with attention to *Cirque du Monde* documents, training sessions in Ecuador, and the *Circulo* foundation. Throughout, we seek to illustrate and make meaning of the pedagogical values and goals embodied through practice. We juggle language and geographical distances, engaging in an ongoing conversation with each other – Lynn, with her Canadian arts education experience, and Benjamin, first a trainer-of-trainers for *Circo Social Tena* and then national pedagogical director of *Circo Social Ecuador*. This chapter depicts our excitement at sharing ideas, listening to each other's passions and enthusiasm, and tumbling across time to find ourselves on the tatami (mats fitted together like puzzle pieces). Our chapter begins with a dialogue stitched together from many conversations as we reflect on pedagogy, what matters, and how best to practice the theories embodied within social circus.

The Conversation

LYNN: Pedagogy – you can't fake it. You have to be present and allow yourself to be vulnerable, to make mistakes, to be blindfolded and trust that the group will take care of you. That's very challenging, for many people, to let go of control ...

BENJAMIN: Because social circus pedagogy is a new pedagogy, it is difficult for instructors. Keeping that pedagogical vision – being in the moment – is always hard. Sometimes you fail and break with the pedagogy – you raise your voice or respond too suddenly with someone who is fragile. There are always flaws, but all we can do is try.

LYNN: Training, as you have told me, has to be ongoing because instructors have to hold close to their heart as well as embody the understanding of what social circus pedagogy is – which is not about achieving expertise but learning through action and reflection. Benjamin, what do instructors pay attention to when they run a social circus workshop?

BENJAMIN: From the moment instructors enter the room, to when they collectively set up the tatami and sit in the welcome circle with their participants, and throughout the workshop, they have to identify the needs and interests of the group or individuals within the group. Instructors have to be alert for moments when an individual or the group is concerned, troubled, or resistant, and if possible, adapt the content of the workshop to address these needs. And of course, after each activity, the instructors encourage discussion about the activities and what was learned, often drawing upon metaphors to apply to the participants' lives and perceptions of the society in which they live.

LYNN: Benjamin, when you were the national director of pedagogy, beyond the training done by the local directors of pedagogy every morning, and when Cirque du Monde wasn't doing their train-the-trainers sessions, how did you train your instructors?

BENJAMIN: I participated in their workshops so that I could see how they applied social circus pedagogy in the activities and how they engaged with their participants. I did not interrupt, I just kept a low profile. But when the instructors finished, I tried to point out their strengths and things to work on. Sometimes, the workshops were too much like a circus workshop; the activities were too difficult or there was not enough attention paid to the meaning of the exercises themselves. So in that sense, I corrected or guided the direction of their instruction. But the principle training was done by the local pedagogical directors.

In social circus pedagogy, our main objective is the social aspects of learning; we focus on what is happening in the small group. How are different participants engaging with each other during an activity? Does an activity exclude any participants? Do the instructors take advantage of all that an activity can offer in the social sense, that is, if we seek contact or an opening, through expression, touch, confidence, looks shared between participants, etcetera, what are we learning about the group? About individuals? I tell the instructors that it is not so important to make five floors of a pyramid but rather that the participants all work and learn collaboratively together.

LYNN: What would you say are the key challenges for instructors?

BENJAMIN: We work in the ideal. I think it depends on the coordinator in charge of the local project. With one coordinator, the focus is tending to the pedagogical objectives of social circus. And then another coordinator listens to what they say in the municipality. 'Oh, I want to have more shows, or more children in workshops, I want bigger tricks,' but they do not hire more instructors. So how can you have participant-centred teaching based on interpersonal relationships if you have thirty people for an instructor? Well, the instructor is not Superman; the instructor is a human being.

LYNN: What I want to know is –

BENJAMIN: Enough talking! In social circus, we learn by doing. Let's join the others on the tatami! Come!

Just as the spirit and intention of individual social circus projects cannot be captured by easy definition, the pedagogical practices are subject to the moment, the place, the context, and the individuals involved. Social circus pedagogy seeks to attune to the needs, skills, hopes, and ambitions of individual participants, as well as the vision, expectations, and ambitions of their instructors, and, as we saw in chapter 3, those of the funders and founders of individual programs, who may have varying objectives. However, social circus has at its heart a desire for social, communal, and institutional change that recognizes equality between and opportunity for all individuals.

Circus arts offer the possibility of accommodating a range of artistic practices and abilities; the juggler, the trapeze artist, the acrobat, the silk climber, the clown, all bring something unique into play. And, wonderfully, all coexist and interact under the circus tent. Circus is an artistic practice with an innate tendency to be inclusive, but is also extremely demanding, thus requiring focus, commitment, and perseverance. With all its gravity-defying action, glitzy costumes, music, and excitement, circus is magic – or as Emmanuel Bochud, current head of *Cirque du Monde,* described at the Art of Changing the World conference in Ottawa (November 2017), circus is the art of "doing the impossible." Circus requires a willingness to learn, to be present in the moment, to be generous in reciprocity. As long-time clown and circus instructor Reginald Bolton writes, "[It is] gratifying that an activity which is so strongly recognised as fun should also present developmental, intellectual and physical challenges, encourage social behaviour more creative and co-operative than competitive, and which has as its end product, an act of donation – of generosity" (Bolton 2004, 188). Bolton identifies six key elements that circus training offers learners. These include opportunities for: a) self-invention, self-design, and individuation; b) fun, play, laughter, and happiness; c) risk and adventure; d) dreaming, [imagination], and aspiration; e) trust, touch, and confidence; and f) hard work, application, and ingenuity (2004, 184–95).

Social circus is a social intervention committed to patience, inclusivity, resilience, openness, and hospitality. It is a pedagogical engagement that seeks individual and communal responsibility in action, a metaphorical and embodied practice of awareness, reflection, dialogue, agency, and empowerment. As a pedagogical and activist venture (Spiegel 2016b, 2016c), social circus is a communal and artistic response to what are recognized as gaps in the social net of society as individuals search for wellbeing, balance, financial and personal security, meaningful work, caring relationships, and opportunity in their lives.

The training, mentorship, and support of instructors requires a pedagogy of sensitivity, flexibility, and responsiveness to the needs of individuals and of the group. The learning relationships created between instructor and participants are delicate; working together requires constant listening to what those present are seeking to say (often inarticulately).

Maxine Greene (1978) cautions educators not to sleepwalk through their teaching but to be wide awake, a moral responsibility, she argues, that requires all educators, particularly those working with youth on the margins, with young children, or with individuals in need, to attend to what they are offering in their teaching, their curriculum, how they are co-creating a curriculum of meaning-making, capacity building, and citizenship. Leaders, coordinators, and instructors need to focus their attention on the *why* of social circus and also ask for whose benefit it exists. For what purpose? What possible new worlds (Varela 1987) might fall into presence on the tightrope? In her book *Bitter Milk* (1988), Madeline Grumet asks whether teachers are to be handmaidens of the state or agents of empowerment. For those of us in curriculum and pedagogy, whether in a classroom or on the tatami, the question is of deep importance. What ambitions and intention have guided and currently guide the pedagogical relationships and practices as *Circo Social Ecuador* is imagined into being?

As discussed earlier in the book, studies of social circus and its impact on children and marginalized youth have escalated exponentially in recent years (Ricken 2001; Sugarman 2001; Bailly 2002; McCutcheon 2003; Bolton 2004; Rivard et al. 2010; Lavers and Burtt 2015; Spiegel et al. 2015; Spiegel 2016c; Funk 2017; Spiegel and Parent 2017), and all speak to the benefits and challenges of circus training as a pedagogical intervention for individual and collective wellbeing and development. Bolton, while acknowledging the benefits, reminds circus trainers not to forget "that an essential and sometimes forgotten element of circus is 'magic' – an indefinable expectation of the unexpected" (Bolton 2004, 197).

As Lynn joins Benjamin on the tatami, she eagerly anticipates the arrival of magic that dwells within each participant, within the gift of social circus, a surrendering of *what is*, a willingness to welcome something new.

Pedagogy as Embodied Theory and Action within Social Circus

There were no social circus instructional handbooks when *Cirque du Monde* began its work with vulnerable street youth. Current head of *Cirque du Monde* Emmanuel Bochud describes those early years: "When we started to do it, we were working with instinct, with our hearts trying to do what we thought was best. And we did that for many many years, and I think we did it pretty well. Because we thought ... then we listened to our hearts and we did things in a very instinctive way. For example, we did a plan, but we never followed it ... because we listened to the spirit of the group. After a while, we invited somebody at *Cirque* to explain what we were doing by explaining how we can relate this to an educational approach that already exists. And then we found four different educational principals that were definitely linked to what we were doing ... It's a mixture of something experimental ... centered on participant conscientization approach" (Interview at Banff, 2015).

According to Bochud, four key principles inform the philosophy of *Cirque du Monde* pedagogy, and are integrated into social circus workshops and train-the-trainers sessions, which may be simply stated as:

- Be in your body
- Be together
- Be learning
- Be in action.

And yet, to state these principles so simply is to lose sight of the complexity and nuance that *Cirque du Monde* brings to these principles. Here, within these four principles, is a social circus pedagogy that is dynamic, embodied, experiential, collaborative, focused on social responsibility, citizenship and democracy, reciprocal care, and support for each other's learning. The body and one's relationship to one's body are central components in understanding pedagogy as an action site of exploration, meaning-making, and performance. Embodied within all four principles is a call for participants to commit to themselves, to each other, to the community, to fully engage and be present in each pedagogical moment.

Inherent in the pedagogy of social circus is the concept of transformation (Miller and Seller 1985; Lange 2004), that lives of individuals and/or groups may be transformed through educational practice. Education becomes a vehicle for change, for putting into practice new ways of being in relationships, new understanding.

Mentorship plays a critical role. Research has indicated that the positive role and presence of mentors and tutors can be beneficial in the lives and learning of individuals (Dubois et al. 2002). Tutoring and after-school enrichment have proven to successfully nurture resilience and academic achievement (Hock et al. 2001). Resilience may be conceptualized as "the capacity of an individual to overcome difficult and challenging life circumstances and risk factors" (Bryan 2005). In Ecuador, social circus seeks to provide rich mentorship, a supportive environment, opportunities for instructors and volunteers, participant-focused approaches, and community building, and requires both individual and communal responsibility.

Social scientist Donald Schön (1991) contributes to our understanding of social circus pedagogy by emphasizing the dialogic relationship between action and reflection. Schön distinguishes between "reflection-in-action" and "reflection-on-action" in the process of learning. "Reflection-in-action" is a key component of social circus, as learners learn through action and then, during debriefing, or what Schön calls "reflection-on-action," think critically about their experiences both during and following, and thus make visible the lessons learned. Participants, with the guidance of their instructor, attend to metaphorical connections between their lived experience and the various activities and interactions that occur during sessions. These reflections are designed to awaken participants to their habits of engagement and relationships, the contexts within which they live, and, through making visible connections, assumptions, and biases, to encourage them to imagine their worlds anew (Spiegel 2016c).

Social circus as an arts-for-social-change enterprise seeks a change in the status of the participants, whether by: a) the adoption of the values inherent in the circus arts and the pedagogy that informs its practices; b) the transformation of participants and instructors as they become professional artists and/or learn to engage in society in meaningful ways; c) acquiring a vision of a world not bound by the dominant values of the society in which they live; and/or d) becoming more socially engaged to bring about this newly envisioned world.

Scholars and practitioners warn that social circus as a policy initiative should neither be perceived as nor burdened by expectations of being the solution to all problems; nor should social circus be fully credited or take complete responsibility for an individual's or group's or community's success (or failure) in pursuing their dreams (Ricken 2001; Spiegel 2014a, 2014b, 2015c; Spiegel et al. 2015). Social, economic, political, communal, and personal factors always need to be considered, intertwined as they are in the lives of those perceived to live on the margins, those who experience trauma, those who are left behind. As Emmanuel Bochud acknowledges, "Sometimes we work with participants who are very vulnerable ... maybe they will have a lot of fun during the circus project and they will get their life together, but two years later we don't always know. Because the fracture [in their lives] is ... sometimes very deep, traumatic ... the trauma is sometimes very deep. Circus is not magic, it's not enough. We need other resources, health clinics, social supervision, community support, school integration, government support, ecetera. ... Social circus is one part of the ecosystem!" It is critical to remember that social intervention work is relational, contextual, and temporal. Social circus pedagogy requires of its participants and instructors (and those supporting these projects), a spirit of compassion, mutual respect, openness, and a willingness to engage, to forgive, to begin anew (Arendt 1958; Gordon 2001).

Cirque du Monde has played a critical role in the pedagogical development and training of instructors in Ecuador, introducing concepts such as train-the-trainers and the seven pillars of foundation of social circus. However, while many influences can be traced to *Cirque du Monde*, *Circo Social Ecuador* as it exists today is born of those who imagined it into being and shaped by those who have shepherded its development; many of *Circo Social Ecuador*'s trainers came from other fields, such as theatre, and locations such as Chile, Italy, and France. They brought their own practices, perspectives, and understanding – particularly those with experience in Augusto Boal's *Theatre of the Oppressed* methods or attuned to the educational philosophy of Paulo Freire's *Pedagogy of the Oppressed*, as discussed later in the chapter.

Social circus offers an opportunity for compassionate action and self-reflection among those whose responsibility is to attend to the wellbeing of individuals who dwell in difficult situations. The concept of *hospitality*, as imagined by Jacques Derrida – the welcoming of an unexpected stranger to our door, whoever that stranger may be (Borradori 2003) has a poignancy here. A community and its leaders are judged by their willingness to engage not only with those in need but also to welcome those who embody difference or the unexpected. In our everyday lives, we can be called to attention in a moment of surprise, astonishment, fear, denial, or resistance by the knocking on our door of a stranger asking permission to enter. Individuals accustomed to who they are or who accept how they are identified by others may fail to recognize and invite the unexpected into the here and now. Individuals, communities, institutions, and governments can react to new situations by exploring new ways of being in the world or, in response to the unexpected, simply reproduce familiar scripts performed in an endless cycling of habits of response, attitudes, and perceptions.

Social circus arrived in Ecuador like a curious stranger with early street circus performers; later it was formally invited into the country because of the enthusiasm of the vice-president. Those who engaged in the creation of *Circo Social Ecuador* were willing to reimagine what was possible. And, as we have seen, there were those who chose either to shut the door, politely but securely, or who invented their own version of social circus (see chapters 3 and 7).

Train-the-Trainer Workshops as Models for Learning

During the early years, bi-annual week-long full-day workshops were offered by *Cirque du Monde* to mentor and support instructors of *Circo Social Ecuador*, to introduce their philosophy, pedagogy, and practices, and to promote social circus as a vehicle for social change. The concept of train-the-trainer as a philosophical and instructional stance is well known in the fields of public health, education, community, and workforce development (Yarber et al. 2015). The objective of train-the-trainers is to share knowledge, practices, and skills that can then be implemented by local practitioners rather than to rely on costly and impractical dependence on outsiders for ongoing teaching.

During *Cirque du Monde* instructor workshops, the trainer models a variety of pedagogical strategies and facilitation skills to instructors so that they can incorporate these into their own teaching. Each activity becomes a metaphor, an illustration of lived experience, an example, modeling what is possible in order to amplify participant understanding.

As an example of how dialogue may be facilitated as a learning strategy, let us attend to the seminar facilitated by Emmanuel Bochud in October

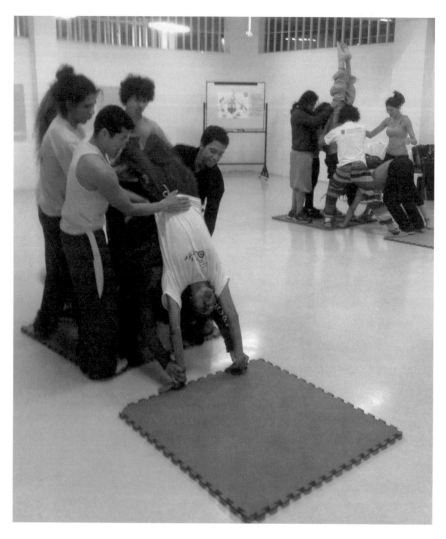

Photo 4.1 A game called "The Islands" that allows participants to live an experience in order to illustrate the themes of social circus. This photo was taken during the basic training (level 1) provided by *Cirque du Monde* in Quito, 2013.

2015 at a focused leadership group gathered to discuss the creation of a network of social circus in Ecuador (see chapter 3). Notice, as you read the transcript below, how Bochud asks questions about what they have done and why, draws on the experiences of the group, clarifies, and paraphrases, skillfully employing well-known facilitation techniques (Hunter [1994] 2007).

PARTICIPANT 1: [We did] the exercise "Puedo? Venga!" so we could start communicating ...

PARTICIPANT 2: And understand each other's availability ...

EMMANUEL: In this exercise we developed a trust atmosphere, learned to respect each other, improved concentration, etc. Thus we learned how to change things, but also we learned about cooperation. Cooperation means to ask for help or permission. May I? Yes, you may. Do you need help? Yes, I do. Can you help me? Cooperation between people and projects is very important. What else did we learn?

PARTICIPANT 3: Interpreting, because we didn't talk anymore.

PARTICIPANT 4: Yes, there was an evolution [through the different activities].

PARTICIPANT 5: The game "*¿A quién le gusta?*" (who likes it?), where we learned about affinities.

EMMANUEL: Affinity! What we have in common! We can concentrate on the positive things we have in common, not only those where we are different. We need to understand that to work as a team we need to know the strengths in each of us. An instructor, a leader, an ambassador can't be a superhero that has everything.

PARTICIPANT 6: All strengths sum up.

EMMANUEL: Exactly, and we need different skills to have a team. We can't have eleven Messis within the Barca, it just wouldn't work. What else did we do?

PARTICIPANT 7: The "focus" game, so we could build up leadership.

EMMANUEL: Definitely leadership. We are going to talk about networks this week, possible networks. It is essential to share leadership, but also it is complex and challenging. Every exercise we practice here to talk about leadership, cooperation, to focus on this energy can be impressed in children using social circus workshops. Working with children so they can find what they have in common is very powerful. Then, they have a break and can talk about skateboarding, music, etc. For example ...

This dialogue demonstrates many aspects of social circus pedagogy. Trainers of social circus instructors (and instructors leading workshops) try not to miss an opportunity to apply the methods and principles they profess, and activities, as illustrated here, serve multiple purposes. If you listen closely to Emmanuel's conversation with the participating instructors, you can see that the group draws many lessons from a single activity. Emmanuel encourages the instructors to reflect on their learning, to identify and speak to the value of the activities they have been engaged in. He invites participation, involving everyone, asking questions until he receives answers that meet his pedagogical objectives (and often some that surprise, which is the gift of the work). He does so by valuing and giving continuity to the group's responses, and without failing to insert a little humour.

During the discussion, Bochud models how to facilitate and engage others in meaningful dialogue. Bochud clarifies the discussion, the overall objective, and any concepts or issues arising so that these are clear for the whole group, thus reinforcing the positive messages and learning that have been transmitted in practice. He concludes by reaffirming their contributions, and models how they may facilitate dialogue and reflection with their own participants. Bochud makes visible the hidden curriculum of the exercise (Giroux and Purpel 1983) and explains to participants that everything experienced during the train-the-trainer sessions is a practice or strategy, model or activity that can be transposed to their own social circus workshops. Group dialogue and reflection, as facilitated here, make transparent the learning strategies employed by *Cirque du Monde*, an approach that is to be implemented in turn by the instructors.

Paulo Freire's (1972) teaching about pedagogy and collective learning is embodied in the practices of *Cirque du Monde*. Freire critiques conventional educational practices; he uses the uncomfortable metaphor of education as a banking system in which the educator deposits his or her knowledge into the heads of students, as if they were empty vessels waiting to be filled. Central to Freire's work is the concept of *conscientization*, or critical consciousness, in which learners become aware of the value of their own experience, perspectives, and knowledge: in which learners move from being consumers to becoming active producers of their own learning, creativity, and critical thought. This pedagogical approach leads to an awakening of their present potential and capabilities.

Freire challenges the conventional authority of the teacher, dismissing the vertical hierarchy of teachers positioned as superior in knowledge and expertise to their students, and proposes instead a relationship of horizontality. He encourages educators to understand that all individuals have experience that is valuable to collective learning. By incorporating the voices, experiences, narratives, and perspectives of learners, educators create a dialogic space in which they create meaning with their students (Freire 1972). Such a pedagogy leads to collaborative learning and peer teaching, resulting in a co-emergent curriculum, and one hopes, mutual respect, support, and reciprocity. *Horizontality* as a pedagogical positioning between participants and instructors can be easily breached (Freire 1972); social circus instructors and volunteers, and those with whom they work, are not infallible. Thus, the responsibility of the educator is to design an environment to welcome, nurture, guide, and facilitate learning and collaboration within the group.

Freire's teachings have influenced social circus projects across the continent of South America and elsewhere in which learning is the shared responsibility of the group. Within social circus pedagogy as imagined and practiced by *Circo Social Ecuador*, we see Freire's concepts embodied in the practices of peer teaching, collaboration, and respect for individual and collective agency and lived experience. Similarly, theatre activist Augusto Boal, also a native of Brazil and a friend of Freire, has played a role in influencing social circus pedagogy and practice, bringing into the work a spirit of questioning, a critique of what is, asking what might be.

Boal's work has had an impact on social circus practice in Ecuador as a number of instructors, particularly those who have experienced Boal's *Theatre of the Oppressed* or forum theatre, incorporate his games and image work into their pedagogical practice. His social critique embraces the questions: "What if?" "How might we replay this situation?" "Who now is the oppressor?" (Boal [1985] 2008). In training, as well as in social circus workshops, participants are invited to explore situations through improvisation, action, and dialogue. Social circus, like Boal's work, calls forth, through our bodies in relationship to each other, that which is unsaid, not known, unsayable (Salverson 2011), along with those situations which we recognize as injustices in our relationships, our political, economic, and social contexts.

In social circus pedagogy, through the use of metaphors, analogies, games, group activities, mind-mapping, and other creative strategies, knowledge is co-created (Bagley and Cancienne 2001; Fels 2009; Peters 2009; Norris 2010) and learning shared. Each exercise, activity, or technique illustrates or speaks to an aspect of personal or group work; an analogy becomes a window on a social objective or value. In social circus, building a human pyramid, juggling balls, and climbing the ropes reveal who we are in relationship to each other and the challenges we face. Here is the heart of social circus practice and pedagogy. Group reflection on these activities is critical. How we engaged, how we cooperated, whether we focused on learning a difficult task with patience or reacted in frustration, whether what we learned we offered to teach others – these are all moments that teach us to be present in the world, and with each other.

We can, from this distance, name the process that has led to the current *Cirque du Monde's* train-the-trainer model as a co-emergent, participant-centred, co-created pedagogy. Social circus pedagogy is dynamic; it encourages adaptability, active listening, reflection, creativity, sensitivity, humour, and responsiveness to the environments within which we live and work, and, most importantly, the presence of those in the room.

In Ecuador as elsewhere, the train-the-trainer sessions are generally conducted in two stages, for a total of eighty hours. Creative activities, dialogue, reflection, questioning, debriefing, and shared learning opportunities are central to instructor trainings, and regularly designed around social, pedagogical, and technical goals. The learning offered by trainers of the instructors and volunteers, in formal and informal sessions, is primarily focused on key principles, learning strategies, facilitation, and reflective practices rather than on circus techniques. Instructors are expected to already have such knowledge and skills when they are selected to lead workshops. The pedagogy of social circus theory and practice is transmitted through readings, mind maps, slide projections, video observation, a variety of activities leading to presentations through group work, and especially, much debate and dialogue, so that the learning is shared, thus inviting communal understanding.

Notably, as we witnessed during Bochud's training session, as well as other workshops we attended in Ecuador, all activities or exercises are followed by group debriefings. Making visible the reasons for, and value of, individual games and activities to participants by engaging them in follow-up debriefing is a critical strategy to facilitate participants' understanding and to consolidate their learning. As shown by Spiegel in an in-depth study of social circus in Quebec (Spiegel 2016c), failure to introduce and debrief such exercises properly can lead participants to feel infantilized, playing games that they associate with children, not young adults.

Today, learning strategies and related activities are available to instructors through *Cirque du Monde's* participant notebooks. There are many resources that may be used during training, such as videos, participant notebooks, and handouts. Antonio Benítez, one of the trainers who facilitated a significant portion of *Cirque du Monde's* training in Ecuador, used handmade mind-maps (photo 4.2) to convey theoretical knowledge in a way that engages participants who, in general, are more interested in technical knowledge or learning through experience.

Photo 4.2 Example of a mental map used in the basic training of *Cirque du Monde* level 2, in Loja in 2014 and in Urcuquí in 2017.

Key issues such as communication and teamwork are highlighted during training sessions, directly, through different activities, or in response to emergent group dynamics. All activities and debriefings are modelled and reflected upon by the trainers and participants. Topics such as "creativity," "facilitation," and "group management" are addressed and modelled with the intention that these will be transferred into practice. Exemplars of good planning and communications prior to training sessions are demonstrated by the design and circulation of official invitations, through registration questionnaires, as well as through personal and group communications regarding the coordination and logistics of the sessions. All of these practices help to ensure that the training is carried out successfully and serve as models for participants as to how to organize and engage in program communications and delivery.

Cirque du Monde trainers pay particular attention to intercultural relationships, as their sessions occur in different parts of the world. Relationships between individuals and groups is a recurring theme in Ecuador, which is a multi-cultural and multi-ethnic country. Participants belonging to very different cultural communities, including diverse nationalities, can be found in social circus projects. Instructors are taught that a coherent way of working with and developing cultural sensitivity is by respecting and nurturing relationships, engaging in shared experiences, sharing stories face-to-face, and addressing intercultural relationships and conflicts through group reflections and dialogue.

Topics such as "youth at risk," "conflict management," and "ethics" are addressed during training sessions to help instructors develop interpersonal skills and to nurture empathy so that they learn how to navigate difficult situations and promote feelings of respect and belonging. *Cirque du Monde* proposes to engage with those at risk who face one, if not more, of the most feared situations such as homelessness, unemployment, drug-addiction, and mental illness. Awareness and sensitivity to the ethics of engagement with populations at risk, and to their needs and experiences, are required; conflict-management strategies help instructors address and tend to the youth and young adults who engage in social circus, or who live in their community.

The Seven Pillars of Social Circus as Enacted in *Circo Social Ecuador*

Cirque du Monde trainers introduced instructors and volunteers in *Circo Social Ecuador* to "the seven pillars," the pedagogical foundation upon which social circus is based. The seven pillars provide a useful frame to look at how social circus structure, pedagogy, and practices have been conceptualized and enacted in Ecuador.

Tandem Facilitation and Team Teaching

Cirque du Monde recommends that a social worker and circus instructor facilitate social circus workshops in tandem, each bringing their unique skills and knowledge, thus modelling collaboration, participation, and a willingness to learn from each other. While the circus instructor may feel at home, the social worker will likely be on a steep learning curve. As Bochud said to us, "The social worker has to participate, has to climb in the trapeze, [has] to do exactly the same thing as the kid. [He or she] is not there to be a policeman to do only conflict management; not at all, you have to participate, you have to show vulnerability to the kids." In other words, the social worker operates from within, engaging with participants

Photo 4.3 Mónica Tapia (social worker, left) and Kalu Arévalo (volunteer, right) showing how "working in tandem" operates, the social worker actively engaging in a *replica* at *Circo Social Cuenca*, 2013.

in the same way as the social circus instructor does: by being present, participating, learning, and sharing. Tandem facilitation is designed to allow the social worker to establish a closer relationship with participants.

The concept of a tandem partnership is based on Freire's horizontality of shared learning and experience rather than on an authoritative model of hierarchy and expertise. By being actively engaged, the participating social worker may more easily navigate barriers to create a different kind of relationship with participants than a conventional one. The tandem model has both benefits and challenges, as Mayra Guzman, a former social worker with *Circo Social Quito* recalls: "When I started working here at the circus, I was told that as a social worker, our role will be to get involved in the circus work of the boys. It was somewhat new to me; it was a completely different population than what I had worked with before ... I had resistance to work on balancing and juggling, I did not see the value ... I had to overcome certain fears, like heights (trapeze) and was very afraid. Now I look back and on a personal level, it helped me overcome some fears, but it also helped me from a professional point of view. It also helped the kids ... For example, [during a workshop] I overheard a boy say, 'I have a family problem,' then I intervened, [I met] with the family, [channeled] the case" (interview, October 2015).

In pairs, instructors and social workers engage in planning, problem-solving, and evaluation; they are in constant communication during training sessions, thus reducing the risks associated with circus practices. Increased and shared attention to issues of physical safety, group management, and relational dynamics are facilitated by tandem teaching. Thus, when two trainers come from the same professional area, complementary profiles are sought based on specialization, style of facilitation, even geographical and cultural origin.

Although perceived as ideal, such partnerships are rare in Ecuador. Most projects do not have the degree of social work participation originally anticipated. The inability to put tandem facilitation into practice has been largely due to the lack of social workers with appropriate profiles, experience, aptitude, and/or training. A call for appropriate training in university programs for social and community workers was heard repeatedly during our research. Javier Figueroa, an instructor at *Circo Social Cuenca,* observed:

> there are young people, adolescents who see social circus as a new strategy of social intervention ... There is much interest especially in universities to take advantage of this [opportunity]. Because people who are already doing social work, who have had ... their specialization credentials; they sit behind a desk, maybe fill out forms, and their work is very, very traditional. This [social circus] process is brand new, and is innovative, therefore requires the social worker to work a little more. We had social workers who did not want, for example, to even take off their shoes to enter the tatami and share with the kids. But young social workers who are beginning to know these new techniques, this new methodology, are interested in learning more and becoming involved ... So I think that in the future, with the theme introduced in universities, if we managed to accomplish this, that would be something, would be very positive.

We see some evidence in Ecuador that social circus is generating a desire for change within the field of social work. Such interest will hopefully encourage professors of social work to expand their range of course content to include, for example, an introduction to arts for social change practices such as social circus.

A Participant-centred Approach

The pedagogical stance of *Cirque du Monde* is innovative, holistic, and respectful of the individual, while simultaneously attending to the dynamics of group learning. John Dewey ([1938] 1997) advocated for an active pedagogy of meaningful engagement. He admonished teachers for simply enabling book-learning; Dewey wanted students to engage in meaningful experiences related to those that they would encounter in the world. Similarly, Hannah Arendt (1958) called upon educators to attend to the activities that they ask of their students. Are these simple tasks that require mindless repetition? Labour required for the work to be done? Or creative critical engagement where agency, meaning-making, change, and renewal is possible?

Reciprocity in learning and agency in action are cornerstones of social circus, recalling Friere's pedagogy of shared expertise and learning. As noted by Bochud, "We learn a lot from the participant. It's the participants who tell us what they need." Sharon McCutcheon, in her research on circus pedagogy, notes that, "Circus tutors need ... most importantly passion, enthusiasm and respect for circus and the innate abilities of young people" (McCutcheon 2003, 127). The pedagogical heart of social circus is the individual and their relationships with others; social circus projects and training sessions commit to and incorporate a participant-centred, co-emergent, and inclusive pedagogy, a concept and practice familiar to educators and curriculum theorists (Davis et al. 1996; Fels and Belliveau 2008).

Sometimes, during a workshop, an instructor encounters what might be perceived as resistance from an individual or an entire group. Rather than becoming frustrated, the instructor's challenge is to figure out what the individual or group needs or wants, and how compromise can be achieved. As Juan Carlos Ortiz, an instructor for *Circo Social Loja* advises, based on his own experience, "If a group clearly prefers to watch the national soccer game, the instructor can bring in a television. Together they could watch the sporting event and then begin the class."

Given that social circus often works with youth at risk, with attitudes and behaviors that can be quite challenging, an instructor needs to be creative, not punitive. Matías Belmar, the pedagogical director from the

Photo 4.4 Alejandra Pacin (instructor) teaches a girl a basic figure on the silks during an open circus, Tena, 2013. Note the knot in the fabric; this facilitates learning and increases risk control.

Fundación Circulo, who was awarded the contract to develop the *Circo Social Ecuador* from the ground up, helped and guided by the vice president's office and *Cirque du Soleil*'s team, offered these two examples of how he managed difficult situations.

> En Cerro Navia [Chile] ... I had students ... from seven to seventeen. Most of them were the children of drug-dealers. They were totally addicted to cocaine paste. There was one student in particular who was very addicted to this cheap drug. One day the community space was occupied so we had to move to the kitchen ... This guy was in the group and he was just going nuts under the effects of the paste. When we got to the kitchen, he started to do acrobatics, totally crazy. I got distracted for one second – as there were about twenty kids in a very small space – and all of a sudden, this guy

Photo 4.5 Open circus in the vice presidency of the Republic of Ecuador, organized jointly by the former pedagogical director of the *Circo Social Quito*, Yacine Ortiz (base), and the former national pedagogical director to combat stereotypes about and preconceptions of the beneficiaries and scope of the project. In the picture, volunteers help an official from the vice presidency to climb, 2013.

grabbed a bread knife from one of the kitchen drawers. 'Hey! Pass me that knife.' And he replies, 'Awe ... Which knife, dude?' 'Enough! The knife that is there!' 'No, dude, I mean, it's all good. Nothing is wrong.' At that point, I had it, so I told him 'Look, do what you want but if you don't pass me the knife, I'm the one who is going to be screwed. All of us will. If I'm screwed, all of us will be screwed.' ... When I explained that he was putting everything and everybody at risk, he finally said, 'Ah OK, dude. You are cool!' And he passed me the knife and he continued doing acrobatics, all good, all peaceful. Everything was cool with him, after that incident he was an ally. He was always an ally.

Here, a participant is called to task by his instructor, who asks him to be responsible to the group, and to not let his actions impact on the wellbeing of others. He is given the opportunity to step forward into the space that the vice president had imagined: a space where participants might learn "to develop self-esteem, trust in others, social skills, the spirit of citizenship, and the expression of creativity and potential." Matias continued, "In this same workshop, there were two kids who fought all the time ... One time they were coming to blows and I had to interfere and split them up. But for some reason, when we did clowning exercises those two were outstanding. They were awesome all the time. And so they started to get together while doing clowning and, in a way, I was fostering this relationship during the workshops. At the end, in the final performance, they both put together the best clowning act of all. And it was wonderful. They were always very good friends, but at the same time they always had lots of conflicts together."

Establishing a Secure and Fun Space

The circus for me, is having [...] found that family warmth that is not commonly found. And here I have found family, camaraderie, I have found a magical world, a world of emotional security, more than anything, a world [....] of sharing, of being very friendly, very open with other people, with some limits for sure, but in general, more than what other people are used to being with each other.

Zoila Castillo, participant, Circo Social Loja

The social, physical, and pedagogical focal point of social circus is the *tatami*. The preparing of the space together offers instructors valuable opportunities to illustrate one of the basics of social circus pedagogy – collaboration. Instructors may use the experience of assembling the tatami as a metaphor for the importance of collaborating, or as an opportunity to gather in those hanging about at the margins, or as a way to create a spirit of belonging and shared responsibility and accomplishment. Typically, the group works as an ensemble to prepare the space, unrolling and piecing together the individual mats, as a collaborative act, a ritual, or a gesture that marks the beginning of the workshop. The tatami space, besides being physical, is temporal; the workshop has a beginning and an end – the physical spaces where most social circus projects are located have schedules for other programs. Thus, the ritual dismantling and storing of the tatami mats mark the end of the session, a symbolic stepping-out into the world.

When adapting a space originally intended for another activity, security and physical safety cannot be neglected. That is why, symbolically and practically, the tatami space has become synonymous with social circus. It clearly defines physical and emotional space that offers, both literally and

Photo 4.6 A demonstration of clowning, *Circo Social Quito,* 2013. Clowning in social circus provides a clear space for expression and creativity. From left to right, Claudia Davila, Johnny Paguay, Diego Martillo, Paula Laverve, and Jorge Hidalgo.

metaphorically, safety, belonging, communal care, and responsibility. By providing a play area, instructors lay the first foundation of a respectful, secure, and fun space in which to play, learn, and build community; the space invites creating oneself anew: "The safe space thus acts not only as a refuge, but also as a context for trying out different possible ways of being" (Cirque du Soleil Cirque du Monde 2013).

Play is recognized as critical to learning (Burell and Perlmutter 1995). Although circus requires rigour, perseverance, and tenacity, in social circus these skills are achieved through activities that are playful. It is through play that we learn most things that will serve us in life; it is through play and reflection that the social circus aims to address the larger issues of life (see photo 4.6).

Circo Social Ecuador ensures that its participants find themselves in a playful and safe space, as is evident in the following testimonials:

"Happiness. Every time I come here I feel very good."

"I would like to say that for many guys, including myself, the social circus is a home / shelter. I do not want it to ever end!"

Photo 4.7 Group of instructors and volunteers discussing pedagogy at the training headquarters of *Circo Social Loja* in 2015.

Therein also lies one of the fundamental differences between circus pedagogy and social circus pedagogy. In social circus, learning the technical or artistic skills of circus is an intermediary step towards more important objectives linked to personal and communal growth and well-being, or what we call social objectives. For this reason, instructors incorporate humour, a sense of play, and care. The objective of social circus is not to create a skilled acrobat but a thoughtful caring responsible citizen, who might also become a skilled acrobat!

The safety, upkeep, and use of the circus equipment must be carefully regulated. This has proven difficult because the equipment for each of the circus activities is costly and must be inspected and renewed regularly. In Ecuador, the National Government made the first purchase of equipment, but maintenance and replacement are in the hands of the municipalities.

Emotional safety is even more complex, and is directly related to the instructor's capabilities, attitudes, biases, sensitivities, and perceptions, as well as those of everyone else in the group. The challenge of creating a welcoming learning space when working with vulnerable populations weighs heavily on the shoulders of those involved.

As in any pedagogical environment, instructors are taught to stay alert to signs of emotional discomfort, bullying, depression, or distress experienced by the participants. Instructors are also expected to offer support by requiring reasonable results in a timely fashion without imposing unnecessary pressures. The stresses and anxieties resulting from academic and/or performance-related endeavours are well documented in education (Ryan and Deci 2000; Reddy et al. 2003), and are best avoided by those leading social circus activities. And finally, as in any pedagogical situation, an instructor can make mistakes in handling difficult relationships, particularly those of a romantic or aggressive nature, which can lead to serious safety and emotional problems for individual participants as well as the group as a whole. The emotional safety of participants is also the responsibility of the institution, which needs to ensure that instructors are adequately trained and supported (Blum 2005).

Challenges to both physical and emotional safety can be further complicated, as we have witnessed in Ecuador, when officials are overly eager to promote social circus within their communities. Instructors may feel outside or internal pressure to have participants perform publicly too early in their training, without proper preparation, or to deliver unnecessarily difficult tricks. The vision of some municipalities has led to projects scheduled with too few workshop hours or excessive demands on instructors, volunteers, or participants. Social circus prioritizes safety and fun to achieve social objectives, in many cases, technical and artistic results are secondary. So it is not surprising that the performances of participants may be of lower quality than expected by the funders, followers, and the general public. This dynamic brings tensions to the projects, to such an extent that *Circo Social Loja* – whose research results were wonderfully positive – was discontinued in 2016 because of a disagreement related to an artistic demand of the mayor. In 2017 the team was restructured with three instructors, retaining only one former instructor.

Creativity and Expression

Creativity and expression are central to art as a valuable and evocative means of communication that invites one into the lives of others (Salverson 2011; Conrad and Sinner 2015; Gonçalves and Majhanovich 2016).

Creativity is the heart of human engagement, relationship, and expression. Creativity allows us to revise our view of life, to face our perceived realities in ways not considered possible, or help find solutions to problems that seemed unsolvable. Creativity has become the poster child of what employers allegedly want in their employees (A Forrester Consulting Thought Leadership Paper Commissioned by Adobe, 2014).

Creativity is the big tent of social circus, a critical dynamic that imagines into being an infinity of possibilities (Duffy 2006). Creativity is of pedagogical importance for instructors and participants alike (Jeffrey and Craft 2004). Instructors must be able to incorporate creativity into their activities through content and delivery, in response, in action, and in resolution of any difficult relationships and/or situations that arise. Instructors need to be creative during their teaching so that they can extract the maximum from each moment.

In order to offer content that encourages creativity, instructors must constantly evaluate and adapt the curriculum; varying methods, games, and exercises is essential to bring diversity to the workshops and encourage participants. Social circus sees creativity as one of the main tools for the development of resilience. Creativity invites participants to change their vision and face reality in ways not considered possible; to find solutions to problems that seem unsolvable.

Instructors and participants learn to express themselves creatively through gestures, facial expressions, and body language. Expression through one's art, through communal engagement and creation, through dialogue and reflection are all ways to inquire, express, and respond to personal and communal challenges. Participant expressions of fear, doubt, anger, dismissal, or confusion require creative and thoughtful response from instructors, whether to change or modify an activity, to introduce a preliminary step, an explanation, a progression, or, in extreme cases, to manage conflicts among participants. The creative instructor is able to adapt to a new space or a sudden change of space; creativity is also in action when instructors find solutions to organizational problems, the unexpected absence of a partner, or a last-minute directive.

While performances or demonstrations by social circus offers tangible evidence of instructors' and participants' creativity, the demand for presentation, as suggested above, can be counter-productive. One pedagogical approach, commonly referred to as "process over product" (O'Toole [1992] 2005; Moody 2002) focuses on the experience of learning as opposed to a final product or, in the case of social circus, choosing not to offer public performances or demonstrations before participants are fully prepared, able, or willing to perform.

Being state-funded, *Circo Social Ecuador* faced particular pressure to perform in order to demonstrate that public monies were being well spent, as explored in chapter 7. The pressure to perform was perceived by many instructors as not only emotionally risky, it sometimes compromised the process by forcing instructors to interrupt workshops so that they or their participants could participate in performances. As in any artistic endeavour, attending to the readiness of young artists is a pedagogical and ethical responsibility. Such a responsibility is particularly the case in social circus, given the emotional complexities of the participants and the challenge of performance.

Respecting the physical and emotional safety of participants, instructors are advised in the train-the-trainer sessions to present initially to a limited public, perhaps peers from other levels or family members. Instructors are encouraged to create routines and acts that are within their participants' reach, focusing on collective moments, limiting solos and duets, consciously attending to objectives linked to shared decision making or the development of personal goals. Progressively, and depending on the readiness of individual groups, circus demonstrations or performances may then become more technically or artistically demanding, allowing spaces for solos, more height in the air, or more complex tricks, and these performances may be opened to the community.

This debate within social circus is not unfamiliar to other arts educators, who also wrestle with focusing on the end product rather than on a student's experience, often short-changing students in order to meet institutional and/or community expectations.

Links with the Community

Social circus creates or recreates links and dialogue between the participants, often young people, and their family or community. It serves as an interface between the community and the participants and invites the community to come and meet these youths so as to change how they are perceived.

Cirque du Soleil Cirque du Monde 2013

No pedagogical endeavour occurs in isolation; an educational venture is intimately linked with family and community, and is strongly influenced by its cultural, economic, and political environment (Benard 1991; Lee and

Photo 4.8 Instructors and volunteers of *Circo Social Cuenca* in 2013, conducting workshops with the children who accompany their parents to work in the *10 de Agosto* market.

Burkam 2002). Outreach with the community is initiated through public announcements of upcoming registration or when organizations are contacted to recruit participants. Social circus is linked with families and friends of participants throughout the process of workshops, as participants share their learning. As discussed in chapter 7, performances create a significant bond with the community.

Engaging in social circus changes the relationships of the participants with each other, with family, and with the community. Social circus helps participants understand that there are multiple ways of engaging in one's community. The impact of social circus on participants' ability to renew and extend their relationships beyond social circus is evident, as seen in chapters 6 and 7.

One way that *Circo Social Ecuador* seeks to bond with the community is through open circuses, a legacy of the strategy proposed by the *Circulo Foundation*. These events consist of large workshops designed for public participation. The community is invited to an event held in a large public space that has been divided into several areas where different circus workshops are held.

Participants are divided into small groups, rotating through each workshop or demonstration until all the groups have briefly tested every practical circus experience. The event usually ends with a short presentation by instructors or, should the open circus coincide with the end of an advanced cycle of trainees, the trainees. The strengthening of the project's link with the community at these events is considerable, and may lead to new ventures.

Partnerships

The "Social Circus Trainer's Guide" emphasizes the importance of partnerships with local community organizations, government agencies, and municipalities. The concept of social circus is itself a partnership between the worlds of circus and social work. As discussed in chapter 3, partnerships have played a critical role in the conception and implementation of *Circo Social Ecuador*, which was initiated as a partnership with *Cirque du Monde*, as well as the *Circulo* foundation. As we have seen earlier, the partnership with the vice president shifted to the Technical Secretariat for Disabilities and Family and, finally, to the *Ministerio de Cultura y Patrimonio*.

Partnerships were created with each of the municipalities that chose to welcome a social circus project. Schools, social foundations, rehabilitation centres, and even shelters for the elderly were among the partners of social circus projects. And, let's not forget that in Ecuador, the multiple training sessions arose through an original partnership between the state and *Cirque du Soleil*; *Cirque du Monde* itself was the result of an alliance between *Jeunesse du Monde*, *Cirque du Soleil*, and dozens of professional social circuses.

Within each social circus project, instructors promote partnerships among and with their participants. The critical importance of partnerships is expressed and experienced in all activities which require teamwork, reinforcing a sense of belonging, fostering camaraderie, responsibility, and collaboration, developing expression and communication, improving self-esteem and the ability to socialize, and teaching how to seek allies to fulfill dreams. Partnership is primarily conceived between the social and the circus, as a pedagogical and activist project.

Duration over Time

Time is a precious ally. The amount of time that participants, instructors, and volunteers are engaged in social circus, during training sessions and workshops, influences the effectiveness of social circus pedagogy, and the overall impact and sustainability of *Circo Social Ecuador* and its influence within a community. Any project, given enough time and support, may achieve more effective results, become more sustainable, or simply reach more people (Shediac-Rizkallah and Bone 1998). *Cirque du Monde* recommends that the duration of workshops for participants be not less than two months. As this social worker explains: "I think in my profession [what matters] ... is the long-term work you do."

Experiential learning requires time for participants to overcome their fears and to learn how to succeed. One participant recalls, "My best experience was to see that fear, that great phobia of heights, because, I had ... a terrible phobia, I was only halfway up – 'Lower me, let me down' I would cry in that moment. But the circus has done that, it has taken from me this phobia that I had, if a little bit, but not like it used to be at an extreme level, now ... is normal."

In Ecuador, each social circus project implemented different lengths of time, ranging from two to four months, for workshop sessions. In some of the projects, the time was extended so that those participants seeking to become professionals might have more opportunity to practice and refine their skills. Because there are no schools or high-level training centres in Ecuador, some individuals remain with their social circus program over long periods in order to continue their training. Commitment to continuous training ensures the sustainability of social circus over time and increases the quality and experience for participants.

Extended participation in social circus workshops has largely occurred in *Circo Social Quito*. *Circo Social Quito* responded to a high demand for professional training by creating independent working groups. Participants, primarily those who became volunteers, were able to take advantage of the space and equipment for a greater length of time, but unfortunately, at the time of our research, there were no sufficiently trained instructors to guide the group's activities or take responsibility for what was done in that space.

Photo 4.9 First demonstration of training social circus instructors and volunteers offered by *Circo Social Tena* in 2012; as with *Cirque du Monde*, the training offered by the vice presidency and the *Circulo* foundation sought balance between theory and practice.

A similar situation existed in *Circo Social Loja*. Participants who aimed to professionalize became part of the volunteer group; they received additional training in circus techniques and social circus pedagogy in the morning, together with instructors. Providing continuous training of instructors and volunteers is a legacy of the original proposal by the *Circulo* foundation. The opportunity for participants to further their training was originally implemented by the resident artist and later by the local educational officer. Until the end of 2013, Cuenca, Tena, Quito, and Loja had all adopted this working model. Since 2014, only *Circo Social Loja* has offered both time and space for the continuous development of instructors' skills and understanding of social circus; at *Circo Social Quito*, training continues to be offered to volunteers but with less emphasis on social pedagogy.

Attention to time is of great importance in social circus – whether it involves instructors (and participants) being punctual or the length of time allowed for learning. Perseverance, self-esteem, solidarity, creativity, autonomy, tolerance of failure, resilience, tolerance for others, the ability to work in teams, anxiety, self-centredness, selfishness, fear of criticism, the fear of failure or fear of heights, are all things that need to be addressed through creative action and positive support, and worked upon gradually until participants experience a real change in their lives and/or perceptions of themselves. Experiential learning (Whyte 1991; Fels et al. 2011) is the cornerstone of the pedagogical approach articulated by *Cirque du Monde*, and time is required for this learning to take hold and have a profound impact.

The training of instructors over several sessions illustrates the importance of time. First, activities are experienced as conceptual relationships between theory and practice, between what is experienced in the training and what is experienced in the individual trainee's workshops, making tangible the differences and relationship between circus objectives and social objectives. Continued association with each other through multiple sessions provides opportunities for instructors to create alliances to meet common goals and to provide each other support.

Commitment to Pedagogy, Commitment to Social Change

Cirque du Monde training sessions are simultaneously an analogy to and a model of social circus pedagogy. They actively engage participants in learning, and by example, model ways and strategies to be employed in social circus projects, thus "enlarging the space of the possible" (Sumara and Davis 1997). To create an intervention that is pedagogical, that invites individual and social change, horizontality, and empowerment, that gives voice, agency, and presence to those who are vulnerable, marginalized, and in need, is the gift and potential of social circus.

In the following interview, Bochud illustrates how *Cirque du Monde* practices many of its own principles in terms of flexibility, adaptability, and learning from experience: "We always assess what we're doing and we always have to adapt and change what we're doing, so the training is something alive, something that is moving. So there is a core that seems to be equal all over the world and that always comes back, ethical issues are one of these things, also security of the participants. Definitions of social circus can have different colours, different variations, but I like to say they have the same art, so there is a common goal, common things. So definitely there's something that stays all the time in the training program but there's many things that change ... new topics or dressing it up ... the topics differ, etc. So yes, we have to adapt it. It's very important." Bochud acknowledges the importance of evaluating the instructors' experiences and perspectives in the training sessions, but he also recognizes that long-term studies on the impact of *Cirque du Monde's* training sessions would be beneficial: "Every time after the training, we do an evaluation of the participants, we do an evaluation with the trainers, and we do an evaluation with the partners, and those three assessment evaluations, we analyze them ... With the participants, a lot of time they really enjoy the training. But for us, it's not enough. You can enjoy it, but does it change anything? We're very good at making training fun, and they think we're nice and we have a nice attitude and everything, but at the end, did they learn something from it? ... The evaluation of the instructor is challenging for us right now and it would be very interesting to evaluate how big an impact our training has on the field six months later or a year later."

What is the experience for participants in a training session conducted by *Cirque du Monde* or by others trained by *Cirque du Monde*? What has learning to juggle or leading a social circus workshop meant for youth and their instructors involved with *Circo Social Ecuador*? Chapters 5, 6, and 7 all speak to the learning and experiences of participants, instructors, and others, thus contributing to an ongoing evaluation of how social circus has been introduced and received in Ecuador.

In a curious way, how our research was undertaken in Ecuador is an evaluative act, as we reflect upon our experiences, gather our interviews, engage in arts-based inquiry, turning to the narratives of those who have participated in social circus for their perspectives. Some things are difficult to evaluate in conventional ways; we have to listen with our hearts. What is the worth of a young adult's self-esteem as he leads a group of teenagers in a discussion on the tatami mat; an instructor's shout of triumph as a participant swirls with confidence in the ribbons; or the feelings of accomplishment among instructors and participants as they listen to the applause of their community? What emerges, for us, as we experience and reflect upon social circus pedagogy is Arendt's question of "Who are you?" and, perhaps more importantly, "Who will I become in your presence?"

Social circus pedagogy embodies "natality," as conceptualized and articulated by philosopher Hannah Arendt (1958); Arendt (1962) asks educators if they love children enough to invite them into the world's renewal, not as we imagine it might become but as they will choose to create it. As Levison writes: "Natality is manifest in the world whenever individuals and groups act in relation to the world in ways that suggest that seemingly intransigent social processes can be changed" (Levison 2001, 17). The invitation of natality, to see ourselves and each other anew, to become that which we are not yet, is not overtly discussed in social circus, but the project itself as a social enterprise embodies natality in its ways of welcoming and empowering those who engage in the project. Those who are committed to social circus see its pedagogical value not as a strategy to remove youth from the streets (albeit, as discussed elsewhere in the book, this is not beyond what some funders see as the main goal of social circus), but rather as a condition of recognition, acceptance, and hospitality requiring new ways of being in relationship together, in family, in community.

Social circus pedagogy meets Dewey's call for experiential learning, a pedagogy that listens to the body as a place of knowing and learning (Snowber 2016). Social circus pedagogy is transformative, seeking to move learners from the transmission model of learning so dominant in conventional education to one that is interactive, embodied, and relational, hopefully transformational, as instructors and participants learn alongside each other. Freire's pedagogy of the oppressed seeks to awaken all of us – educators, politicians, social and community workers, and youth – to the wealth of experience and potential within each one of us.

How wonderful, then, that through the Ecuadorean government's desire to put *Buen Vivir* into action, a national social circus was conceived! Social circus is perceived by those who engage in its practice as a pedagogical vehicle of social change and an opportunity to nurture and facilitate engaged citizenship. Therefore *Circo Social Ecuador*, and all who support this political and social endeavor, have been tasked by the government (whether the government is aware of it or not) to question and reimagine *what is.* Hannah Arendt (1961) calls upon educators to conserve that which is perceived as most important, as the fate of the world passes from one generation to the next. What, we wonder, are the critical values to be transferred from Ecuador today, to its youth of tomorrow?

Postscript

"Lynn, come, join me on the tatami. The next activity will help us prepare for our next performance."

The teenagers and young adults walk around the space with little enthusiasm or energy, some with hands in pockets, others distracted by their own affairs. As Benjamin guides them through his activity, I follow along, hoping to blend into the group, keeping a low profile.

"Everyone, as you walk, be present, attentive, awake. Follow your own direction, see where it goes. And listen. The faster I clap, the faster the speed."

Benjamin claps and everyone walks faster, the energy in the room increases.

"Now, get in a circle. Here's a ball to throw to each other. Don't let it touch the ground."

He tosses the ball to someone who mimes juggling, pretending to almost drop the ball. Laughter. We toss the ball to each other, leaping high to catch it, our laughter increases, the pace accelerates, we throw the ball recklessly, not checking if the other person is ready to receive it – the ball lands on the floor.

"No problem.'" Benjamin retrieves the ball. "This time let's pass the ball as if the ball is something beautiful that you want to pass to the other person."

This time the ball is passed calmly, gently, with affectionate gestures. The pace slows down, interest dissipates. Benjamin intercedes.

"The ball is a metaphor for our show. When you throw the ball make sure that the person you are throwing it to is making eye contact with you. Use the *jonglage* technique, launch the ball in an arch."

The pace increases but this time everyone looks at each other's eyes before passing the ball, we communicate back and forth across the room and toss the ball high. Then, Benjamin releases two more balls into the group!

"All the balls are equally important, just like all the acts of a show. Each ball is what one wants to put in the show and each is nourished by what follows the next. We all need to help to make the show work, it is our common dream, our project."

The three balls circulate, everyone concentrating, but again a ball falls. Benjamin retrieves the ball and launches it into the air, saying, "As in life, sometimes things fall, relationships break, projects fail. Understand that if you fall, that experience is teaching us something; I need to pay more attention, I should perhaps better establish if the person is ready to receive my gift, my dream, or I need to be more attentive when someone is willing to give me something or is asking for help. The more the ball falls, the more we learn. Each time we learn a better technique to pass the ball, a better way to communicate with others, to tell each other what we need or asks us to understand."

Beyond teaching the techniques required for juggling, body awareness, mindful attention, and eye contact, the activity brings everyone together. We learn collaboration, teamwork, focus, patience, perseverance, and –

oops! another dropped ball! – to find within ourselves, with the support of others, the resilience to try again when we stumble. On the tatami, under Benjamin's guidance, we prepare for the show that is our life, shared with others, in this moment.

The simple act of throwing and catching a ball becomes both metaphor and practice for creating a show, being present in our relationships, attending with care to those standing in the circle, playing in exploration, in learning, in a shared journey. Social circus pedagogy is a pedagogy for living life well. *Buen Vivir*. Here on the tatami is the heart of social circus pedagogy.

5 Through Their Own Bodies, Eyes, and Voices: Social Circus, Social Inquiry, and the Politics of Facilitating "Collectivity"

JUDITH MARCUSE, LYNN FELS, KATHERINE M. BOYDELL, AND JENNIFER BETH SPIEGEL

In community-engaged arts practices, facilitation is always embedded in a social politic. The facilitator never brings a pedagogical vision into action in neutral conditions; the burdens carried by those in the room become core elements of community arts practice. Social circus, as we saw in the last chapter, embodies a pedagogy that holds much in common with Freire's "pedagogy of the oppressed" and Boal's "theatre of the oppressed," navigating trust, risk, and play. While debriefing sessions between participants and instructors are a key component, social circus is not a verbal, logic-based activity, but rather an affective, embodied, and reflective process. How, then, does one glean the experiences of those involved, and what politics are involved in doing so?

Any method of inquiry is beholden to its own framework, each deriving from its own series of epistemological and ontological roots. Arts-based inquiry opens up ways to explore the richness of health and social interventions, programs and supports, and invites multiple levels of engagement that are cognitive, sensory, emotional, and aesthetic (Cox and Boydell 2016). Arts-based research embraces a variety of forms: i) *"performative"* including theatre (Belliveau and Lee 2016) and dance (Boydell 2011; Snowber 2012, 2016),

ii) *"visual"* including film (Tilleczek and Loebach 2015), photography (Wang et al. 2000), and drawing (Guilleman 2004), and iii) *"literary"* including poetry (Prendergast et al. 2009) and fiction (Richardson 2000). In addition to engaging in a variety of media, arts-based researchers employ a variety of practices, theories, and forms of knowledge-representation and mobilization (Boydell, Gladstone et al. 2012), such as a/r/tography (Springgay et al. 2005), social construction frameworks (Boydell 2011), embodied inquiry (Snowber 2012, 2016), performative inquiry (Fels 1998, 2012), and numerous other approaches.

These methods of research recognize personal, emotional, experiential, and embodied expressions of knowledge as effective strategies to engage communities and to communicate to a variety of audiences (Boydell, Jackson et al. 2012). They offer participants and researchers opportunities to pose new questions, attain deeper understanding, and enhance knowledge translation through creative modes of engagement. Collaborations between artists, facilitators, and researchers offer thought-provoking possibilities for crossing interdisciplinary boundaries, transcending the potential constraints of conventional modes of dissemination, and developing innovative ways of working together (Cole and Knowles 2008; Gwyther and Possamai-Inesedy 2009; Boydell 2011). As such, these techniques represent ways to encourage individuals (particularly young people) to share stories and experiences (Boydell 2013; Baker et al. 2015).

Arts-based methods offer particularly relevant techniques through which to look at social circus, as this practice is itself an embodied art of inquiry that seeks social change at individual, communal, and political levels. When combined with other more conventional methods of inquiry detailed in chapter 2, arts-based research opens a particular way for participants to explore and speak "in their own language."

Several forms of arts-based research were used in this study to reflect on the processes, tensions, and impacts of *Circo Social Ecuador*, including theatre-based facilitation, photo-voice, and performative inquiry, as well as video. The first three methods formed the subject of workshops with Quito's social circus community, whereas videography allowed the recording of workshops for their participants as well as informing the researchers' own reflections and ethnographic study (unpacked most extensively in chapter 7 of this book). This chapter focuses on what was learned through these workshops and the implications for understanding the politics of enabling the collective experience.

Initiating Collective Community Research through Performative Inquiry

Through their training and experience, instructors make visible the lessons of social circus and communicate their metaphorical relationship to individual lives and relationships. The work is embodied, collaborative, and interdependent, challenging participants to reimagine their roles in the world, what they have to offer, and who they might become. Social circus offers new ways of engagement to those relegated to the margins of society, inviting them into meaningful participation and presence. As discussed in the previous chapter, this is why instructor training, not only in technical skills, but also in social pedagogy, is crucial.

Performative inquiry is a particular form of research that invites participants, through role drama, image work, improvisation, and other arts activities to attend to "stop moments" – moments that "tug on our sleeve" (Fels 2012). A stop moment is an interruption, an embodied pause in action. These are the "moments of risk, moments of opportunity," which awaken participants to the choices and habits within the relationships and actions in which they engage through performative play and everyday living (Appelbaum 1995). A space of recognition is opened, whether within a co-created moment or upon reflection; we, as participants, as researchers, perform that which we may have not yet recognized or named. Performative inquiry invites a reflective, critical, and creative lens of inquiry, recognizing that the act of creating or performing is, itself, an action site of embodied knowing, inquiry, and learning. This performative space, which theatre director Peter Brook (1968) refers to as "the empty space," is a liminal space of inquiry, a generative space within which stories may be told and learning released through play.

Performative literacy – the ability of the researcher and participants to be able to embody, perform, and "read" the scene, tableau, and dramatic action that is offered, both known and not-yet realized – is critical to meaning-making. Thus, in any arts-based inquiry, the facilitator requires both a high level of performative literacy and the political and personal insight to recognize the possibilities of metaphor and analogy. They need to be able to read between the lines of what is presented and what remains unsaid. Both physical literacy and creative expression are strongly cultivated in social circus participants (Spiegel 2016; Spiegel and Parent 2017; Besone 2017; Kriellaars 2013). Physical expression is thus an ideal medium through which to explore in a manner that is commensurate with the participants' own practice.

Building on these strengths, in Quito in February 2015, six of the seven authors of this book participated in a three-day workshop along with other members of the Universidad Andina Simon Bolivar (UASB)-based research team. The goals and format were collectively generated in keeping with the principles discussed in chapter 2. Individuals invited to attend this workshop were drawn from the most advanced group of participants and volunteers from *Circo Social Quito*, as well as the three instructors, the local coordinator, and the municipal official managing the program. Research activities were co-designed with the editors, Canadian cultural studies scholar Jennifer Spiegel and former Ecuadorean instructor, performer, and pedagogical director of social circus Benjamin Ortiz Choukroun, who together also oversaw and/or co-chaired the events. In conversation with the research team, senior Canadian social-arts practitioner Judith Marcuse planned and facilitated the theatre-based exercises and photo voice debriefings, with the exception of the final stage of photo voice exchange which was led by the participants themselves with instructions from Spiegel and Ortiz. Annalee Yassi, Arturo Campaña, and Lynn Fels all participated and contributed insights throughout, each offering sessions on particular techniques that would be utilized in the research – Yassi and Campaña together providing an overview of the quantitative methods, and Fels introducing the ideas behind the use of photovoice. Spiegel also shared visuals and insights from her work in Quebec, while Ortiz brought depth to discussions of social circus pedagogy. Maria José Breilh, the Ecuadorean research coordinator, both participated and translated; Bayron Torres videotaped the entire process and helped initiate participants into the art of photography. In essence, the research team attempted to model collectivity in the design of the workshop itself.

On the first day of the workshop, Dr Jaime Breilh, the rector of UASB, the university where the workshop took place during the first two days, welcomed the participants. Everyone gathered in a circle. Participants' familiarity with each other and their high levels of physical and performative literacy made it possible to move quickly through the early moments of the workshop. After introductory remarks, Marcuse invited each person to create a simple gesture and a sound that expressed what they were thinking and/or feeling. The whole group then copied each person's gesture and sound. This process was repeated around the circle until everyone had "spoken." Each person was then asked to share their name, one thing about themselves that they thought would be of interest to the others, and the best thing that had happened to them during the last week. The best things tended to be about family, work-related developments, and their recent technical accomplishments in circus.

These introductions were followed by an activity called "popcorn" – an easy way to elicit a quick reading of individual sensibilities. Participants were asked to volunteer single words that described social circus for them. An asset of this non-ordered, spontaneous process was that the activity offered a low-pressure situation in which people could speak whenever ready. While scarcely recognized as a research method by most participants, the exercise revealed deeply held values. Responses from the group included: "team," "emotion," "heart," "body," effort," "sovereignty," "work," "structure," "movement," "family," "hug," "solidarity," "touch," and "love"; some of these words were repeated by more than one participant. No one threw out a word carelessly. The word "fun," interestingly, was not mentioned, which suggested to the researchers that for these participants, despite its aura of playfulness, social circus is a serious undertaking and commitment.

The workshop continued with a series of games and debriefing sessions. A Boal-inspired exercise was conducted in which participants were asked to walk around the room at a speed with which they were comfortable; the only instructions given were to avoid collisions, to fill empty spaces, and to pay attention to what they, themselves, were doing while being aware of others' patterns around them. This exercise became increasingly challenging when participants were asked to repeat the activity with arms fully spread out to the side (see photo 5.1) and then, linking elbows, repeating the walking process in pairs (see photo 5.2), then in groups of three, four, and five. Participants were then asked to take part in three stages of analysis, first describing their experience doing the exercise, then reflecting on that experience, and finally exploring what that experience implied in terms of their thoughts and feelings about social circus. Participants talked about the need for collaboration and attention to the space around them as well as how different personalities were revealed as they chose to lead or to allow themselves to be pulled in different directions. Thus, the activity became a series of metaphors about the group's dynamics, including issues of independence, co-dependence, and compromise, along with the need for trust and thoughtful awareness of others.

PARTICIPANT 1: When I go with other people, my attention is wider and my hearing increases. I have to be aware of my mates and

Photo 5.1 People walking with arms spread during the "Fill the Empty Space" exercise, Day One of the workshop held at the Universidad Andina Simon Bolivar (UASB), Ecuador, in 2015.

Photo 5.2 People walking in twos, the second of four stages of the "Fill the Empty Space" exercise, Quito, Ecuador, 2015.

listen to where they are going and also, I would guide them if other groups come.

PARTICIPANT 2: When I am alone, I feel very comfortable because I can go to the places I like. In a group you have to compromise sometimes, because one always wants to be a leader, but sometimes you have to compromise. And in a group, I think that if you let others take you away, you can close your eyes and won't crash into anyone, because maybe somebody else is directing, and you trust in them.

As debriefing continued, the focus of the conversation turned to leadership, decision-making, awareness of the necessity for compromise, following expectations, pedagogical and institutional ethics and the multiple ways that individuals "step into leadership." Some participants focused on the act of choosing partners and learning to become inclusive:

PARTICIPANT 3: When you need to make a group, first you see who you are going to pick, who you are going to hug, who is by your side, because that was the order ...

PARTICIPANT 4: When one is starting the work in circus, for instance, if somebody arrives with her little brother, she always picks that little brother to work with her. It is a matter of affinity. At the beginning when you start working, one searches for trust, but then in the process one gains trust and one can work with whichever partner.

The relationship between learning to work inclusively and overcoming one's own fears was highlighted.

PARTICIPANT 5: When we first started doing this kind of exercise, I could not talk with my partners. When I needed to do something in front of everybody, I was very nervous, it was something traumatic for me. When we started doing these exercises in groups, it helped me feel included. An opportunity to have physical contact with somebody who I can talk to later, with whom I can relate and talk. Also, when we did presentations and we moved around the spaces, it helped me explore my creativity. It helped me confront my fears.

One participant spoke about the activity as a metaphor for addressing the broader issue of adaptation – how individuals have to meet the requirements and goals of the institution within which they work. This comment quickly led to a conversation about expectations and ethics, leading toward a politic of social circus organizations and the tensions therein.

> PARTICIPANT 6: It is about adaptation ... The important thing is to assume the role, when one is inside the institution of *Circo Social* one is part of *Circo Social* and takes on the goals of *Circo Social* even when the goals are not yours, even when the goals are against yours, you have to take on the goals because you are in the institution ... What is important is to achieve goals (to fill spaces, to not bump in each other) ... determined by the ethics of the institution.

The debriefing of this activity made visible the competing goals within participants' experience of social circus – between those wanting to become "technical" circus artists and those engaged in social circus as an agent of social change. One participant wisely suggested that these goals did not have to contradict each other, that the pedagogy of social circus required technical skills.

> PARTICIPANT 7: In my experience, if you are only a person who practices the technique as you are told to, then you are wrong and you are destroying somebody. In reality, that could be clarified by saying that both things (technically and socially) make you a better person. And I think discipline is something that makes you change a lot, both ways. So if on this side or this other there is no discipline, then nothing happens.

> PARTICIPANT 8: I only want to emphasize that whether it is social or whether it is technical circus – in both ways, if you make an abstraction of the process, if you analyze [it ... from either angle, as a 'social' or 'technical' circus metaphor] any way [through circus] you are getting better as a person.

Benjamin Oritz spoke about how this activity presented a valuable learning opportunity in terms of being able to articulate the difference between *social circus* pedagogy and *circus* pedagogy to the researchers – and perhaps even to some of the participants – who may not yet have been completely familiar with this difference.

Imaging the Personal and the Collective: The Surfacing of Political Rifts

In a series of exercises and dialogues, individual participants moved from creating abstract still and silent shapes to small and larger group images that reflected myriad aspects of topics explored in the workshop. Dancer and curriculum theorist Celeste Snowber (2016) reminds us of the power of the body as an action site of inquiry and knowledge: "The body is a vehicle of exploration, an action site of knowing, which leads us to creative expression and understanding of what is not yet articulated."

This exercise began with an illustration that the same body image can have different meanings for each person and that what each person sees, therefore, is "correct," drawing out the importance of positionality not only in considering the spectators' experience of a work of art but also in the act of analyzing research data (Diamond 1992). A "complete-the-image" theatre game followed in which one person offered a shape with their body that was then "completed" when a second person joined with their own shape, creating a "story." The first person then left, and another joined to create a new, two-person image and story. Meaning shifted rapidly as one body replaced another, reframing the body that remained. This process was repeated until, after the group had created many diverse images, the two-person image was expanded to create multi-person images specifically focused on social circus. Collective images were deconstructed by everyone in the room exploring the "stories," including interpretation of each person's shape, the relationships between people as implied by their use of space, and other details such as who was making or avoiding eye contact. These group images were then activated with movement, sound, and spoken words. Later in the workshop, participants also explored how they might move from current perceived realities to an "ideal" image ... all expressed through the body.

Participants initially created very positive images – of mutual support, new ways to learn, collaboration, community, a sense of family, and cooperation. Later images revealed concerns, in some cases illustrated underlying issues. Responses to general questions such as: "What do you see?" and "What does this image make you think about?" became more detailed and nuanced as the group explored the metaphors contained within the images themselves and in further interpretation of those images. Eventually, a quiet tension in the room implied that there was more to explore beyond the mostly positive discourse that we had heard earlier in the day. The tensions between technical and social circus goals suggested earlier began to become clearer, as did serious concerns about structural problems with the program, including the safety of circus equipment, interpersonal issues, and a lack of clarity about both individual roles and leadership.

Throughout this introductory day, various research methodologies were explored. The participants were invited to provide input to the survey being designed and suggest how to circulate it; previous ethnographic research with a social circus organization in Quebec was presented, opening a conversation around similarities and differences; and discussion occurred about a video of a theatrical circus performance directed by one of the social circus instructors in which many in the group had participated (this will be discussed further in chapter 7). The day ended with an exercise inviting the sharing of thoughts and feelings. This exchange was not a dialogue; sharing was optional. It was designed as a way for participants to gain some closure at the end of what had been an intense and somewhat challenging day. To conclude the workshop, participants bowed to each other sequentially around a circle. This simple ritual brought the group together to acknowledge the contributions of each person and to express respect for each other.

As researchers, we knew there was much more to explore the following day. As participants are invited to engage in exercises and games, the responsibility of workshop facilitators is to explain and promote processes for personal safety such as respect, mutual care, and confidentiality, especially as the exploration of issues deepens. The facilitator's role is thus to frame the inquiry with a series of activities and questions. Pablo Helguera identifies key principles of facilitation: collaboration, accountability, and expertise; the ability to frame the work within a socially engaged art project without dictating what issues are to be explored; nurturing a collaborative relationship with participants; and creating a collaborative environment, all "within the realities and possibilities of the environment that he or she is working in" (Helguera 2011, 57). Helguera's four levels of community participation and control – nominal, directed, creative, and collaborative – provide a gradient for understanding principles of ownership and agency at work in social arts practices. In the case of our research workshop, the facilitator helped the participants to frame their experiences as research; she also managed what emerged through the inquiry through a series of reflective questions and dialogue, inviting all to participate: researchers, instructors, volunteers, and *Circo Social Quito* administrators. The politics of positionality was unavoidable, challenging the team to focus on flattening the hierarchy as much as possible.

Work resumed the next morning. After a simple physical warm-up to help bring the group back together after an overnight recess, a mini-workshop on performative inquiry and how to attend to "tugs on the sleeve" or stop moments was offered to help participants approach their experiences, as social circus practitioners often do, deeply in their bodies. Participants were reminded to attend to how we see, hear, and respond to spoken communication and what is revealed through our bodies; to pay attention to and to reflect upon those moments in which action is desired; and to ask the questions: What if? What happens? What matters? So what? Who cares? It is critical to remember that moments that arrest our attention are embedded within the social, communal, political, economic, and institutional contexts within which our explorations take place. Throughout the workshop we listened to the voices of all participants (Freire 1972), those who spoke and those who remained silent, seeking awareness of power dynamics (Foucault et al. 2008). We trusted that the work itself would reveal insights into the relationships within and the workings of *Circo Social Quito*.

With this orientation completed, the image-making exercises initiated the first day of the workshop continued. In another exercise, working silently and in pairs, "sculptors" shaped their partners, described in this exercise as "clay," to create two images ... one for practice and another that described a moment in which they felt unhappy, oppressed, or unsatisfied while involved in social circus activities. Then roles were reversed, giving everyone an opportunity to reflect on and create an image expressing personal experiences they wished to share.

One stop moment that gave rise to rich discussion and helped shape subsequent research was an image created by a group of participants (photo 5.3). One of the researchers, who happened to be wearing a suit, was positioned at the centre of the image, looking as if he was about to execute a circus move with the assistance of those surrounding him. Four very different interpretations of that same image were offered, each about issues of power and control related to the bureaucratic administration of the *Circo Social*. One interpretation was about lack of consultation with participants, while another was about how the practices of social circus could inform better social policy. A third interpretation featured collaboration across class differences, while a fourth explored a strongly felt precariousness of the entire program. These interpretations, although not the original intent of the image's creators (which was about people supporting each other), would lead to the exploration of very serious issues the next day.

Photo 5.3 An image created during the first day of the workshop at UASB, Quito, February 2015, sparking discussion of the various interpretations of the issues portrayed.

In another tableau, one person was seated on the floor asking for help (photo 5.4). Another figure, standing apart from but facing the group, looked aggressive, his face in a silent, angry shout (not visible in the photo). One standing figure was precariously balanced, his legs crossed, arms also crossed pointing in opposite directions. Another figure, quite close to the others, was hunched over, heavy with weight or depression, while close by, someone else was looking for direction. Yet another figure pointed ahead with one hand while his other hand covered his eyes, and another looked like he was working very hard. Few people were looking at each other. At this point, the facilitator asked everyone to move in stages toward what they wanted. Some participants looked as if they were clear about their desires; others followed. A few moved away from the group. It was clear that there were unresolved issues, conflicting ambitions, and desires embodied within the statues created.

There appeared to be common agreement and support for the principles and goals of *Circo Social*, although as dialogue continued, a rift between

Photo 5.4 An image created by workshop participants late in the first day of the workshop in Quito, in 2015, which expresses their concerns about *Circo Social*. From right to left, Nancy Jaramillo (coordinator), A. Campaña (researcher), Adrián Llumipanta (volunteer), Soledad Contreras and Mario Sánchez (instructors), Stephen Mier (head of youth programs for the Municipality), Arianna Páez (volunteer), and Josué Tapanca (participant).

various participants' perspectives about the program surfaced. By the end of this session, the atmosphere was less than celebratory. Some people appeared to be closing down; their arms crossed, their eyes averted. There was less laughter. The day's work ended with a brief exercise reflecting on what had happened, using both words and gestures. Something was simmering beneath the words and gestures, visibly embodied but unspoken.

Facilitation and the Politics of Purpose: Critique, Celebration, Transformation

The palpable tensions surfacing raised anew the question of purpose: the purpose of social circus, the purpose of the research, and how to facilitate ethically in moments of conflict. While the first two days were held at the university, the third day was at the venue of *Circo Social Quito*, the site of Quito's old, unused airport (photo 5.5). The shift from the university to

Photo 5.5 A hangar at the old airport in Quito served as the main venue for *Circo Social Quito.*

the field brought home the implications of the research and the political nature of what was unfolding.

We began the third day by assembling and cleaning the modular tatami, mats needed to make the concrete floor of the hangar safer for our work. This simple and almost daily preparation for members of *Circo Social Quito* became a research activity as questions of who was leading, who was participating, and how well the group was working together swiftly surfaced. Reflecting on this mundane activity, one of the instructors spoke beautifully about collaboration, responsibility, and learning to work together, something everyone experienced or could reflect upon as the researchers and participants collectively connected the pieces of the tatami. However, as we sat in our welcoming circle, the tension became acute. What was happening? It was time to build on the insights and conflicts revealed in the workshop process. Rather than leading us into the next arts-based activity, Marcuse invited the group to speak to how they were feeling – to surface issues that were clearly straining relations among those present.

Photo 5.6 Mural beautifying the venue of *Circo Social Quito*, February 2015.

There was increasing tension as participants started to talk more candidly about issues, including a sense of payment disparities and unfairness.
Then, one member of the group revealed that he had just learned that *Circo
Social Quito* was going to lose their home in the hangar because it was in an
area slated for development. This was shocking news for the group, most
of whom had volunteered many hours to clean and beautify the space.

The senior municipal official responsible for managing the local social
circus program was present, as was the recently appointed psychologist responsible for coordinating *Circo Social Quito*. Both had taken part in some
of the activities during the previous two days. After a much-needed break,
the officials attempted to clarify the situation, presenting a graphic plan
for the proposed new space (much smaller than the hangar) and explaining
the bureaucratic structures that restricted their decisions. This candour
diminished anger and led to some moments of perceived reconciliation
and a sense of common cause. The participants' commitment to and care
for their work was clearly evident, as was the sense that some people felt

Photo 5.7 After tensions had surfaced on the previous day of the movement/
theatre workshop, a game of exchange using an imagined ball of energy was used
to refocus, energize, and positively reconnect the group at the venue of *Circo
Social Quito*, 2015.

that their efforts were not valued. There were tears, a desire to speak to individual situations, strong feelings expressed, and some brave individuals
spoke candidly about what mattered to them based on their experience
and perspective. The rumours, infrastructure problems, lack of resources,
and perceived inequity of opportunity and remuneration made it difficult
for the group to move forward as a team into an uncertain future. As we sat
on the tatami mats in a circle, the participation of the administrator and
psychologist, and their willingness to engage in difficult dialogue, sharing
their own stories and perspectives, enabled the whole group to begin to
listen to each other and the challenges each faced, diminishing the distance between them. Some individuals who had been in conflict eventually
hugged each other.

The plan that day had not been to discuss the impending space crisis,
but the convergence of personnel brought together by the workshop made

Photo 5.8 An image from one of the short scenes created on the last day of the movement/theatre workshop in Quito, to deepen perceptions of the concerns of the participants and to explore positive new directions. In this scenario, people are either unable or unwilling to hear or listen to each other.

it both possible and necessary to address their shared challenge then and there: How were they to move forward together, with the possibility of severely reduced space and consequently, limited programming?

The group was asked if everyone was willing to continue with the day's research activities. Everyone agreed. To refocus the group and encourage a more positive energy, the facilitator introduced a new exercise. An imaginary ball of energy was sent and received by participants – at first with only hands and arms and then increasingly involving more of the body, as participants improvised the rules of the game (photo 5.7). A sense of release was created.

It seemed that everyone wanted to regroup in a more positive way. The group was asked to offer three still single-person shapes, each one quite different from the other, that expressed an element of their experience of social circus. The remaining participants were then asked to stand with

Photo 5.9 In the second scene during the last day of the workshop, the group forms a supportive structure to allow instructor Soledad Contreras to climb to the top for a "wider" view.

the person whose shape most resonated for them. The three groups each then created three-minute performance pieces that expanded on the central ideas of the shape. Laughter filled the space as people worked together, suggesting a sense of relief as everyone returned to creative processes. When called together to share their images, all were attentive, and generous in their receptivity.

The scenes were each performed twice and then discussed by the whole group, providing an analysis of key moments when crises or transformation occurred or solutions were found. Tension and resolution were evident in all three offerings. As shown in photo 5.8, the actors in the first scene are listening intently, hands cupping both ears, trying to understand each other. Other people enter the playing area separately, each person isolated and very active, not paying attention to anyone else ... on the phone, dancing, trying to figure something out, late for an appointment, waiting impatiently for someone. Chaos ensues as they begin to talk, to shout, each isolated in their own space, ignoring each other. The noise level keeps rising. Eventually, one person shouts: "Enough!" Everyone freezes, and they slowly turn to look at each other.

In the second image, one person wanders about the stage on his own. A group enters, led by someone who is marching everyone forward. There is disagreement, and another person leads the group in another direction, this time using a silly walk, which everyone copies. A third leader has everyone crawling in yet another direction. The person who has been on his own (his headstand was the core image) then joins the "lost" group, and they begin to create a supportive structure that enables the smallest person to climb to the top, becoming a lookout (photo 5.9). She scans the horizon, and points in a new direction. As she points, all eyes follow her suggestion. There is calm.

In the third image, one participant flies into the performance space, mimicking an airplane. (Laughter erupts as a real airplane flies overhead!) Three more figures enter singing "Hi ho, hi ho, it's off to work we go!" Two figures arrange themselves into a mirror structure; a third then climbs on top to create a simple pyramid. The structure is presented to the audience as if a great feat has been accomplished (photo 5.10).

In helping the group reflect on all three scenes, the facilitator was able to take into account the tensions expressed before this artmaking began, concerns which became embedded within the scenes themselves. In the first scene, in which the group of participants intermingled in a chaotic pattern, shouting, ears covered, not listening to each other, meaningful

Photo 5.10 The third scenario explored contrasting concepts of flying freely and of "hard work."

communication was impossible. The failure of the figures to communicate became increasingly difficult to witness, until finally someone yelled for everyone to stop. True listening, as we witnessed and experienced, began in the scene and continued during debriefing.

In this moment, the researchers and participants were deeply involved in the exploration and shared reflections that revealed the internal relationships, tensions, and the politics we were investigating. We learned about the resilience of our participants, who were willing to engage in our research despite having just heard the heartbreaking announcement of the impending loss of their beloved hanger which, for some, was perceived as a home, a place where they could be themselves, where what mattered to them was keenly felt and expressed. And here, despite the misunderstandings and conflicting ambitions, listening was happening in ways that mirrored the always-imperfect sharing circles of social circus itself. While as researchers we could not resolve their grievances, the differences between participants seemed negotiable. The psychologist responsible for the program had asked earlier that morning, "Can we work together? Can we work this out?" Here at this juncture, the politics of facilitation became palpable, as did the politics of research itself. The role of the facilitator was critical in allowing space for these encounters, in guiding the process from critique to celebration of what was important. Here the university-based researchers were not simply passive observers but rather active participants in the analysis of images and dialogue. Dialogue became research: by identifying – first through creative exploration and expression, and then through discussion and reflection – what action was needed to strengthen the program in a manner that took into account all the competing visions in the room.

The second scene, which elicited great laughter, illustrated what happens when a group is led by first one leader, then another, then another, everyone mimicking each other's movements without clear communication, meaningful objectives, or shared expertise. Only when the group stopped and recognized the futility of their actions did meaningful action and shared leadership come into play. Through embodied consultation, they built their pyramid, each participant standing as a support for the others, so that the figure on the top could see beyond the previous frenzied movement of bodies. In performance, the possibilities became clear. Participants were encouraged to look again and again at what had been created (each scene was repeated twice).

Interestingly, the group that created this second scene involved researchers, participants, the psychologist, and the administrator responsible for *Circo Social Quito*; their scene was representative of the struggles within the group, and of *Circo Social Quito's* relationship with the municipal government. A possible resolution was reached in their collective creation: the offering of collaborative skills and strengths so that the whole group could see beyond the current struggle. The critical importance of flexibility and compromise, the security that comes from working together, was revealed in the scene. Subsequent communal and individual understanding was enriched as participants shared their perspectives. The facilitator encouraged the debriefing to continue until the concept of compromise, interestingly, was introduced by the municipal official.

In debriefing the third and final scene (involving the circling airplane and ending with the pyramid), individual participants saw multiple meanings. But they all agreed that the airplane – performed at the hanger that had become the program's home – was a metaphor for social circus. This image was a gift to the collective to fly us beyond the tensions on the tatami, as were all of the contributions.

Each of these three scenes illustrates key issues needing to be addressed by the group: to listen to each other, to communicate, to participate in a shared vision, to work together, to compromise, to recognize and celebrate the hard work and success that they had already accomplished, and to go forward with confidence that they would do so again. The facilitator played a critical role in inviting meaning-making from those participating in and watching each scene. What matters in this kind of workshop is not guessing what the scene is about but eliciting multiple meanings or interpretations, which, in turn, offer possible understandings of what we see, and what we think may be happening.

In chapter 2, we draw upon Masny's use of rhizoanalysis as a tactic to engage in research differently (Masny 2013; Boydell et al. 2016); rhizoanalysis is equally helpful in understanding the value of arts-based inquiry. In Deleuze and Guattari's (1987) conceptual proposal, a rhizomatic process uses a multiplicity of expanding and overlapping connections rather than working from a fixed centre. What becomes obvious as one rereads the transcripts and watches the videos is the engaged participation of researchers and participants in the debriefing of the scenes that we had engaged in; the workshop became a site of convergence where multiplicity, connectivity, rupture, and mapping of the state of social circus could be explored. These workshops were designed to introduce the participants to arts-based research. They offered all of us an opportunity to witness what was created, to "read the data" through viewing and debriefing, and in so doing, come to understand the issues, to identify what mattered. We were blessed by the generosity and expertise of our participants as they created the tableaus and scenes, making visible what mattered to them, through their bodies, in their hearts, with playful, intense creativity.

All participating recognized and respected that individuals were struggling to find common ground, struggling to hear each other, struggling to be present to each other's needs, and together witnessing the vulnerability with which they revealed what they cared about. We learned how deeply *Circo Social* members invested themselves in their commitment to work whatever their motivations, whether or not they were hoping for a new career (and hence frustrated about the lack of resources, expertise, skill levels, and equipment). We were touched by the tenuousness of the relationships; by the release and opening of what mattered to each individual.

Cracks were revealed on the tatami, such as the lack of resources and the fragility of the endeavour, but also the strengths that had led to such as commitment to social circus for what it offered and promised.

Although we had experienced the group unraveling and then regrouping in order to participate in the research, the group was divided in a serious rift between what was perceived as inequality of authority and opportunity, perceived dishonest engagement, mistreatment and inadequacy of equipment, unshared priorities, and unfair distribution of compensation. But they had moved forward in their understanding of the issues and each other.

As our creative collaborations and shared reflections make visible all the ways that we might come to know and re-create the many possible worlds in which we might live, the line blurs between research and life.

Returning and Re-framing: New Visions of Singular and Collective Impacts

When it comes to social constructs ...
Foucault reminds us to look to the systems,
rather than the individuals.
Systems gain authority and power from social constructs,
often disguising inequities and imbalances.

Varela 1987

Foucault (1975) wrote to issues of power, encouraging us to attend to the many possible worlds we create through language, through social constructs, through systems that perform us. *Circo Social Ecuador* is but one possible world: a fragile ecological system, originally a politician's vision, now being played out in multiple ways by instructors, volunteers, municipal officials, psychologist, participants, each performing within the confines of the social and institutional scripts imposed, as individuals improvise, making the seemingly impossible possible. Arts-based research invites the researcher, the municipal official, the clown, the juggler, the volunteer, and the instructor to engage together on a horizontal plane of imagination and authorship, embodied, negotiated, and navigated, through play, through honest efforts to communicate. Arts-based research invites us to share and then to reflect on what we have created together and what remains unsaid.

And yet, we must never forget that we too, as researchers, educators, citizens, are governed by institutions, by hierarchies of knowledge and status and differences in power concerning who structures, frames, and disseminates knowledge to and for whom (Foucault 1975; Fels 2009). Thus, arts-based facilitators have a responsibility to attend to their biases, prejudices, and perspectives, and to be mindfully aware of the context within which they are working; they must "listen to what is in the room," as Patti Fraser advises (in conversation, 2017). They need also to be aware of what has not yet been revealed, the gaps in their own perspectives and experience, seeking always to "enlarge the space of the possible" (Davis et al. 1996). "What artmaking has to offer is not accurate representation but rather the complication of readings so that we can ask new questions. It is when we position ourselves in those tentative locations, and when we insist on making them concrete experiences, that interstices become locations of meaning" (Helguera 2011, 71). Throughout the workshop, the facilitator engages in multiple roles: "teacher, leader, artistic director, boss, instigator, and benefactor ... but the artist cannot disappear ... The expertise of the artist lies in being a non-expert, a provider of frameworks on which experiences can form and sometimes be directed and channeled to generate new insights around a particular issue" (Helguera 2011, 54).

An activist facilitator or arts-based researcher can encourage issues to emerge from the shadows and inspire a level of desire and commitment that leads to future and sustainable engagement beyond the time limits of their own project. The artist/facilitator thus needs to pay attention to power dynamics and the tensions within the room; provide access to counselling or other support services when appropriate; develops deep listening abilities, including "reading the body"; builds on participants' physical and emotional interactions; and offer activities that respect difference while providing space for everyone's voices, including contentious opinions. These and other dialogic and communication techniques skills open spaces for candour and risk-taking while providing safeguards for participants (Marcuse 2015). Yet it is always difficult to figure out whose needs take precedence and how to level and energize the space for the sake not only of product, but also for the sake of future relations.

In this spirit, the following year, some of the original researchers returned. Though precarious, the program had not yet been moved to another location. We returned to inquire more deeply with our participants into the impacts of social circus on their lives, visions, and engagement with their own realities. Many of the same long-term participants and volunteers were present, but there was also a new cohort who had recently joined the program. This time the workshop focused on the use of photovoice, a research technique to which participants had been offered a theoretical orientation by research team-member Fels in the first series of workshops. This second workshop process, spurred by ongoing questions surfaced in Spiegel's ethnographic inquiry, consisted of two preparatory sessions, each with different participants, over two days and, a few days later, a third session that brought everyone's photos together for all to view and discuss. The aim of this process was to gain an understanding of how participants experienced life in their communities (however they interpreted that word) and the relationship of their "outside" lives with their experience of social circus.

In the preparatory sessions, as a warm-up, participants were introduced to a quick series of activities to help them learn to "read" images and to reflect on their daily experiences outside of circus. The first exercise focused on how the same image (in this case, through a "complete-the-image" process) could be interpreted in many different ways, a process akin to the one facilitated during the previous workshop. In the second exercise, each person led their partner through a typical day in their life by briefly describing their activities while also physically leading them through each moment. The partner then acted out what they had learned about that day for the whole room. This interactive process led to conversations about their daily routines inside and outside of their circus activities.

This exercise introduced participants to the relationship between performative and visual literacy. By asking participants to physically experience and "perform" a typical day, it created a bridge between the physical languages of circus, the embodied experiences of daily life, and the work of "seeing" that is core to photography. This activity was followed by instruction on the use of the cameras; participants were asked to choose two photographs to share from a suggested maximum of thirty images. As instructed, they took photographs of objects, people, or places that symbolized aspects of their lives that were important to them, whether positive or negative, and were urged to reflect on and then take photos of what mattered to them in their daily experiences outside of circus.

When the two groups came together in the final session, their photos had been printed and spread out on the floor for everyone to see. The facilitator led individuals and the group to discuss possible meanings, both literal and metaphorical, of each image. Questions such as "What do you see?" and "What does this image make you think about?" led to detailed dialogue about each image as well as exploration of tangential but related topics.

In most cases, time constraints dictated that only one of the photos taken by each person was presented in the individual groups during the workshop. When the group had explored at least one image taken by each participant, each photographer then explained the thoughts and feelings that led them to take the photo and then choose it to show others. Discussion was animated, with many people talking at once and exchanging perceptions in small groups. To allow for further elaboration, we provided audio-recorders for pairs of participants to interview each other about their photos the following week, exploring in depth what the images meant to them. While the formal research team had set the terms of the exercise, the invitation was for the participants to ask the questions that they felt were pertinent.

Many themes that were identified focused on the importance of being part of the *Circo* community as central to participants' sense of well-being, acceptance in society, comfort in their body, and ability to express themselves; the importance of mind/body connections to self-acceptance was highlighted. The photographs taken by participants spoke to the joy derived from social circus and the sense of accomplishment that comes from the hard work of mastering techniques; the desire to "go far"; artistic expression; spirituality and reflective insight; friendship and team work; the strength that comes through struggle; and the importance of family. Several photographs reflected the quest for re-affirming identity and re-discovering their roots. A valuing of the "social" within social circus was core to all, although "social" meant different things to different people, ranging from a strengthening of interpersonal and family bonds, to development of a greater sensitivity to social inequities such as homelessness, to respect for indigenous traditions. Regardless of the pedagogical goals (emphasizing the social over professional development, as explained in chapter 4), every person in the workshop wanted to have circus continue in their lives in some form. Even new participants voiced concern about the legitimacy of social circus as seen by others and fears that they were seen to be doing unimportant work, as discussed in chapter 7. The latter was experienced at both the micro and macro level from family disapproval of participation to the disapproval of policymakers who did not understand the benefits of this form of circus training.

The politics of facilitation are as critical to arts-based research as they are to the facilitation of the arts-based workshops; the goals and ambition of each are designed to call forth learning, insights, and the production of an equitable collectivity through embodied reflexive practice. Yet bias, ambition, concerns, hopeful offerings can be suspect – such is the challenge of arts-based research. Various structural pressures made visible the ongoing struggle between social circus instructor-facilitators whether to prioritize social goals over technical goals, or vice versa; the tensions were palpable, as were the heartfelt desire to engage and to speak to what mattered. The richness and specificity of each participant's response made possible an enriched analysis of what social circus means for those engaged, and how it is experienced. Contributions by those who participated, referenced in other chapters of this book, offer valuable insights into the pedagogy, policy, impacts, and structural and contextual tensions of the process. Yet, the images and explanations generated are also testaments in their own right, eloquent in meaning both individually and collectively.

In lieu of a conclusion, we invite readers to reflect on these contributions on their own terms and to allow both images and words to inform the reading of this book, keeping in mind that even here, as participants contribute "in their own words" and "through their own eyes," the politics of facilitation and our imperfect capacity to navigate the tensions and ambitions of research cannot be effaced. The physical expressions, images, and texts of participants are the ultimate legacy of these collective, arts-based processes and the social transformation that these make possible.

Photo 5.11 "I took this picture because we were very tired from working on the stilts but we still wanted to get a picture, as we were really happy." *Natalia Casillas*

Photo 5.12 "This is the place where we work ... a place where we always share with many artists from different backgrounds. This is the only place we can be who we really are. Every time we have to put on a show, they tell us how to do it, but in this place [the picture] is who we really are. Everyone has their own role and style ... This is the place where we slowly started to grow in the circus. This is where we developed our skills ... People walking on the street will stay and watch if they like it. It's not like a paid show, where you go in and watch. You almost have to stay for the whole show since you already paid. In this case it's different. If they like you they will stay, if not, they'll leave ... I also think that, thanks to the circus, many people have been able to overcome some bad things. It helps you live in a different way ... Sometimes there are people that stop and tell you 'I did not know you were from Ecuador'; they like it and are surprised about that. Other people have very stressful lives or jobs but they go to 'La Ronda' for a little while, watch the show for a bit and they leave happier, they forget about their problems, at least for a moment ... I love to watch their expressions. When I see they look happy, I continue to work on that; if I see other reactions then I switch to another routine. I present in a different way to please the majority of the audience. It has to be fun for them and for me." *Alexander Gomez*

Photo 5.13 "This [landscape] is what I see every time I leave my home. Down here is my house, at the front the Panecillo monument. [This image relates to social circus] because throughout life we must deal with our environment and also find many paths, know which one to choose, and the type of people we engage and socialize with ... There are amazing things human beings can accomplish, like put a statue at the top of the mountain. Stand on other people's arms and maintain your balance, which is very hard to do. The circus, life, the picture I took here are all very real; there are many difficulties in life and we must deal with them."
Jorge Hilaldo

Photo 5.14 "I took a picture of a mask and juggling sticks, which was on a shelf above my bed. Juggling is very hard for me because I don't have good coordination and it's very complicated for me. So I put that image right above me so I can visualize it and think that I can become a great juggler. I know that is not my favourite thing to do and I am not that great at it, but I want to be better ... The mask you use when you go out on stage, play a different role is like going to another world. It's a different world being on stage, so that's what the mask represents ... Sometimes it can be very frustrating not being able to do certain tricks. It's a big challenge for me, juggling. That's why I took it; every day is a challenge for me. So watching those images in my room every day reminds me to do it better each day, train very hard." *Natalia Casillas*

Photo 5.15 (*opposite, above*) "This photo makes me think of two phases – two life styles. One about the university role and the other about what we do here at the circus. What I wanted to show, what is part of my life: university, the silks, my body ... And the university, which is very 'square.' Here I get to be myself; I am more relaxed." *Estefanía Casillas*

Photo 5.16 (*opposite, below*) "I took this picture because this person loves what he is doing; this is the first sticker I received during a circus conference, where I fell in love with what I do now." *Alexander Gomez*

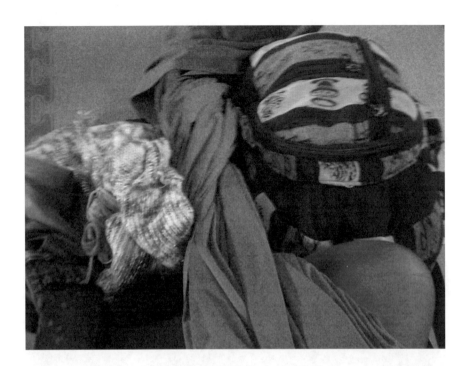

Photo 5.17 "I took this picture because I was by myself on the road and stopped to take a rest. I felt a passion for what I was seeing at the moment, to see my friends and travel companions and see how far I can go." *Juan Pizarro*

Photo 5.18 "Everything that I am involved in with art has to be present – part of you – you just can't study only one thing without art ... your body, your feelings. Art is how you are able to express your feelings." *Ana Morales*

Photo 5.19 (*opposite, above*) "I took this one because I believe that we came from heaven and we return to the sky. It represents everything, the good, the bad. Sometimes there are sunny days and others are cloudy. I think that's what I like the most in this world." *Micaela Ruiz*

Photo 5.20 (*opposite, below*) "I took this picture because it represents the distribution of all my time: university, circus, sleep, eat, everything in general." *Mickael Enríquez*

Photo 5.21 (*above*) "Cats are always telling us something; they show us to be more audacious, more cautious, and more mysterious. I believe these are all important things to learn from cats and apply them to our lives. They are very independent but at the same time they are very lovable." *Estefanía Casillas*

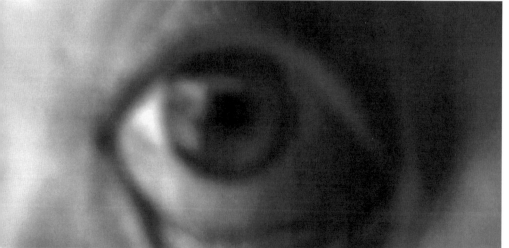

Photo 5.22 (*opposite, above*) "I took the picture when I was at Casa de la Cultura playing soccer alone and at the time it was raining. The ball rolled over a small passage where the water was running, and I saw the bird. I saw it and asked myself, how did it get there and it just died? No one knows when you are going to die." *Richard Quintana*

Photo 5.23 (*opposite, below*) "[I took this picture] because a look represents everything. In a look I can show a lot of joy, a lot of sadness, being annoyed, happy, or not. It represents how I look, how I visualize many things." *Pablo Muñoz*

Photo 5.24 (*above*) "My picture is about a group of friends - classroom friends. That day we were celebrating, being together. My message is about unity, teamwork ... The picture is about a group of people jumping together, equally, that's all. They are happy." *Pablo Muñoz*

Photo 5.25 "These kids were at an artistic event in the south part of Quito. Despite the shows and good artist performances going on, the kids started spontaneously to work together, in groups ... They started to build the first pyramid, all the kids were gathered as if they were doing communal work (*minga*) to form this pyramid. They were not concerned that the train was about to come by and that would make the pyramid fall. As you can see in this picture, they built it again. I like the moment when something breaks. When something that you build falls apart, you can rebuild it again without any concern ... This means a lot, because it provides a lesson to me. When this type of situation happens, when we have problems, sometimes things that are in place can fall apart so easily. Then we must reconstruct, we must use the same passion, enthusiasm as before. Have fun and don't be afraid ..." *Fernando Rodriquez*

Photo 5.26 "I took this photo because this knot was supporting many anchors around it and it was the centre of everything. How you see it here, it's falling apart, but it's due to the strength and how it's being pulled from all different directions ... Colleagues, teamwork [make it stronger], release some weight, and maybe another person takes over if someone feels too tired." *Jorge Hidalgo*

Photo 5.27 "The one I took is a mother with her two children. The mother is combing her daughter's hair while the boy is patiently waiting, observing how his sister is getting her hair done. This picture was taken in Latacunga. I wanted to take lots of pictures from the community wearing their traditional dresses. The mothers make sure their young daughters continue to wear those traditional outfits. I wanted to capture how a mother interacts with her children. At that moment it was something very important, the relationship between mother and child or father and child. What a mother is able to teach her kids, how the children learn from her, and how the children feel about her. I believe the relationship kids can have with their families is the most important thing, the only one that supports you firmly – an unconditional support. Before social circus, when I saw a similar situation, I was not interested ... nothing special. This time I was able to feel something different, appreciate their corporal movements. I was interested to see how with their bodies they were able to express their feelings. At the same time, I wanted to share something inside of me with them so they could take a special feeling with them. This comes from the point of view that these are the people I want to know better, get involved with them, learn more about their values, their way of thinking. Now [since I joined social circus] every time I go out and walk, I am very interested in people's facial expressions. I like it because the mother is so spontaneous; usually people avoid those types of activities [combing hair] in public. In some way, she has the freedom to be herself and do what she wants and needs to do." *Karla Barbosa*

Photo 5.28 "The picture I took is a girl who is surrounded by plants ... That girl is my younger sister, Raquel. I took that picture because we went on holidays, we are from the province of Carchi, and my parents are from there. So we went there during the break and visited the countryside, where we saw a small school. This school was founded by my grandmother's grandfather. Right next to it, there was a nice picturesque view of the highlands and the typical plants. So I took Raquel's picture there, it was like getting connected to our own roots, understanding that you come from a different place, further away. Sometimes things are not always in the city but also in the countryside ... About the picture, sometimes it is important to listen to the stories that come from the past, we just don't know." *Mikaela Ruis*

Photo 5.29 "I did not take the picture, someone else did, but it represents a man on stilts dancing to band music during a parade in Quito's colonial city centre. It represents lots of happiness, and when you look at the outfits and the typical band, it sends a message that the typical 'banda de pueblo' [band which plays typical tunes] is still alive in our daily lives and could animate any kind of party and be the leader of the parade." *Juan Pizarro*

Photo 5.30 "It's part of the culture. People judge you, but they don't provide any help/support. The important part was that when I took this picture, the police were going by and they did not see it as a risk. This man was at risk, he could be hurt, he could vomit and choke ..." *Fernando Rodriquez*

The Impact of *Circo Social Ecuador* and Other Community Arts on Health: A Longitudinal Comparative Quantitative Analysis

ANNALEE YASSI AND ARTURO CAMPAÑA

We must not allow the concept of social determinants of health to become banal, co-opted or reduced merely to smoking, sedentary behavior and poor nutrition, when what we need is to recognize that behind those symptoms and effects lies a social construction based on the logic of a globalized hegemonic culture whose ultimate goal is the commercialization of life itself.

ALAMES et al. October 2011

There have been extensive calls for rigorous evaluation of community arts programs, especially over the past fifteen years (Belfiore 2002; Newman et al. 2003; Putland 2008; Galloway 2009; Belfiore and Bennett 2010). There has also been increasing attention to the role of community arts specifically in promoting health (Cox et al. 2010; Stuckey and Nobel 2010; Clift 2012). But what is "health," and how can it be promoted? Adopting the philosophy of *Buen Vivir* (Good Living) as a guiding principle for a new society necessarily leads to recognizing that a healthy, inclusive, harmonious, social, and naturally sustainable life – different in essence from that based on the principles of individualism, inequality, exclusion, and the exploitation and hoarding of natural resources – is possible and desirable. *Buen Vivir* also implies that the health of individuals is determined by processes that shape their social group's "ways of living," and, in turn, their personal "lifestyles." Ultimately, these social processes define the dynamic relationship between the individual and the collective, and the dialectic between health and disease.

The focus among health scholars and decision-makers on social determinants of health (Marmot et al. 2008; World Health Organization 2008) has been a useful evolution from the biomedical model of health wherein illness was seen largely as a function of an individual's genetic make-up. Nonetheless, many scholars in the Global North (Birn 2009; Navarro 2009; Krieger et al. 2010) in addition to the Global South (Breilh 1979, 2011, 2012; Guzmán 2009; CEBES 2010; ALAMES 2011), prefer the term "social determination of health," proposed decades ago (Breilh 1979), to convey the notion that individual (or even group) risk factors do not just happen but result from processes at the societal level. The argument that ecological sanity and social justice is key to health was also advanced in the Global North over thirty-five years ago (Hancock 1983) and was embedded in the Ottawa Charter for Health Promotion (World Health Organization 1986). Indeed, the dialectical relationship between the health and health-related lifestyles of individuals (at the micro scale), their ways of living as a social group (meso scale), and the socioeconomic processes driving these forces (macro scale), has been increasingly well documented, even if not widely applied (Yassi et al. 2017). In effect, the social determination and "collective health" approach, in contrast to the more traditional social determinants of health analytic framing, focuses attention not merely on the discrete social factors or conditions that impact health and wellbeing (e.g. nutrition, housing, education, income, etc.), but rather on the structural processes at the societal level that lead to these social inequities, and the interrelationships among these (Breilh 2008). We have embraced this understanding of what determines health.

The overall objective driving this study was to better understand the complex ways by which social policies, as well as associated interventions employing the arts (sociocultural interventions), intercede in the dominant modes of constructing ways and styles of being at both individual and collective levels (see also Spiegel et al. 2018). As such, our investigation was not merely descriptive of changes – in attitudes towards fitness, eating habits, and substance use; in access to housing, education, and employment; or even in personal growth, social inclusion, and social engagement – in those who participate in social circus and other community arts. Rather, we were interested in the relationship of these indicators to a proposed post-neoliberal vision of a better life promoted through developing artistic capacities, a sense of community, and social integration (see Spiegel 2016c, for example).

Social circus aims explicitly to work at the psychological, emotional, and affective levels to improve the personal growth and social inclusion of participants as well as their social engagement. According to *Cirque du Monde*: "In this approach, the primary goal [of social circus] is not to learn the circus arts, but rather to assist with participants' personal and social development by nurturing their self-esteem and trust in others, as well as by helping them to acquire social skills, become active citizens, express their creativity and realize their potential. Social circus is a powerful catalyst for creating social change because it helps marginalized individuals assume their place within a community and enrich that community with their talents" (Cirque du Monde, Cirque du Soleil 2014).

In this chapter, we quantitatively assess the extent to which claims about personal growth – "the desire or capacity to change and develop one's self" (Robitschek 1998) – and social inclusion – "the means, material or otherwise, to participate in social, economic, political and cultural life" (Huxley et al. 2012) – as suggested by the above quote, are being met in *Circo Social Ecuador*. In addition, we specifically examine changes in attitudes and practices related to diet, fitness, and consumption of harmful substances – in other words, what some population health researchers have been referring to as behavioural risk factors for ill health (Marmot et al. 2008). Again, we stress that our focus is not on individual risk factors per se, but on the extent to which *Circo Social Ecuador* has been intervening with regard to such indicators and the relationships amongst them.

Importantly, this chapter aims to investigate the question "Why circus?" by comparing not only the impact of social circus on subpopulations within and across the various municipal programs, but also between social circus and other community arts and cultural programs for youth. While assessing the impact of social circus requires a critical mixed methods – indeed rhizomatic – approach (see chapter 2), this chapter contributes to the analysis through an extensive survey, building on work conducted in Quebec (Spiegel and Parent 2016, 2017). Specifically, we seek to:

1 facilitate a better understanding of who participates in social circus, characterizing not only their demographics but also their "ways of living" compared with youth who enroll in other arts and cultural activities;
2 measure the impact of social circus on personal growth, social inclusion and social engagement, including changes related

to schooling, employment, and housing; here we compare the impact of social circus to that of other arts and cultural activities, as well as exploring differences among the various programs and the relationship among these variables and constructs;

3 explore lifestyle changes, focusing on health-related attitudes and practices (including diet, fitness, and substance use in particular), as well as perception of wellness; here we embrace the term "lifestyles" as a collective attribute, "not just as the behaviours that people engage in, but rather, as the relationship between people's social conditions and their social practices" (K.L. Frohlich et al. 2001);

4 analyze the impact of characteristics beyond the programs themselves (age, gender, socioeconomic strata), and whether the individual serves as a volunteer;

5 examine individuals who reported negative impacts and seek to understand what might explain this; and finally

6 outline the implications of our findings.

Our Methodology and Rationale

To understand the impact of social circus, as well as to ascertain what was unique about this sociocultural intervention, we conducted a survey of not only participants but also a comparison group of youth in other arts and culture programs run by the municipality in four youth centres across metropolitan Quito. We were particularly interested in the constructs of personal growth (Robitschek 1998) and social inclusion (Huxley et al. 2012; Coombs et al. 2013), based on previous research conducted by our team on the impact of social circus (Spiegel 2016c), the observations of other social circus researchers (Hurtubise et al. 2003; Avrillon 2011; Bessone 2013b), and the explicit objectives of the national government described in chapter 3.

THE QUESTIONNAIRE: Our questionnaire, shown in the appendix, was designed specifically for studying social circus, adapting and enhancing the questionnaire used in Quebec (Spiegel 2014b; Spiegel and Parent 2016, 2017). It documented:

- Participant demographics, including not only age and gender but also the socio-economic position of the respondent or their family, based on the Social Insertion Index (INSOC; Breilh et al. 2009), an indicator designed to analyze the social determination of health

(Breilh et al. 2014). We did not ask about ethnicity, as this is a fluid concept in Ecuador, and, as such, not recorded even in the census. We did, however, ask about maternal language. Further questions were included about education, housing, employment, and economic resources, as well as satisfaction in these regards.

- A set of sixteen questions measuring self-perception of self-confidence, ability to relate to others, willingness to change, self-esteem, self-control, and optimism, derived from validated questionnaires designed to measure personal growth (Robitschek 1998). The questions were analyzed not only individually but also as a "scale" reflecting the single construct "personal growth."
- A set of nine questions derived from validated questionnaires designed to measure social inclusion (Huxley et al. 2012), including employment, accommodation, access to community services, and sense of group belonging. This set was also measured as a scale, this time for the construct "social inclusion."
- Satisfaction with lifestyle, including diet, physical exercise, and drugs and/or alcohol, as well as satisfaction with physical, financial, and emotional health; and
- Social engagement in society beyond their current arts or cultural activity.

Most questions used a five-point Likert scale (Sullivan and Artino 2013) in which participants were asked to indicate the extent to which they strongly disagree (1) to strongly agree (5) with the statements in the questionnaire. We added questions that asked participants to suggest their own words to characterize their emotions, and we provided space for comments throughout the survey, as well as two final open-ended questions to allow participants to elaborate on the impact of social circus on their families and community.

STUDY DESIGN AND DEFINING THE STUDY POPULATION: The difficulties in researching changes over time (longitudinal studies) with people who do not remain at the same address and/or keep the same email or phone number, have been noted by other researchers (Booth 1999; Benoit et al. 2005). Nonetheless, our intent was to minimize "survivor bias" – the studying of only those who stay in the program and more likely to feel positively towards it. We therefore sought to survey all participants who had enrolled in programs of *Circo Social Ecuador* since its inception in 2011.

After obtaining permission from the national and local authorities as well as approval from research ethics boards, we created databases from whatever records existed (see chapter 3 for description of changes in the programs over time, summarized as well in Spiegel et al. 2018). We indeed used multiple strategies to try to reach as many as possible former as well as current participants.[1] As only 45 respondents completed the question-naire online in the first few weeks of the study (as not everyone has easy internet access or saw the online requests), further efforts included indi-vidual phone calls and site visits (Cuenca, Loja, and Quito).[2] Overall, we obtained 424 survey responses from 254 *Circo Social* and 170 *Casa Metro* participants aged 12 to 39. We also had responses from 68 respondents in younger or older age groups that we collected to analyze separately.

To avoid an extensive number of people who are "lost to follow-up" – a problem that has plagued other longitudinal studies of arts-based activities with street-involved youth (Hampshire and Matthijsse 2010), and other dif-ficulties associated with administering questionnaires at the beginning of a program and trying to link these to answers many months or even years later from the same people (Howard 1980), we used a retrospective "post-then-pre" questionnaire (Rockwell and Kohn 1989) in which respondents were asked to rate their feelings or experiences on each indicator as it is now (post-participation), and think back to how these were before partici-pation in their program.

Of the 254 questionnaires completed from social circus participants, 132 were from youth, young adults, and adults participating in *Circo Social Quito*. As described in chapter 3, this comprised instructors who also ex-perienced the social circus process, as well as volunteers, *replica* partici-pants, and participants training regularly at the municipal venue, includ-ing those involved in specialized workshops at the *Circo Social Quito* site. It also included participants in *replicas* held at community organizations and institutes such as *Honrar la vida*, a foundation serving a marginalized com-munity, *Ecuasol*, an educational French-Ecuadorean foundation serving young people from another vulnerable neighborhood, and social circus in the *Virgilio Guerrero* social rehabilitation centre for male juvenile offenders.

For *Circo Social Loja*, 58 questionnaires were completed by respondents from the *Los Chilalos* therapy centre (housing male adolescents in conflict with the law or who have had drug addiction), the Municipal Therapy Re-lief Centre (serving young adult males with drug and alcohol addictions), and participants as well as volunteers and instructors training at the *San Juan de Jesus* convention centre.

For *Circo Social Cuenca*, 76 questionnaires were collected – including 12 from participants under age 12 and 22 from participants over 39 years old. Respondents included ex-participants from this program as well as from young people from disadvantaged neighborhoods belonging to the *Fundación Mejores Días*, a group of elderly men and women who access social circus through the services of *Fundación Gerosol*, the "Caterpillar Group" (boys and girls who had belonged to different art groups in previous years and were invited to a more advanced program), and youths who participated in workshops in the municipal installations of *Circo Social Cuenca* at *Parque La Florida*.

Circo Social Tena, as explained in chapter 3, operated only from 2012 to 2014; however, we were able to track down 9 participants through social networks and through the Internet. We were not able to obtain permission from the municipality to conduct the survey for *Circo Social Guayaquil*, and therefore had only one respondent who identified this program as their main social circus experience.[22]

While our denominator data are unreliable, and therefore response rates by site cannot be provided, we note that we surveyed all the sites associated with *Circo Social Ecuador* and believe that our sample is relatively representative of all social circus participants aged 12 to 39. As noted above, responses for those over 39 (n=29) and under 12 (n=21) were also collected, but those results, of course, were not incorporated in our comparative analysis with youth in other arts and cultural activities.

Our comparison population of 170 youth participating in different activities included 63 involved in collective creative practices that were generally more physically demanding, such as personal defense, dance, break dancing, capoeira, and parkour, as well as 104 participating in other cultural activities that were generally less physically demanding, including music, guitar, percussion, art, language studies, and other activities.

For most analyses, we compared social circus participants to all participants in *Casa Metro* programs. When studying the impact on physical fitness, we separated the programs into those more physically demanding and those that are less so. Similarly, to study social inclusion, we separated out programs that, according to the literature and our interviews with the *Casa Metro* director, attracted participants because of their more collective and (less mainstream) pedagogical approach – specifically parkour and capoeira (Atkinson 2009). In their study entitled "'If I Climb a Wall of Ten Meters': Capoeira, Parkour and the Politics of Public Space among (Post) Migrant Youth in Turin, Italy" (2016), De Martini Ugolotti and Moyer discuss youth engagement with capoeira and parkour as the media through which struggles about belonging and citizenship take place. They describe how participants "challenge dominant regimes of representation, while also attempting to improve their life conditions and reach their personal goals." Gilchrist and Wheaton (2011), portraying parkour more as a sport than an art, discuss how the perceived success of parkour is related to "the culture and ethos of the activity that is more inclusive, anticompetitive and less rule-bound than most traditional sports, and to its ability to provide managed risk-taking." They note the strong social and emotional bonds that develop between these committed participants "often described as subcultural communities or neo-tribal affiliations – linked by shared attitudes, values, and ways of life" (Wheaton 2007). We were, therefore, particularly interested in these groups due to the similarities with the aims and pedagogy of social circus (see chapters 3 and 4).

For questions related to employment and income, we eliminated those under age 18. For most comparisons between social circus programs, we grouped together those with fewer respondents, either because they were no longer targeting youth as the key group of beneficiaries (Cuenca), or were no longer operating at the time of our survey (Tena), or had had a different political philosophy from that of the national government (see chapter 3) and did not agree to facilitate distribution of our survey (Guayaquil).

STATISTICAL ANALYSIS: To see if the questions related to personal growth and social inclusion respectively were internally consistent, i.e. that they measure the same thing, we conducted the Cronbach's Alpha test (Bland and Altman 1997)[3]; results indicated that we could consider these sets of questions as "scales" rather than as individual questions. We used the SPSS, R statistical software version 3.2.4 and Tableau version 8.1.4 to ascertain statistical significance, defined in this study as having a less than 5% likelihood of being chance findings, using various techniques to ensure a high level of rigour in our analysis.[4] In the figures and tables presenting the results, we have indicated which statistical tests supported the specific analyses discussed.

We also calculated the correlation between our scales, and (conducting linear regression) explored the relationship between personal growth and social inclusion, as well as (conducting linear modeling) examined the influence of the various demographic and other variables. To adjust for significant differences in demographics amongst the participants in different programs, we used "propensity matching" (Ho et al. 2007; Austin

2011; Randolph et al. 2014), creating a new database consisting of pairs of participants from the two programs being compared matched by relevant variables, e.g. age, gender, and social class.

Results

Who Participates? Marginality and Diversity

We confirmed that social circus serves highly diverse groups of all ages, genders, and social classes. Table 6.1 summarizes characteristics of respondents aged 12 to 39 in each of the municipal programs as well as in *Casa Metro*, showing that even among the youth and young adult group there is considerable diversity.

GENDER, MATERNAL LANGUAGE AND AGE: Our respondents included 148 women and 273 men. In Loja, over 81% of respondents were male – significantly higher than the other programs, where the male to female ratio equaled 1.6. While sex and gender are important in the arts, we found no significant differences in outcome by gender.[5] It is noteworthy, though, that in 2016, with the additional focus on aerial dance (including use of silks, as well as hoops and other hanging equipment), the proportion of females (52%) exceeded males for the first time since the program began, as will be discussed in the next chapter. While the cohort seemed to be highly diverse, only 7 respondents reported a maternal language other than Spanish: one indicated French, and 6 indicated Indigenous languages: Kichua, Achiar, Chicham, or Pai Co.

The age distribution of registrants from *Circo Social Quito* in 2015 and 2016 is also shown here in figure 6.1 along with that for our sample in Quito, indicating that our sample of respondents was an adequate reflection of age groups overall. We did not have information on age and gender for all registrants in other cities or for other years, but we have no reason to suspect that our respondents are atypical of the populations from which they were drawn.

As was shown in table 6.1, 184 of our respondents in the 12 to 39-year-old group were aged 18 to 22, constituting the largest group overall. It is noteworthy that 52% of the "youth/young adult respondents" from Cuenca were 12 to 17 years old, as this program specifically targets younger people, and is significantly different from the others in this regard, as was noted in chapter 3. For *Casa Metro*, over half (58%) of the respondents were in

Table 6.1 Demographics, modes of living, as well as baseline personal growth, social inclusion, and social activism of respondents, by program (ages 12–39)

		CSE: Quito N=132	CSE: Cuenca N=42	CSE: Loja N=58	CSE: Other N=22	CM N=170
Age group						
12 to 17	N=108	19.7%	52.4%	37.9%	4.6%	23.1%
18 to 22	N=184	39.4%	19.1%	37.9%	18.2%	58.1%*
23 to 27	N=90	28.8%	21.4%	12.1%	36.4%	16.9%
28 to 39	N=39	12.1%	7.1%	12.1%	40.9%*	2.5%*
Sex						
Female	N=148	37.9%	38.1%	19.0%	36.4%	36.9%
Male	N=273	62.1%	59.5%	81.0%	63.6%	61.9%
Social class						
Professional/technical	N=129	38.6%	28.6%	13.8%	27.3%	31.3%
Small business	N=126	29.6%	33.3%	25.9%	36.4%	30.0%
Working class/self-employed	N=111	23.5%	26.2%	46.6%	13.6%	23.1%
Financial support						
Self-supporting	N=87	31.1%*	16.7%	22.4%	45.5%	9.4%*
External support	N=289	66.7%	73.8%	70.7%	40.9%	90.6%
Marital status						
Single	N=337	72.7%	52.4%	82.8%	72.7%	93.1%
Married/civil union	N=33	7.6%	4.8%	17.2%	18.2%	4.4%
Separated/divorced	N=6	2.3%	0.0%	0.0%	4.5%	1.3%
Baseline score %						
Personal growth	N=403	63.1%	62.1%	55.5%†	70.8%	65.0%†
Social inclusion	N=402	60.0%	61.9%	47.6%†	64.0%	61.3%
Social activism	N=373	52.4%	60.9%	48.5%	56.2%	46.9%†

* Chi-squared tests show that the proportions for this characteristic for this program (*Casa Metro, Circo Social Loja*, etc.) are significantly different from other programs, with 95% confidence.

† T-tests show that baseline score for this program is significantly different from other programs.

Note: Proportions may not add up to 100% as some data are missing for each question.

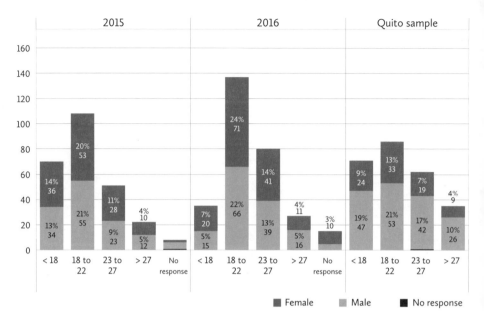

Figure 6.1 Age range and gender proportion comparison between participants in *Circo Social Quito* in 2015 and 2016 and participants aged 12–39 who completed the survey

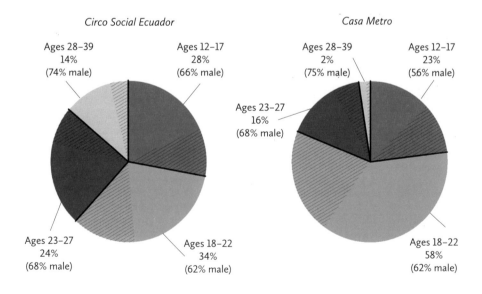

Figure 6.2 Proportion by age range of *Circo Social Ecuador* and *Casa Metro* program respondents (ages 12–39)

the 18 to 22 age group, with some younger and some older, but with very few over age 27. Pie charts of the age distribution in *Circo Social Ecuador* and *Casa Metro* respondents are shown here (figure 6.2), noting the gender comparability of the two groups within the various age groups.

SOCIAL CLASS CHARACTERISTICS: As shown in table 6.1, based on their family background, 129 participants were in the "professional or qualified technician" group – i.e. families with higher income; 126 participants were in the "workers without specific qualifications, artisans, and small traders" group – families with middle income; and 111 participants were in the "workers and self-employed" group – families with lower income. We ascertained that Loja's respondents comprised a significantly higher proportion of participants from families with lower income (p=.0003), with a significantly smaller proportion of participants belonging to the professional class (p=.004).

We found that people in the higher-income group (professional or qualified technicians) had significantly higher initial starting points – i.e. higher baseline scores – than the middle-income and lower income social groups. Specifically, for "personal growth," the highest income group had statistically higher baseline levels than the middle group (p=.03) and lowest social class group (p=.008) – a finding that is consistent with what other researchers have noted, for example that self-esteem levels are higher in the economically better-endowed social group (Richman et al. 1985; Twenge and Campbell 2002). There was also a difference in "social inclusion" with the "high income/professional or qualified technicians" group having a statistically higher baseline than those who came from families who were "middle income/labourers, workers, self-employed" or "lower income/unqualified employees, artisans, small traders" (p=.005 and p=.003 respectively).[6]

SCHOOLING, SELF-SUPPORTING, INCOME AND WORK: A large proportion of our youth and young adult respondents (44%) were still in school, while 25% had completed school at the beginning of the study; 8% reported having dropped out of school before beginning their arts activity. One fifth (87 out of 424) of the respondents were self-supporting, with *Circo Social* having a higher proportion of self-supporting members (p < .001) when compared with *Casa Metro* – a difference that we ascertained was not attributable solely to age. As a main target group for social circus is precisely street-involved youth – including young people who perform their circus skills at traffic lights for a living – it is not surprising that these people are less likely to be dependent on their families for financial support compared to *Casa Metro* participants in the same age group.

Impacts on Ways of Living: Personal Growth, Social Inclusion, and Social Engagement

To turn to our second question, related to impact of the programs, we documented changes on key indicators of personal growth, social inclusion, and social engagement post-participation in social circus compared to prior to beginning the program. As shown in figure 6.3, for the "personal growth scale," aside from two questions ("Feel non-judgmental [positive] towards people who think differently from you" and "Often feel successful"), all the other indicators increased between 16% and 24%, with an overall increase of 17.5%. For the "social inclusion scale" (figure 6.4), two of nine questions increased by 17% and 14%, while the changes for all other questions also increased significantly but by less than 13%, for an overall increase of 12.3%. Similarly, the increase in social engagement (figure 6.5) was significant, with question increases ranging from 12% to 24%, resulting in an overall 21.4% increase. Given the importance of social engagement for collective health (Wilson et al. 2008), this finding is noteworthy, and consistent with what was learned from other aspects of the research (see chapter 7) and studies elsewhere (Kawachi and Berkman 2001; Bennett 2005; Cherry et al. 2013).

The results also documented that "personal growth" is important for "social inclusion" and vice versa, with the linear regression models showing a strong correlation between these two measures (figure 6.6). While the impact of the programs was greater on personal growth than on social inclusion, in addition to these two measures being highly correlated, each also contributes to the impact on the other measure as well.

PERSONAL GROWTH, COMPARING ACROSS PROGRAMS: What is clear from figure 6.3 is that while both social circus and *Casa Metro* programs showed overall benefit post compared to pre, the results for social circus were significantly better (17.5% increase versus 14.2%, p=.033) with the difference reaching statistical significance for four of the questions: "feel non-judgmental towards people who think differently" (p=.006), "often feel successful" (p=.026), "comfortable interacting with people who are different" (p=.043), and feel self-confident" (p=.007). The better outcomes for social circus compared to *Casa Metro* held true even taking differences in age,

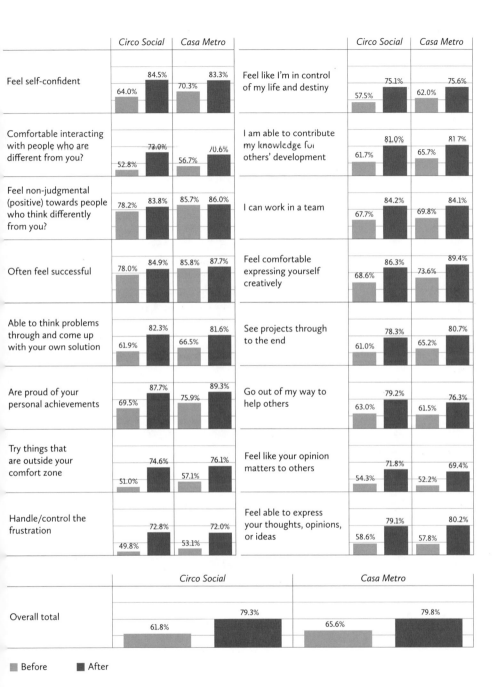

	Circo Social	Casa Metro		Circo Social	Casa Metro
Feel self-confident	64.0% 84.5%	70.3% 83.3%	Feel like I'm in control of my life and destiny	57.5% 75.1%	62.0% 75.6%
Comfortable interacting with people who are different from you?	52.8% 73.0%	56.7% 70.6%	I am able to contribute my knowledge for others' development	61.7% 81.0%	65.7% 81.7%
Feel non-judgmental (positive) towards people who think differently from you?	78.2% 83.8%	85.7% 86.0%	I can work in a team	67.7% 84.2%	69.8% 84.1%
Often feel successful	78.0% 84.9%	85.8% 87.7%	Feel comfortable expressing yourself creatively	68.6% 86.3%	73.6% 89.4%
Able to think problems through and come up with your own solution	61.9% 82.3%	66.5% 81.6%	See projects through to the end	61.0% 78.3%	65.2% 80.7%
Are proud of your personal achievements	69.5% 87.7%	75.9% 89.3%	Go out of my way to help others	63.0% 79.2%	61.5% 76.3%
Try things that are outside your comfort zone	51.0% 74.6%	57.1% 76.1%	Feel like your opinion matters to others	54.3% 71.8%	52.2% 69.4%
Handle/control the frustration	49.8% 72.8%	53.1% 72.0%	Feel able to express your thoughts, opinions, or ideas	58.6% 79.1%	57.8% 80.2%

	Circo Social	Casa Metro
Overall total	61.8% 79.3%	65.6% 79.8%

■ Before   ■ After

Figure 6.3 Mean personal growth scores comparing *Circo Social Ecuador* and *Casa Metro* (ages 12–39) before and after participation

† Paired t-test shows the average participant response improved significantly with 95% confidence.
* T-test shows that the average change between programs is significantly different, with 95% confidence.

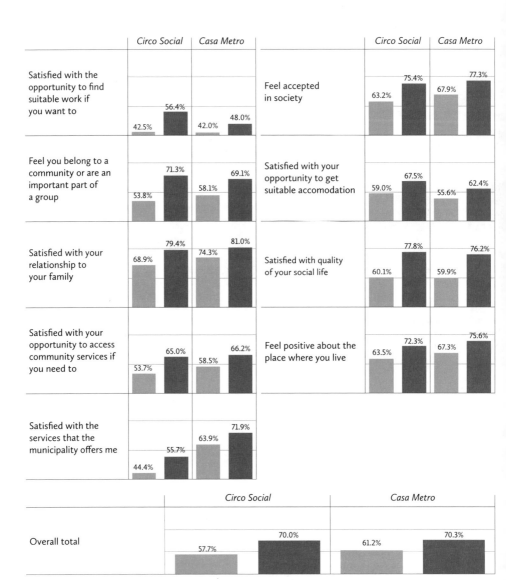

	Circo Social	Casa Metro		Circo Social	Casa Metro
Satisfied with the opportunity to find suitable work if you want to	42.5% / 56.4%	42.0% / 48.0%	Feel accepted in society	63.2% / 75.4%	67.9% / 77.3%
Feel you belong to a community or are an important part of a group	53.8% / 71.3%	58.1% / 69.1%	Satisfied with your opportunity to get suitable accomodation	59.0% / 67.5%	55.6% / 62.4%
Satisfied with your relationship to your family	68.9% / 79.4%	74.3% / 81.0%	Satisfied with quality of your social life	60.1% / 77.8%	59.9% / 76.2%
Satisfied with your opportunity to access community services if you need to	53.7% / 65.0%	58.5% / 66.2%	Feel positive about the place where you live	63.5% / 72.3%	67.3% / 75.6%
Satisfied with the services that the municipality offers me	44.4% / 55.7%	63.9% / 71.9%			

	Circo Social	Casa Metro
Overall total	57.7% / 70.0%	61.2% / 70.3%

■ Before   ■ After

Figure 6.4 Mean social inclusion scores comparing *Circo Social Ecuador* and *Casa Metro* (ages 12–39) before and after participation

† Paired t-test shows the average participant response improved significantly with 95% confidence.
* T-test shows that the average change between programs is significantly different, with 95% confidence.

gender, and social class into account, as well as baseline values. Specifically, the improvements in personal growth for the questions "feeling confident" and "feel non-judgmental (positive) towards people who think differently" remained significantly higher among social circus participants than *Casa Metro* participants (5.3% and 4.7% higher respectively). Changes in physical health, emotional health, and comfort with body expression were also significantly higher even when adjusting for differences in age, gender, and social class.

To explore possible explanations for these findings, we looked at the data for various programs in more detail. For 12 to 39-year-olds as a whole, we found that *Circo Social Loja* participants showed significantly greater improvement (23.2%) compared to *Casa Metro* or other social circus programs (14.3%), but not significantly better than *Circo Social Quito* (17.6%). However, focusing only on 18 to 39-year-olds, the Cuenca group (which had only 27 respondents in this age group) did indeed show a 15.2% increase, *not* significantly different from the responses in Quito or Loja for 18 to 39-year-olds. Both *Circo Social Loja* (20.2% increase) and *Circo Social Quito* (18% increase) showed results that are statistically significantly better than the *Casa Metro group* (13.5% improvement). We will return to the impact of age group later.

When we separated the *Casa Metro* group into those activities with greater physical demand and those with lesser demands, we found that the less physical group showed a 12.2% increase compared to a 16.5% increase for the more physical group (p=.054). Adjusting for differences in age, gender, and social class, the difference possibly attributable to physical demands of the program was even more significant, with participants enrolled in more physically demanding group activities (social circus, dance, parkour, capoeira) having a significant 5.2% *greater* increase in their personal growth compared to those in less physically demanding activities (p=.019). The importance of physical demands for personal growth is a subject of interest to many researchers, noting, for example, the value of sports in improving self-esteem (Ekeland et al. 2005; Slutzky and Simpkins 2009).

SOCIAL INCLUSION, COMPARING ACROSS PROGRAMS: For the "social inclusion" scale, both *Circo Social* and *Casa Metro* participants rated each of the indicators significantly higher after participation in the program (P < .001), as shown in figure 6.4. A large difference existed between the two groups in "sense of group-community belonging," where the changes in social circus and *Casa Metro* participants were 17.5% and 11% respectively, with the gain in social circus being significantly greater (p=.016). Given the importance

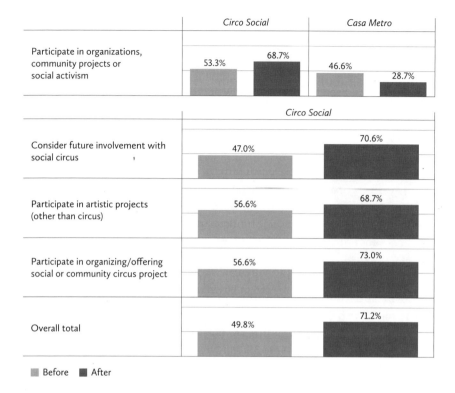

	Circo Social	Casa Metro
Participate in organizations, community projects or social activism	53.3% 68.7%	46.6% 28.7%

	Circo Social
Consider future involvement with social circus †	47.0% 70.6%
Participate in artistic projects (other than circus)	56.6% 68.7%
Participate in organizing/offering social or community circus project	56.6% 73.0%
Overall total	49.8% 71.2%

■ Before ■ After

Figure 6.5 Mean social engagement scores comparing *Circo Social Ecuador* and *Casa Metro* (ages 12–39) before and after participation

† Paired t-test shows the average participant response improved significantly with 95% confidence.
* T-test shows that the average change between programs is significantly different, with 95% confidence.

Note: There were 26 of 254 (10.2%) *Circo Social Ecuador* survey respondents who reported lower scores in social activism after involvement in social circus; there were 21 of 254 (8.2%) survey respondents who reported lower social inclusion scores after involvement in social circus.

of community-building in the pedagogy of social circus (see chapter 4), this result was quite reassuring.

The greatest difference in the two programs, however, was for the question regarding "satisfied with the opportunity to find suitable work," where the social circus group had a marked and statistically significantly better outcome than *Casa Metro* (13.9% improvement versus 6% respectively; p=.011). This finding is important given the situation of precarity discussed in chapter 7.

The "satisfaction with municipal services" was considerably lower amongst social circus participants than among *Casa Metro* participants at baseline, with an average score of only 44.4% among social circus

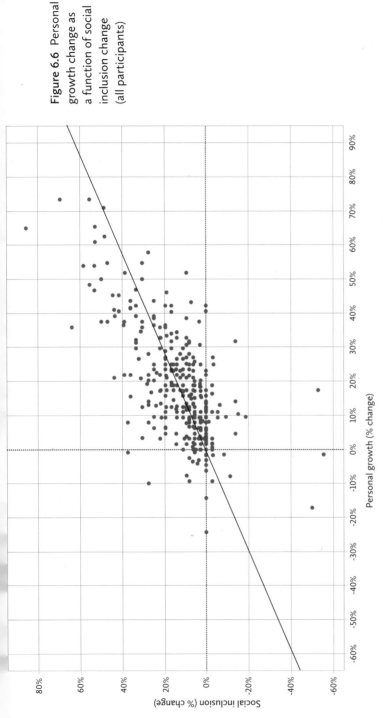

Figure 6.6 Personal growth change as a function of social inclusion change (all participants)

This linear model shows that all participants, regardless of their change in social inclusion, would expect to see a baseline increase in personal growth of 7.0% to 9.8%. Additionally, for each 1% increase (or decrease) in social inclusion, we expect to see a supplementary 0.62% to 0.76% increase (or decrease) in personal growth. We also created another graph, to assess the converse – the impact of personal growth on social inclusion. That linear model showed that all participants, regardless of their change in personal growth, would expect to see a baseline increase in social inclusion of -1.4% to +1.8%. Additionally, for each 1% increase (or decrease) in personal growth, we expect to see a supplementary 0.62% to 0.76% increase (or decrease) in social inclusion. The Pearson correlation coefficient shows a positive correlation between the two variables with coefficient 0.689 (p < .001).

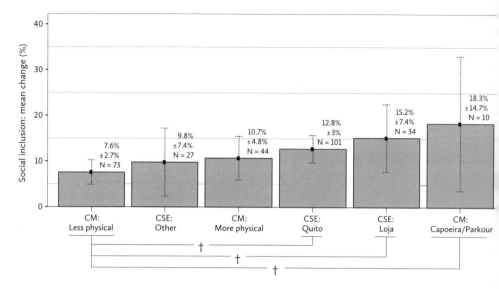

Figure 6.7 Social inclusion change pre- versus post-participation by program, with *Casa Metro* activities grouped by physical demand (ages 18–39)

† T-test shows a significant different between groups, each individual t-test having 95% confidence; none of the differences reach statistical significance for the age group 12-39, nor using the more rigorous Tukey test, nor when controlling for differences in baseline values within the groups. (It is noteworthy that *Circo Social Loja* had significantly lower baselines compared to all other groups except the capoeira/ parkour group.)

respondents, compared to 63.9% for *Casa Metro* participants. There are, of course, multiple interpretations for this, some of which are explored in chapter 7.

We also tried to understand the extent to which the differences in social inclusion in our study could be related to the physical demands dimension noted in the data for personal growth, or whether the non-mainstream nature of the programs themselves is what mattered for this indicator. As shown in figure 6.7, the combined data from the capoeira and parkour participants 18 to 39 years old showed much greater growth in social inclusion (18.3%) compared to the other physical activity groups of *Casa Metro* participants (which showed a 10.7% increase for social inclusion) and significantly more so than the less physical group (7.6% improvement). Although not statistically significant (given the small numbers involved), the combined parkour/capoeira group reported better results than any of the social circus programs with respect to promoting social inclusion.

We would have liked to analyze the parkour/capoeira group separately from the other physical activities in *Casa Metro*, adjusting for all the variables that could account for the differences observed, but the numbers were too small to show significant differences for this indicator. Nonetheless, we note the observation offered from research in Quebec: "Leveraging the collective highly physical performative art form of circus with its distinct appeal to 'marginal' members of society ... contributed to catalyzing the creation of communities for those primarily identifying as alienated 'outsiders'" (Spiegel and Parent 2017). As such, our data support the view that pedagogy matters; the Loja program, with its strong social circus pedagogy (more instructors per participant, better instructor training, more focused target group – see chapters 3 and 4) showed better results than the other social circus programs.

Our data also suggested that the physical demands of the program mattered – social circus and the physical *Casa Metro* programs showed better results than the less physical art forms. And our data also showed that parkour, capoeira, and social circus had the best results for social inclusion, supporting the contention that "counter culture" association plays a role in the attractiveness of such programs to marginalized youth, as argued with respect to parkour and capoeira (De Martini Ugolotti and Moyer 2016), as well as regarding social circus (Hurtubise et al. 2003; Avrillon 2011; Bessone 2013a; Spiegel and Parent 2017).

For the questions on the social inclusion scale pertaining to "feel positive about the place where you live" and "opportunity to get suitable accommodation," both groups had the smallest increase compared to other indicators. We also asked these questions independently of the validated scale to check for internal consistency of responses and found results that were indeed quite consistent with those above. Table 6.2 shows housing, income, and job characteristics before and after participation according to the various programs.

There was a greater proportion of those in *Circo Social* that "rent for accommodation (with or without housemates)" when compared to *Casa Metro*, both at baseline and after the program (p=0.01). *Circo Social* participants had a higher proportion of people in less stable housing options (on the street, living with friends, in a shelter) than *Casa Metro,* where there was a greater proportion of participants living with their parents. These proportions remained similar before versus after the program, suggesting that the programs did not have any significant impact on housing.

Table 6.2 Housing, income, and work at baseline and after participation, by program (ages 18–39)

		CSE: Quito N=106	CSE: Loja N=36	CSE: Other N=31	CM N=131
Housing					
Have my own place (with	Before	3.8%	0.0%	0.0%	6.1%
or without roommates)	After	6.6%	5.6%	0.0%	6.9%
With partner/children	Before	0.9%	5.6%	3.2%	0.0%
	After	3.8%	8.3%	3.2%	0.8%
Rent a place (with or	Before	14.2%	5.6%	12.9%	3.8%
without roommates)	After	15.1%	5.6%	19.4%	3.8%
Sleep at a friend's place	Before	3.8%	2.8%	0.0%	0.8%
	After	1.9%	0.0%	3.2%	1.5%
Live with own parents/family	Before	60.4%	47.2%	54.8%	60.3%
	After	62.3%	41.7%	45.2%	58.8%
Sleep in shelters or	Before	0.9%	2.8%	0.0%	0.8%
on the street	After	0.0%	0.0%	0.0%	0.0%
Income					
Little to no income and	Before	21.7%*	19.4%	22.6%	40.5%
it is fine for me	After	10.4%*	13.9%	3.2%	28.2%
Little income and would	Before	24.5%	30.6%	38.7%	18.3%
like to have more	After	21.7%	25.0%	38.7%	25.2%
Fair income and content	Before	19.8%	13.9%	12.9%	9.2%
with the amount	After	22.6%	16.7%	19.4%	7.6%
Fair income but would	Before	15.1%*	2.8%	0.0%	5.3%
like to have more	After	28.3%*	8.3%	16.1%	12.2%
Work					
Have a job, and am glad	Before	21.7%	22.2%	19.4%	18.3%
	After	26.4%	25.0%	22.6%	12.2%
Have a job but do not like it	Before	10.4%	8.3%	12.9%	6.9%
	After	5.7%	2.8%	9.7%	6.9%
Do not have a job, but	Before	33.0%	22.2%	41.9%	37.4%
would like to have one	After	37.7%	27.8%	35.5%	48.9%
Do not have a job, and do	Before	13.2%	2.8%	3.2%	9.2%
not want/can't have one	After	5.7%	2.8%	0.0%	9.2%

* Chi-squared tests show proportion change (before/after) is significant with 95% confidence.

Note: Proportions may not add up to 100% as some data are missing for each question.

Of those who had dropped out of school, 50% returned to or finished school after involvement with *Circo Social* and a further 33% said that they would like to return to school, with no significant difference between *Circo Social* participants and the comparison population. Although limited, other studies on outcomes for youths involved in arts and cultural activities have also reported a positive correlation between such participation and academic success (Heath and Roach 1998; Eccles and Templeton 2002). Results from other studies also suggest a reduction in school dropout and juvenile offending (Posner and Vandell 1994; Baker and Witt 1996).

Importantly, both *Casa Metro* (p=.03) and *Circo Social* (p=.01) showed an increase in the numbers of participants stating that they had "a reasonable income" after participation. This could mean that the skills refined in the program led to more job opportunities and greater earnings. When we examined the results for those 18 years old and over, there was a significant increase of 45.9% in people reporting "fair income" for *Circo Social*. While *Casa Metro* saw an increase of 5.3%, the baseline proportion of people reporting "fair income" in *Casa Metro* had been only half of that for *Circo Social* (14.5% vs 28.7%, respectively), so there was much more room for improvement in *Casa Metro* than in *Circo Social* – yet improvement in income-related satisfaction did not materialize to the same extent.

There was, nonetheless, a significant overall increase (p=0.02) in those who said: "I have no job but would like to have one." Importantly, while there was no difference between *Casa Metro* and *Circo Social* at baseline, at the end of the program a greater proportion of *Circo Social* participants said "I work and I am happy" than *Casa Metro* participants (p=0.0006). This suggests that *Circo Social* is particularly successful at providing job skills. It may also reflect the fact that *Circo Social* participants depend to a larger extent on their own work for income rather than on contributions from their families (38.3% of those over 18 years old reporting as self-supporting) compared to participants in other activities (12.2% self-supporting) (P<.001).

SOCIAL ENGAGEMENT – COMPARING ACROSS PROGRAMS: Applying the social determination of health approach means that to be "healthy," participants in social circus ought to be able to serve as active agents of change. This also harkens back to the stated *Buen Vivir* goals for this program and its post-neoliberal vision. We observed, in this regard, that social circus participants did significantly improve on all aspects of social engagement, as was shown in figure 6.5.

It is not surprising that the greatest increases related to interest in pursuing social circus itself (23.6%), then in organizing social circus in communities (16.4%), with some increased interest in other arts (12.1%), but also increased interest in social activism more generally (15.4%).

The only one of the four Social Engagement questions relevant to *Casa Metro* participants pertained to social activism: "I participate in organizations, community projects, and social activism." The other questions in this section explicitly related to engagement in social circus, for which the questionnaire was designed. For *Casa Metro,* the score on social engagement after participation was statistically significantly lower than before – a decrease of 17.9% (p < .001). A possible interpretation could be that *Circo Social* pedagogy explicitly gears the participants towards the social role of the arts and therefore entrenches an attitude of greater community involvement than do other activities. Possibly participants of *Casa Metro* are more interested in achieving objectives tied to the art form rather than in other social actions or social activities. For this indicator, parkour and capoeira participants did not significantly differ from other *Casa Metro* participants, and therefore are not presented separately.

Using the propensity score-matching technique (comparing 59 participants from Loja with 59 participants from other social circus programs matched by age, gender, and social class), participants from Loja still showed an 8.7% significantly greater change in social inclusion. The Loja group also showed a 7.4% greater improvement in personal growth compared to other social circus participants; and a 16.4% greater change in social engagement.

Impacts on Lifestyles and Personal Wellness: Diet, Substance Use, Fitness, and Wellness

Table 6.3 shows the results for diet, substance use, and fitness by program for *Circo Social Ecuador* and by level of physical activity in *Casa Metro.* Figure 6.8 shows these results graphically for the *Circo Social* participants.

DIET: With respect to diet, at baseline, about a quarter of all respondents considered their diet balanced and providing adequate nutrition (22%); this number climbed to 28% after participation. Conversely, 31% of respondents indicated having a non-balanced diet before the program; this number dropped to 21% after. This indicates that the proportion of those who acknowledged having an inadequate diet decreased by 10%. *Circo*

Table 6.3 Attitudes and practices related to diet, substance use, and physical fitness at baseline and after participation, by program (ages 12–39)

		CSE: Quito N=132	*CSE: Loja* N=58	*CSE: Other* N=64	*CM: More physical* N=75	*CM: Less physical* N=92
Diet						
I have a balanced diet that provides me with the nutrition I need	% Before	25	16	33	13	18
	% After	30	22	34	27	24
I do not have a healthy diet but would like one	% Before	20	19	17	24	27
	% After	30	17	17	24	33
I don't think my diet is well-balanced and it is fine for me	% Before	34*	22*	31	31	30
	% After†	21*	7*†	16	24	30
Substance Use						
Consumes drugs and/or alcohol habitually	% Before†	9	22†	6	7	5
	% After†	5	16†	3	5	3
Consumes drugs and/or alcohol occasionally	% Before†	25	26	23	12	9†
	% After	19	19	23	9	13
Does not consume drugs or alcohol	% Before†	45	31†	48	52	67†
	% After	57	38†	50	63	68†
Fitness						
Little exercise and fine for me	% Before	20*	28*	14	28*	30*
	% After	5*	10*	0	5*	11*
Little exercise and would like to feel more fit	% Before	33*†	14	22	21	29
	% After†	17*†	26	18	10	41†
Reasonable exercise and glad with my fitness	% Before	17	21	19	11†	16
	% After	23	17	18	21	18
Reasonable exercise and would like to be more fit	% Before†	11*	2†	22	9	4*†
	% After†	27*†	5†	9	26	13*
I am more flexible and, strong and have greater body awareness*	% Before	2*	0*	2	7†	0
	% After†	17*	16*	25	9	1†

* Chi-squared tests show proportion change (before/after) is significant with 95% confidence.

† Chi-squared tests show proportion between program locations is significantly different with 95% confidence.

Note: Proportions may not add up to 100% as some data are missing for each question.

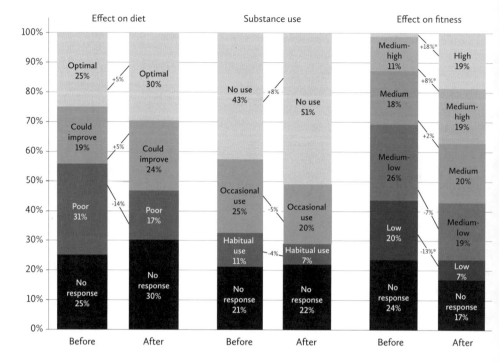

Figure 6.8 Attitudes and practices related to diet, substance use, and physical fitness at baseline and after participation for *Circo Social Ecuador* respondents (ages 12–39)

Chi-squared tests showing proportions before and after are significantly different with 95% confidence.

Social participants (31%) indicated having an unbalanced diet before social circus without wanting to improve it, and this number dropped significantly to 16% after participation (p < .001). For *Casa Metro*, 31% of participants indicated having an unbalanced diet before participation, and this number remained fairly steady after participation (27%). This may reflect an increased awareness of healthy eating instilled through the *Circo Social* program, as has occurred in other community arts programs (Colby and Haldeman 2007). However, adding together the percentages of the indicator "I do not think my diet is balanced but is fine for me" and "I do not have a healthy diet but would like to have it," we see that a large number of people still reported poor nutrition (53% at baseline and 46% after the program). This high percentage reveals an alarming problem documented by others. In Ecuador, 2012 data indicated that 25% of children under age 5 were stunted and 8.6% were overweight, with malnutrition and obesity coexisting in the same households; diet-related diseases, such as hypertension and diabetes, were the second highest cause of death; anemia is rampant; and experts studying the situation have concluded that malnutrition is a major public health issue in Ecuador, just as it is in other developing countries (Peñafiel Anchundia 2017).

DRUGS AND/OR ALCOHOL USE AND ADDICTION: The relationship between mental health and addictions has been well established, with youth who have previous history of trauma (such as sexual abuse or family violence) more likely to suffer from mental health and addiction issues (Unger et al. 1997; Kilpatrick et al. 2000; Boles and Miotto 2003; Keeshin and Campbell 2011). Importantly, research has documented the positive impacts community arts programs can have in addressing problems of substance use in youth (Grunstein and Nutbeam 2007), reporting increased self-esteem and reduced consumption of harmful substance; indeed the relationship between self-esteem and substance abuse is well documented (Kilpatrick et al. 2000; Parker and Benson 2004; Alavi 2011). Our questions regarding drugs and alcohol were designed to assess the respondents' satisfaction with their own use of drug and alcohol, not the amount of use per se. *Circo Social* participants had a higher proportion of substance use at baseline compared with *Casa Metro* participants; and conversely, *Casa Metro* had a higher proportion of participants who abstained from substance use at baseline. These differences were significant (p-value < .001). *Circo Social* also had a higher proportion of regular substance users at baseline compared to *Casa Metro*, but numbers were small (p-value = .085). Overall, after participation in any of the community arts and culture programs, there was an increase in the proportion of participants who reported that they were abstaining from substance use (p-value =.047). *Circo Social* participants saw a significant increase in those abstaining from any substance after the program (p-value =.03), and the proportion of habitual substance-users also decreased from 11% to 7% (p=.126). *Casa Metro* saw the proportion of habitual substance-users decrease from 6% to 4% after the program. At the end of the program, *Circo Social* had 3% more people who said they were habitual drug users, but that difference was not significant.

FITNESS: Overall, there was an increase in physical fitness reported by both *Casa Metro* and *Circo Social* participants (p < .001). For the question "I would like to feel more fit," the less physical *Casa Metro* group saw a significant 23.5% increase (p=.006), and a 10.0% reduction in the proportion

Table 6.4 Energy, perceived physical health, perceived emotional health, and comfort expressing with body at baseline and after participation, by program (ages 12–39)

		CSE: Quito N=132	*CSE: Loja* N=58	*CSE: Other* N=64	*CM: More physical* N=75	*CM: Less physical* N=92
Energy	Before	65%	56%	67%	69%	67%
	Change	+22%*	+28%*	+19%*	+19%*	+19%*
Physical health	Before	61%	55%	65%	67%	68%
	Change	+19%*	+24%*	+14%*	+15%*	+8%*
Emotional health	Before	58%	50%	64%	68%	68%
	Change	+21%*	+33%*	+18%*	+19%*	+11%*
Comfort expressing	Before	57%	54%	61%	68%	67%
yourself using	Change	+29%*†	+29%*	+24%*	+22%*	+12%*†
your body						

* Paired t-test, adjusted using Holm-Bonferroni method, shows change is significant with 95% confidence.

† Tukey range tests shows that respondents from *Circo Social Quito* had a 17.0% greater change that the less physical group from *Casa Metro*, significant with 95% confidence.

of people reporting little exercise. At baseline, there were no significant differences between *Casa Metro* and *Circo Social*. After participation in the activities, there was a significant 19.5% greater proportion of participants from *Circo Social* who selected "I do a lot of exercise" or "I'm more flexible" than those from *Casa Metro* overall (p < .001). A total of 55.7% of *Circo Social* participants reported an improvement in fitness after participation, which is greater than the *Casa Metro* "less physical" group by 19.5%, and greater than the *Casa Metro* "more physical" group by 6.6%. These results resonate well with the wealth of literature on dance and fitness (Cruz-Ferreira et al. 2015; Higueras-Fresnillo et al. 2015).

PERCEPTION OF WELLNESS: There were significant increases in how participants rated their "energy," "physical health," "emotional health," and "comfort expressing yourself using your body," after participation in the activity (all with p-value < .001; see table 6.4). However, while at baseline *Circo Social* participants reported significantly lower physical health than participants in physical activities at *Casa Metro,* 60% and 68% respectively (p=.004), after participation, *Circo Social* reported a significantly greater increase in physical health than *Casa Metro* participants, +19% and +12% respectively (p=.01).

Also very important was the observation that at baseline, participants in *Circo Social* had rated their "emotional health" lower than did *Casa Metro* participants in both the more physical (p=0.02) and the less physical activities (p=0.007) groups. All groups saw an increase in emotional health; however, the average increase in emotional health in *Circo Social* participants was 12.3% greater than those from the *Casa Metro* less physical group (p=0.002). The data suggest that *Circo Social* had better resources for emotional strengthening compared to *Casa Metro*. The significant difference held true even restricting the analysis to the paired database (181 social circus with matched 181 *Casa Metro* participants) – in which social circus participants had a 6.8% greater gain in physical health (p=.016), a 7% greater gain in emotional health (p=.025), and a 9.3% greater comfort with their bodies (p=.001) compared to *Casa Metro* participants. It is also noteworthy that *Circo Social Loja* showed a 14.2% greater improvement in physical health and 18.6% greater improvement in emotional health compared to other social circus participants, when taking differences in age, gender, and social class into account.

Individual Variations: What Might Explain These?

CONDITION AT ONSET: A particularly important question from a policy perspective is whether people who are most "in need" benefit the most. When we consider where people started from on the various questions – their "baseline score" – we find that participants with lower starting points (baseline ≤ 3 on a 5-point scale) had a significantly greater improvement than those with higher starting points (baseline > 3) in "personal growth," "social inclusion," and "social activism." In particular, *Casa Metro* participants with lower starting points saw a 45% greater improvement in "personal growth" (p < .0001), a 10.5% greater improvement in "social inclusion" (p=.0004), and a 36.7% greater improvement in "social activism" (p < .0001) compared to those who started at a higher level. Similarly, *Circo Social* participants with lower starting points saw a 54.8% greater improvement in "personal growth" (p < .0001), a 17.5% greater improvement in "social inclusion" (p < .0001), and a 35.4% greater improvement in "social activism" (p < .0001). It is difficult to determine whether this is due to the program having a greater impact on low-baseline participants, or the limitation of a 5-point Likert scale to measure improvements in participants who already had higher baselines (the ceiling effect). We found it particularly interesting that even when adjusting for baseline values, social circus participants achieved better results than *Casa Metro*. Moreover, when comparing *Circo Social* participants with *Casa Metro* participants while controlling for baseline score, the starkest difference was indeed for social activism.

IMPACT OF AGE: Another issue that is of particular importance is the age groups targeted. Earlier, it was noted that Cuenca focused on those under 12 and over 40 to a greater extent than the other programs, due to the particular needs in their communities. As shown in figure 6.9, those aged 14 to 25 had a statistically significant better outcome for personal growth than those who were older or younger. It may be that this age group is more amenable to the modalities of social circus compared to those younger or older. Importantly, though, the impact on the other age groups was also positive. Also significant is that among all the 14 to 25-year-olds, social circus had a significantly greater impact than *Casa Metro* activities overall.

INTERSECTIONAL ANALYSIS (GENDER, CLASS, MATERNAL LANGUAGE): People in lower social classes had greater gains in social inclusion and personal growth compared to participants from higher class backgrounds; this was significantly so for personal growth. However, people from lower social classes had significantly lower baseline values (were more in need), as noted above. As such, the finding can be said to be reflective of "need" rather than "social class" per se. We also note that females, whether in a lower or higher social class, did not gain as much from the program as their male counterparts. As the differences did not reach statistical significance, the importance of this finding is speculative. Interestingly, while only 6 people self-identified as having an Indigenous maternal language: Kichua, Achiar Chicham, or Pai Coca (4 male, 2 female), and the baseline (starting point) for social inclusion indicators for these 6 was about the same as for the others, the improvement for the 6 Indigenous participants was more than double that of the 359 who reported Spanish (or in one case, French) as their maternal language (22.7% versus 11%, p=.094). While the numbers are too few to draw conclusions, given that many social circus programs worldwide are specifically targeted for Indigenous communities, this finding merits further attention, as does the gender of participants.

IMPACT OF VOLUNTEERING: The other factor that we found made a significant difference on outcomes was whether participants became volunteers or not. Indeed, we found that the 66 volunteers who responded to

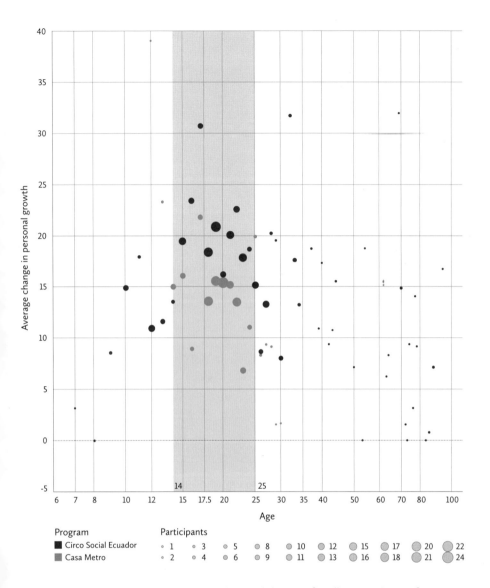

Figure 6.9 Average change in personal growth by age, for all respondents of all ages

Each point represents the average change in personal growth for all participants of a given age, separated by program, with the size of the dot relating to the number of people in that category. The *Circo Social* 14–25 group had a significant 7.3% greater improvement in personal growth when compared to the remainder of the *Circo Social* group (p < .001). The *Circo Social* 14–25 group also had a significant 5.4% greater improvement in personal growth when compared to *Casa Metro* respondents of the same age range (p=.004).

Note: The x-axis (Age) uses a logarithmic scale.

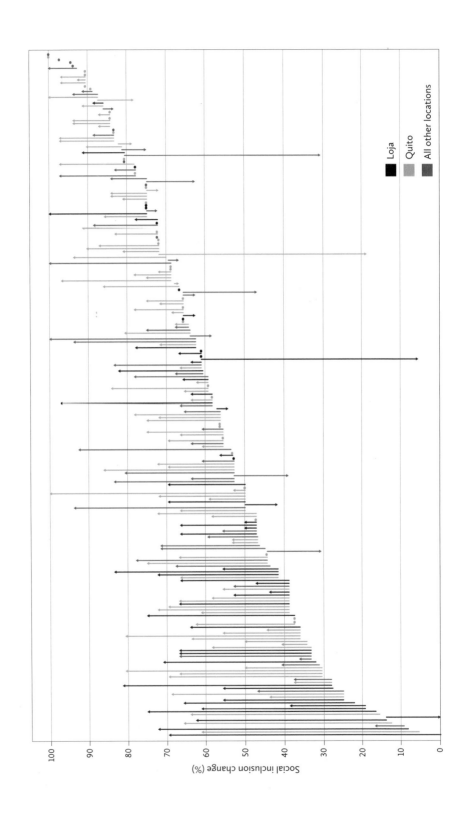

the questionnaire had a 6.3% greater improvement in personal growth and a 6.6% greater improvement in social inclusion than the 158 respondents who were not volunteers, i.e. did not work in the social circus workshop *replicas* with children, perform shows on behalf of the municipality, etc. (p=.035). The survey was also completed by 30 instructors (former participants and/or volunteers); although this group did not have significantly larger changes than other respondents, their final score for personal growth was 9.7% greater than other participants (p=.001). Whether participants became volunteers because they had achieved such positive results and wanted to share the program with others, or whether volunteering contributed to the larger benefit they derived from the program, cannot be determined from the quantitative data (but see chapter 7 for analysis based on the qualitative and triangulated data).

Negative Transformations:

Figure 6.10 shows the magnitude and direction of change for each social circus participant, with respect to "social inclusion." (We also did a similar graph for "personal growth" and "social engagement," and *Casa Metro* as well; available on request.). We can see from figure 6.10 that 21 participants (8.2%) moved in the negative direction for "social inclusion." 14 participants of the total 254 (5.5%) reported their "personal growth" post-program as worse than before they started. For "social engagement," this number was 26 (10.2%). The comparison numbers and percentage of participants who had negative experiences for the other art forms were 10 of 170 (5.9%) for "personal growth" and 11 (6.5%) and 69 (40.6%) respectively for "social inclusion" and "social engagement." We can thus see that, while the majority of participants benefitted from the program, there were exceptions. A few participants indeed had quite negative experiences, especially with respect to the social inclusion indicator, as was shown in figure 6.10.

Figure 6.10 (*opposite*) Individual social inclusion change for *Circo Social Ecuador* participants

Each arrow represents a single respondent, with the tail of the arrow representing the baseline value and the head of the arrow representing the value after involvement in social circus. The length of the arrow, therefore, indicates the degree of change.

A similar graph for "personal growth" instead of "social inclusion" shows 14 of 254 (5.5%) survey respondents who reported being worse after involvement in social circus; in those cases, the degree was much less than the degree of negative change for social inclusion shown here for those who had negative experiences.

The characteristics of the participants with negative experiences, either in the personal growth index or in the social inclusion index, were analyzed qualitatively using the open survey questions. The in-depth qualitative study presented in chapter 7 provides additional analysis in this regard.

There were 6 participants who had negative results on both scales, of which 5 were from *Circo Social* and one was from *Casa Metro*. In *Circo Social*, 2 were young males (13 to 23-year-olds) from Cuenca and 2 from Loja, and one was a female in her mid-20s from Cuenca. The single one from *Casa Metro* was a teenage male whose activity was listed as "study." The *Circo Social* participants who did not improve on either scale had marginally negative results in personal growth (below -10%) and slightly more substantive reductions in social inclusion.

Interestingly, 2 of these participants had positive evaluations of the program, despite their own situation having gone in a negative direction. One young man from *Social Circus Loja* wrote, "I entered this center against my will. However, it is an excellent organization that helps young people and adults, planting [good] things in their life, improving them as people and letting them express their qualities and talents." The participant of *Casa Metro* who reported negative results on both scales mentioned teamwork and social life: "I'm not very friendly ... Teamwork is bad, one works better." As this respondent's activity was sedentary and not group-oriented, the lack of improvement was consistent with the hypotheses of this study.

There were 18 participants (9 from *Casa Metro* and 9 from *Circo Social*) who improved in the social inclusion scale but regressed or remained unchanged in personal growth. Again, the declines in question were minimal, mostly less than 5% for *Casa Metro* and less than 10% for *Circo Social*. It is interesting to note that for 12 of the 18 participants who improved in social inclusion but not in personal growth, their baseline for personal growth was high (above 4 out of 5 points), adding to the evidence that, in general, this program has more benefits for those most in need. The data also suggest that those who already have strong self-esteem and do not appear to have much to gain in personal growth can still gain in social inclusion. Of 12 participants in social circus who did not report improvement in personal growth, 2 experienced gains in social inclusion of above 25%. These 2 participants had relatively low baseline values for social inclusion prior to starting social circus, despite high baseline scores for personal growth.

Finally, 26 of the participants improved, remained unchanged, or did not respond to the personal growth index, but experienced a decline in social inclusion; 16 were social circus participants almost evenly distributed across the sites (5 Quito, 5 Cuenca, 3 Loja, and 3 "other"). These participants tended to have average initial scores (3.65 of 5 points). The 10 *Casa Metro* participants in this group had slightly higher baseline rates (averaging 3.84 out of 5 points). No one commented on discrimination or lack of acceptance in their program or in society. On the contrary, one teenage *Casa Metro* capoeira participant mentioned that the program positively impacted his life, despite overall deterioration attributed to other factors: "The best memory of my life was to meet those of capoeira group [...] On several occasions I tried to commit suicide, but there has always been someone who did not allow me to do it."

It appears that the two questions from the social inclusion scale that related to family and housing problems explain why he was quite satisfied with the program but still experienced an overall decline on the social inclusion scale. While the government had made considerable investments in healthcare and education, as discussed in chapter 3, clearly housing problems persisted.

Implications

There have been several large longitudinal studies of community-engaged arts with comparison groups (Hampshire and Matthijsse 2010); however, no large comparative quantitative studies of this magnitude previously examined the use of circus arts as a sociocultural intervention. The research presented in this chapter not only constitutes the first large quantitative longitudinal study of the impacts of social circus that included comparison groups but also, along with a study also directed by our lead editor, Jennifer Spiegel, in Quebec (Spiegel and Parent 2016, 2017), one of the only studies of social circus to date that specifically examined the indicators of personal growth, social inclusion, and social engagement – constructs closely related to mental health and social well-being. Given the goals of this program, and their relationship to *Buen Vivir* in particular, the results are certainly noteworthy.

Aside from this study's contribution to understanding the role that social circus and other community arts programs can play in promoting positive change in personal growth, social inclusion, and social engagement, it also adds to the nascent literature on the impact of social circus more generally. There are numerous results from our survey that are noteworthy for community arts practitioners and scholars, as well as those interested in the impact of social circus and other community arts for promoting individual and collective health – or in the case of Ecuador, for promoting *Buen Vivir*. We summarize some of these findings below:

First, all the community arts programs studied produced significant improvement in personal growth and social inclusion, as well as some benefits in changing unhealthy habits or attitudes with respect to diet, exercise, and substance use. In other words, community arts helped mitigate ways of living and lifestyles associated with ill-health. These results resonate with well over 50 other studies evaluating community arts programs (http://ascevaluation.ca/), strengthening the conclusion that such programs can be highly effective in promoting collective health.

Secondly, we found that social circus was particularly valuable with respect to many outcomes related to mental and social wellbeing – in some cases, significantly more so than other community arts activities. Moreover, programs that provided extensive training to an adequate number of instructors and targeted youth and young adults in need (namely Loja, see chapters 3 and 4) had greater impacts than those in which the social pedagogical approach was less firmly entrenched or in which the target groups were more diffuse. The "sense of group-community belonging," as well as the more instrumentalized outcome of "opportunity to find suitable work" also showed a statistically significant greater impact in social circus than in other programs. Thus it could be concluded that, in terms of traditional social inclusion indicators (such as satisfaction with employment opportunities), as well as indicators of healthy lifestyles (such as attitudes and practices towards diet, physical fitness, and substance use), *Circo Social Ecuador* showed marked positive impact. While other studies have examined attributes related to participation in the job market (Jermyn 2001; Newman et al. 2003; Mzaku 2014), our study of *Circo Social Ecuador* also showed changes in social engagement/social activism as well as employment and income generation. Our results suggest that social circus can serve as a means for promoting collective values and collective health by fostering the values of *Buen Vivir* that the program aimed to encourage.

Thirdly, we found that community arts programs that had an orientation towards collective physical activities tended to be more like social circus with respect to the various outcomes studied. The importance of collective rather than individual creation has been the subject of discussion in the literature (Guetzko 2002; Newman et al. 2003; Khan 2013), as has the importance of community physical activity and physical arts for youth (Gardner et al. 2008). The fact that the more physical *Casa Metro* group produced more impressive results is consistent with the connection between physical activity and wellbeing observed for centuries, and the well-documented association between aerobic exercise and mental health (Biddle 2000; Stathopoulou et al. 2006). Indeed, holistic concepts of wellness, including *Buen Vivir,* comprise mental *and* physical components. Dance has historical roots among Indigenous people and has been a healing ritual for thousands of years to further the emotional, cognitive, physical, and social integration of the individual (American Dance Therapy Association 2012). Even in low intensity forms, group dance has been shown to reduce mental stress (Hanna 2006; Johar et al. 2016). There is also much theorizing about the role dance can play in social transformation. Recently, Prickett (2016), explored how Martin analyzed dance's power as a social kinesthetic or "the capacity to move an idea in a particular direction through the acquired prowess of bodies in action" (Martin 2004, 48). Kiez (2015) documented the positive impact of circus arts on physical literacy; Loiselle (2015) revealed the potential of social circus for physical rehabilitation for youth with physical disabilities; and Baumgold (2017) explored the synergistic relationship between circus arts and occupational therapy. The fact that our data showed that participants in social circus as well as in the more collective physical activities in *Casa Metro* had greater improvement in social inclusion than those in the less physically demanding programs adds to the literature in this regard.

Fourthly, and perhaps even more important from a policy perspective, our results suggest that the social context of the art form also matters. What we learned is that participants in social circus in Ecuador are not dissimilar to participants elsewhere; in the four programs studied in Quebec, home of *Cirque du Soleil* and its social circus arm, *Cirque du Monde,* "more than a third (36.7%) did not have their own place nor lived with their families before joining circus: 11.2% were living in government-provided care such as youth detainee centers or foster families, 10.2% were sleeping at a friend's place, and 5.1% were living in shelters or on the street" (Spiegel and Parent 2017). It is worth reiterating that the marginality associated with circus is itself attractive to alienated youth (Spiegel 2016c). As noted by Spiegel and Parent (2017), based on their research in Quebec as well as studies elsewhere (Hurtubise et al. 2003; Avrillon 2011; Bessone 2013a), circus emerged from a tradition of street performance and provided livelihoods to those outside mainstream workforces, and, as such, assists marginalized youth to explore their own strengths and interests in an appealing and culturally appropriate manner.

In this regard, within our comparison group, we were particularly interested in the participants who enrolled in capoeira and parkour. Capoeira emerged as an Afro-Brazilian art form practiced mostly by enslaved people that combined music, dance, and acrobatics with martial arts, the latter hidden, having been prohibited by slave-owners. While parkour did not emerge from centuries of history but rather became popular in the late 1980s (De Martini Ugolotti and Moyer 2016),[7] it too was rooted in rebelliousness, encouraging practitioners to use all available urban obstacles to move from one point to another in the fewest number of movements while trying to avoid touching the ground, and paying attention to the fluidity and simplicity of movements. Much more has been written about both capoeira and parkour than about social circus. However, at least on the surface, these art forms seem to share many attributes of social circus, including raising body awareness and consciousness of emotional reactions, perseverance to overcome physical limitations, managing risk, as well as a history of association with resistance and agency (Fuggle 2008). More research is needed to tease out the relative importance of the "collective" ethos versus the "counter-culture historical association" or the "physicality" of the art form, and the interaction of these attributes.

A fifth important finding is that, while engagement in social circus resulted in benefits in all three main areas of focus (personal growth, social inclusion, and social engagement), there was improvement in personal growth and social inclusion but not in social engagement for participants in other community arts programs. While there may be a selection bias such that those people most drawn to social engagement are particularly attracted to social circus (our data showed a significantly higher starting score in social engagement for social circus participants compared to *Casa Metro*), the greatest benefits are still at the level of the individual. Nonetheless, as discussed by Spiegel (2016), as well as in the next chapter, in theorizing the relationship between community arts and social transformation, separating the individual and the collective is itself problematic. Moreover, our data did show a strong impact of personal growth on social inclusion and vice versa.

Sixthly, we found that people in the lower social classes had the lowest baseline levels for personal growth and social inclusion. This is consistent with Bourdieu's theory about the relationships among economic capital, cultural capital, and social capital (Buys and Miller 2009; Hampshire and Matthijsse 2010; Spiegel 2015c). This observation calls for heeding the call by health promotion scholars to take an approach that offers programs for all but also pays special attention to those most vulnerable (Frohlich and Potvin 2008). Indeed, an important revelation from our study is that while people at all levels showed improvement, the participants who started at lower baselines benefitted most. This finding supports the policies of many social circus programs targeting the most marginalized (see Spiegel 2016). Participants in Ecuador are not dissimilar to those elsewhere, such as in the four programs studied in Quebec (Spiegel and Parent 2017).

While the targeting of the most marginalized is not unique to social circus, or arts-based programs more generally, that this group benefits the most is not a universal finding. For example, a longitudinal study with comparison groups to measure social capital and wellbeing in participants of a UK government-sponsored choir (Hampshire and Matthijsse 2010), found that for girls from relatively privileged backgrounds the experience was largely positive, providing opportunities to develop social capital, make new friends, and build confidence. However, others' experiences were more ambiguous and suggested risks such as disconnecting from ex- isting networks of friends. The authors concluded that arts projects can have a positive impact on young people's social and emotional wellbeing but that it cannot be assumed that all changes will be unequivocally good or straightforward. Our own findings echo this observation; while the vast majority of our respondents reported change in a positive direction, some did not. Joining social circus can exacerbate ostracization from family who do not approve of the lifestyles traditionally associated with circus arts. Attention to such potential consequences is important.

We offer a seventh observation, this time with respect to age – namely that while the results for our small older cohort (over 39 years old) were also quite positive, as were the results from children, they were less dra- matic than those of young adults and youth. The analysis showed that par- ticipants between 14 and 25 years old benefitted most. This finding may have implications for policies with respect to which group to target for social circus programs. However, the literature suggests that this age group is highly impressionable, and therefore almost any program shows greater benefit in this group than most other age-groups. Indeed, our *Casa Metro* cohort in this age range also benefitted the most, albeit there were few participants of other ages. The fact that those under 12 and over 39, and indeed the elderly, all also showed positive results is important. There is considerable concern in the literature about policies that focus too heavily on youth to the exclusion of other age groups – what is referred to as "aging out" of social services. We thus hasten to add that while our study focused on youth, the benefits accrue to children, adults, and the elderly as well.

Finally, we note that the greatest benefits accrued to participants who also served as volunteers. Whether they volunteered because they were so satisfied with social circus pedagogy that they wanted to share it, or whether their greater gains occurred because they volunteered, cannot be determined from our quantitative data, but perhaps is moot. From a policy perspective, this finding suggests that this component of the program, in which youth and young adult participants are asked to volunteer to work with marginalized children, can be seen as a strength of the program, notwithstanding the very real concerns about exploitation and precarity discussed in the next chapter.

There are obvious limitations in any study such as this. Despite our efforts to contact those who left the programs, our study still suffers from some degree of survivor bias, volunteer bias, and reporting bias. Additionally, the questionnaire was designed for social circus and there are, no doubt, attributes of other community arts programs that were not captured. Also, the study was observational in nature – there was no attempt to control who entered the social circus programs, thus there is obviously some self-selection at play. (See discussion in chapter 2 on the decision not to conduct a randomized controlled trial.) Despite such limitations, the consistency of our quantitative findings with the qualitative findings presented elsewhere in the book, in conjunction with support from studies conducted elsewhere, is noteworthy.

Importantly, neither social circus nor any arts programs can alone address the social processes that drive health inequities. We noted, for example, that program participation resulted in no improvement to poor housing, but given the situation in Ecuador, this should not be surprising. According to the National Social Housing Program, 45% of the 3.8 million Ecuadoreans live in inadequate housing (Ministerio de Desarrollo Urbano y Vivienda 2016). This includes 1.37 million households residing in dwellings whose tenure is insecure, built with inadequate materials, with a lack of basic sanitary services, or with problems of overcrowding, sharing of more than one household, or living in makeshift housing units. Thus, it would have been unrealistic to expect that in a period of four years or less (since social circus began), participants could substantially improve their housing situation.

We also saw that serious problems in nutrition also remained, despite impressive improvements in personal growth and social inclusion. We can say that changes were made in healthy lifestyles (e.g., fitness, substance use), tied to changes in ways of living (social inclusion and engagement), but the macro forces at play, as we saw in chapter 3, remain largely intact, perpetuating threats to health that characterize this economic system.

The understanding of the "social determination of health" model suggests that while programs such as social circus can help "change mentality" that mires individuals in unhealthy "styles of living," and foster "ways of living" of groups tied to social inclusion, critical activism is still needed to combat the societal social processes that perpetuate health and social inequities.

This large longitudinal comparative study has thus added considerably to the body of literature on arts for social change, providing strong empirical evidence regarding the personal and social value of community arts, and particularly social circus and other programs that embrace collectivity as an integral part of its pedagogy. To better contextualize these findings, we turn to the next chapter.

Appendix – Survey Questionnaire

Many people around the world are excited about social circus and want to learn more about how participating in social circus can affect people's lives. This questionnaire is part of a study being conducted by a team of Canadian and Ecuadorean investigators from the University of British Columbia, Concordia University, Simon Fraser University, and University of Toronto in Canada, and the Andean University Simon Bolivar in Quito. This questionnaire will take approximately 20 minutes to complete. There are no penalties for not completing the whole questionnaire, but, of course, we would be grateful for your time in sharing your experience and opinions with us. By completing the attached questionnaire you are consenting to participate, knowing that your confidentiality will be completely respected. Thanks for helping us understand the impact of social circus.

PART 1: YOUR EXPERIENCE WITH SOCIAL CIRCUS

1. Which social circus did you attend? If you belong or belonged to 'Other' specify which. If you belong to more than one, select which you participated the longest (Quito, Loja, Cuenca, Tena, Guayaquil, Other (please specify))

2. When you participated in social circus, you did it as...? (Participant, Volunteer, Instructor, Trainer)

3. PROGRAM		4. ACTIVITIES	
Which social circus program is yours?	*Mark one*	What activity do you enjoy most?	*Mark one*
Instructor training	❏	Juggling	❏
Semillero 1 (introductory level 1)	❏	Acrobatics	❏
Semillero 2 1 (introductory level 2)	❏	Partner Acrobatics	❏
Semillero 3 1 (introductory level 3)	❏	Clowning	❏
Artistic group	❏	Aerials	❏
Virgilio Guerrero Program	❏	Balancing objects	❏
Other (specify):	❏	Other (specify):	❏

5. How often do you practice
social circus?
Indicate the number that applies

How many weeks per months
(average)?

_____

How many times per week on
average?

_____

How many hours per day on average?

_____

Other (specify)

_____

6. Since when have you been
doing social circus? *Mark the box
beside the year you have begun*

2014 ❑

2013 ❑

2012 ❑

Other ❑

_____

7. How did you feel about social circus BEFORE you started social circus? *(Mark all that apply)*:

Suspicious	❑	Confident	❑	Inspired	❑
Excited	❑	Annoyed	❑	Nervous	❑
Proud	❑	Scared	❑	Other (explain)	❑

_____

8. How do you feel about social circus NOW *(Mark all that apply)*:

Suspicious	❑	Confident	❑	Inspired	❑
Excited	❑	Annoyed	❑	Nervous	❑
Proud	❑	Scared	❑	Other (explain)	❑

_____

PART 2: YOUR PERSONAL GROWTH SINCE YOU STARTED SOCIAL CIRCUS

For each statement, tell us how you remember feeling *BEFORE you started social circus*, and *how you feel NOW* by circling how much you agree with the statement.	Strongly DISAGREE	Disagree	Neither agree nor disagree	Agree	Strongly AGREE
	①	②	③	④	⑤
a) Feel able to express your thoughts, opinions, or ideas					
BEFORE?	1	2	3	4	5
NOW?	1	2	3	4	5
b) Feel like your opinion matters to others					
BEFORE?	1	2	3	4	5
NOW?	1	2	3	4	5
c) Able to think problems through and come up with your own solution					
BEFORE?	1	2	3	4	5
NOW?	1	2	3	4	5
d) Try things that are outside your comfort zone					
BEFORE?	1	2	3	4	5
NOW?	1	2	3	4	5
e) Feel judgmental (negative) towards people who think differently from you?					
BEFORE?	1	2	3	4	5
NOW?	1	2	3	4	5
f) Often feel like a failure					
BEFORE?	1	2	3	4	5
NOW?	1	2	3	4	5
g) Comfortable interacting with people who are different from you?					
BEFORE?	1	2	3	4	5
NOW?	1	2	3	4	5
h) See projects through to the end					
BEFORE?	1	2	3	4	5
NOW?	1	2	3	4	5
i) Feel self-confident					
BEFORE?	1	2	3	4	5
NOW?	1	2	3	4	5

PART 2/CONTINUED

j) Are proud of your personal achievements

BEFORE?	1	2	3	4	5
NOW?	1	2	3	4	5

k) Feel comfortable expressing yourself creatively

BEFORE?	1	2	3	4	5
NOW?	1	2	3	4	5

l) Go out of my way to help others

BEFORE?	1	2	3	4	5
NOW?	1	2	3	4	5

m) Feel like I'm in control of my life and destiny

BEFORE?	1	2	3	4	5
NOW?	1	2	3	4	5

PART 3: HOW YOU FEEL ABOUT YOUR RELATIONSHIP TO SOCIETY/YOUR COMMUNITY SINCE STARTING SOCIAL CIRCUS

For each statement, tell us how you remember feeling BEFORE you started social circus, and how you feel NOW by circling how much you agree with the statement.	Strongly DISAGREE ①	Disagree ②	Neither agree nor disagree ③	Agree ④	Strongly AGREE ⑤
a) Satisfied with quality of your social life					
BEFORE?	1	2	3	4	5
NOW?	1	2	3	4	5
b) Feel positive about the place where you live					
BEFORE?	1	2	3	4	5
NOW?	1	2	3	4	5
c) Satisfied with your relationship to your family					
BEFORE?	1	2	3	4	5
NOW?	1	2	3	4	5
d) Feel you belong to a community or are an important part of a group					
BEFORE?	1	2	3	4	5
NOW?	1	2	3	4	5

PART 3/CONTINUED

e) Satisfied with the opportunity to find suitable
work if you want to?

BEFORE?	1	2	3	4	5
NOW?	1	2	3	4	5

f) Satisfied with your opportunity to get suitable
accommodation

BEFORE?	1	2	3	4	5
NOW?	1	2	3	4	5

g) Satisfied with your opportunity to access
community services if you need to? (example:
healthcare, legal advice, social services, etc.)

BEFORE?	1	2	3	4	5
NOW?	1	2	3	4	5

h) Feel accepted in society

BEFORE?	1	2	3	4	5
NOW?	1	2	3	4	5

PART 4: ABOUT YOU

a) Your gender: Men ❑   Women ❑   Transgender/Other ❑

b) Your age _____ years old

c) Your first language

Spanish ❑   Kischwa ❑   Shuar Chicham ❑   Achuar Chicham ❑
Paicoca ❑   Tsafiki ❑   Other _____ ❑

d) The main earner in your household is: (*Mark one box*)

1. Yourself	❑	5. Close relative who lives with you	❑
2. Your mother	❑	6. Close relative who does not live with you	❑
3. Your father	❑	7. Non-relative who lives with you	❑
4. Your spouse or partner	❑	8. Non-relative who does not live with you	❑

e) The occupation of _____ (main earner) is:

(Check only the most important option, i.e. the one that generates more revenues. In cases where the main earner has two occupations that generate exactly the same income, put the letter to which the second occupation corresponds beside 'second occupation').

a. Professional or technical	❑	i. Laborer	❑
b. Employee at a private company	❑	j. Freelancer (maid, unpaid family worker)	❑
c. Public employee	❑	k. Retired	❑
d. Private employee, no professional title	❑	l. In the police force or military	❑
e. Public employee, no professional title	❑	m. Farm worker	❑
f. Artisan	❑	n. Income from property rental	❑
g. Small business owner	❑	o. Unemployed	❑
h. Owner of an industrial or commercial company	❑	Second occupation	❑

f) What is the role of the main earner in his/her work? *Mark only one answer.*

Performs the job	❑
Directs and organizes the work of others	❑
Performs AND directs the work	❑
Not applicable	❑

g) What is the most important source of revenues for the main breadwinner? Mark only one answer.

Property rental	❑	Salary as a laborer	❑
Informal wage, per day or week	❑	Salary as a farm worker	❑
Private business	❑	Salary as a maid	❑
Private employee, no professional title	❑	Sales	❑
Public employee, no professional title	❑	Fees for services	❑
Retirement pension	❑	Donations from relatives or other people	❑
Salary as a public sector employee	❑	Government subsidy	❑
Salary as a private sector employee	❑	Charity	❑

PART 5: HOW YOU FEEL ABOUT YOUR EDUCATION, JOB, HOUSING, LIFESTYLE

For the following questions, tick ONE box for BEFORE and ONE box for NOW

a) **Housing:** Among the choices listed below, which best represented your situation BEFORE starting social circus, and which best represents your situation NOW?

	BEFORE	NOW
Have my own place (with or without roommates)	❏	❏
Sleep at a friend's place	❏	❏
Live with own parents/family	❏	❏
Sleep in shelters or on the street	❏	❏
Other (please state)	❏	❏

b) **Education:** Among the choices listed below, which best represented your situation BEFORE starting social circus, and which best represents your situation NOW?

	BEFORE	NOW
In school, or taking courses of some kind	❏	❏
Finished school with no desire to seek further education	❏	❏
Dropped out of school with no desire to seek further education	❏	❏
Dropped out of school and interested to go back and/or seek other professional training	❏	❏
Other (please state)	❏	❏

c) **Education:** Among the choices listed below, which best represented your situation BEFORE starting social circus, and which best represents your situation NOW?

	BEFORE	NOW
Have a job, and am content (the hours I work and the type of work)	❏	❏
Have a job but do not like it (would like more hours or a different job)	❏	❏
Do not have a job, but would like to have one	❏	❏
Do not have a job, and do not want/can't have one	❏	❏
Other (please state)	❏	❏

d) **Financial situation:** Among the choices listed below, which best represented your situation BEFORE starting social circus, and which best represents your situation NOW

	BEFORE	NOW
Little to no income and it is fine by me	❏	❏
Little income and would like to have more	❏	❏
Fair income and content with the amount	❏	❏
Fair income but would like to have more	❏	❏
Other (please state)	❏	❏

e) **Use of substances:** Among the choices listed below, which best represented your situation BEFORE starting social circus, and which best represents your situation NOW

	BEFORE	NOW
I use alcohol or drugs occasionally and it is fine by me	❏	❏
I often use drugs and alcohol and it is fine by me	❏	❏
I use alcohol or drugs occasionally and I would like to reduce or quit	❏	❏
I often use drugs and alcohol and I would like to reduce or quit	❏	❏
I do not use drugs	❏	❏
I do not use alcohol	❏	❏
Other (please state)	❏	❏

f) **Fitness:** Among the choices listed below, which best represented your situation BEFORE starting social circus, and which best represents your situation NOW

	BEFORE	NOW
Little exercise and fine by me	❏	❏
Little exercise and would like to feel more fit	❏	❏
Reasonable exercise and content with my fitness	❏	❏
Reasonable exercise and would like to be more fit	❏	❏
Other (please state)	❏	❏

g) **Diet:** Among the choices listed below, which best represented your situation BEFORE starting social circus, and which best represents your situation NOW

	BEFORE	NOW
I have a balanced diet that provides me with the nutrition I need	❑	❑
I don't think my diet is well-balanced and it is fine by me	❑	❑
I do not have a healthy diet but would like one	❑	❑
Other (please state)	❑	❑

PART 6: YOUR ENGAGEMENT IN SOCIETY SINCE STARTING SOCIAL CIRCUS

Think back to when you started social circus. *BEFORE you started social circus, how likely were you to have these social engagements; and how likely you feel these are for you NOW*	Very likely	Likely	Maybe	Unlikely	Definitely not
a) Consider future involvement with social circus?					
BEFORE?	1	2	3	4	5
NOW?	1	2	3	4	5
b) Participate in organizations, community projects, or social activism (examples: human/civil/animal rights groups, anti-racist organizing, community radio etc.)?					
BEFORE?	1	2	3	4	5
NOW?	1	2	3	4	5
c) Participate in artistic projects (other than circus)?					
BEFORE?	1	2	3	4	5
NOW?	1	2	3	4	5
d) Participate in organizing/offering social or community circus project (examples: advisory board; organizing an event; become an instructor)?					
BEFORE?	1	2	3	4	5
NOW?	1	2	3	4	5

PART 7: YOUR WELLNESS

For the following questions, mark which expression is closest to what you feel:

a) How would you rate your overall energy level?

BEFORE

NOW

b) How would you rate your overall physical health?

BEFORE

NOW

c) How would you rate your overall emotional health?

BEFORE

NOW

d) How would you rate your comfort expressing yourself using your body?

BEFORE

NOW

PART 8

Is there anything else you want to tell us about how **your** experience with the social circus impacted **your own life**? (*you can use this space and the back of the page*)

PART 9

Is there anything else you want to tell us about how **your** experience with the social circus impacted **your family or your community**? *(you can use this space and the back of the page)*

Would you like to be contacted by the research team for a brief interview about you experience in social circus?

Yes	
No	

Please put the last three digits of your phone number, so that the survey can be anonymous but nonetheless retains a method of recording responses.

Thank you for taking the time to fill out this questionnaire! Your opinions and experience are extremely valuable!!!

NOTES

1 In the case of Quito, we obtained access to handwritten registration cards
   and created a database of some 605 people who had registered in *Circo Social
   Quito* since 2015; email addresses were available for only 229 and phone
   numbers for 310. We then sent emails to the 229 participants, providing
   them with a web-link where they could complete the questionnaire confi-
   dentially. However, a very large proportion of the email messages came back
   as no longer in operation. We advertised the existence of the study through
   Facebook, also providing the link. We also attempted to reach people by
   phone, but this too yielded limited success as the phone numbers were often
   no longer operational or were simply not answered.

   For Cuenca, the new coordinator did not have access to previous records,
   nor knew if previous records had been kept or, if so, where they could be
   found. Although we were able to obtain a database with 373 participants
   since 2015, most were under 18 years old.

   For Loja, the database contained 121 people in 2016. In order to maximize the response rate of those we were able to reach either through email,
   phone, or in person, we offered incentives for completing the questionnaire
   consisting of a draw for one of five pairs of tickets to the rehearsal for the
   first *Cirque du Soleil* performance in Ecuador (November 2015), and one set
   to the actual performance. As all current participants received a ticket to the
   rehearsal, we made this incentive available only to previous participants who
   were no longer in the program; 30 respondents entered this draw. Many discussions occurred amongst team members as to the most ethical way to ask
   for names and provide incentives, issues also explored by other researchers
   (McKenzie et al. 1999; Smith 2008).

2 We sought permission to distribute questionnaires to participants in the
   social circus program in Guayaquil, but it did not materialize; the program in
   Tena no longer was operational by the time we started the survey (Spiegel et
   al. 2018 for more details.) The program at Yachay, not officially part of *Circo
   Social Ecuador*, had not yet begun when our survey was conducted.

3 The Cronbach alpha score goes from 0–1, and scores greater than 0.7 are
   considered to be acceptable as a reliable scale (DeVellis 2012). We also did
   normal probability plots to confirm that the distribution of the data was not
   skewed.

4 We used Paired t-tests to determine the significance of differences between
   the pre and post responses; the Tukey's range test takes all these paired tests
   into account simultaneously so that the entire family of pairs in a scale has
   only a 5% chance of resulting in a false positive, rather than each question
   having a 5% chance. We used the Pearson chi-squared tests to determine the
   significance of differences when testing proportional changes; for example,

in testing changes in the proportion of people who reported having a balanced diet, using substances regularly, or being satisfied with their fitness level. We used "one-way ANOVA" to determine which of the factors had a significant impact on the scales.

5 The questionnaire asked people to self-identify by gender; it did not ask about sex.

6 While all respondents aged 12 to 39 were included in the above analysis, the fact that Cuenca's target population is children requires a separate commentary. *Circo Social Cuenca* conducted a socioeconomic survey in 2014 and found that only 54.6% had their basic needs met. *Circo Social Cuenca* also conducts an initial assessment of the self-esteem of participants, obtained through a self-administered questionnaire. 44% of the 61 participants in 2015 scored as having "low self-esteem." Importantly, in females the level of low self-esteem reached 60.8%, while in males it reached 37.8%, a difference of 23%.

7 In their study entitled "'If I Climb a Wall of Ten Meters': Capoeira, Parkour and the Politics of Public Space among (Post)migrant Youth in Turin, Italy," Ugolotti and Moyer (2016) discuss youth engagement with capoeira and parkour as the media through which struggles about belonging and citizenship take place. Through nine in-depth interviews with *capoeiristas* and *traceurs,* and with eight street educators working with migrant youth in Turin — a population they state is portrayed as "a population to be controlled and contained," they argue that "youth make use of their bodies through capoeira and parkour practices to contest and re-appropriate public spaces, thereby challenging dominant visions about what constitutes the public, how it should be used and by whom."

7 Creativity in Precarious Conditions: Embodied Social Transformation in a Changing Socio-political Landscape

JENNIFER BETH SPIEGEL

One October evening in 2015, in a public square at La Ronda, the heart of Quito's cultural centre, youth and instructors from the city's social circus program begin to congregate. They set up a sound system. They do their make-up. Just as night begins to fall, a *murga* begins – a short procession of music and colourfully clad artists. Some are on stilts, some wield hula-hoops, others juggle. A night of circus festivities has begun that will continue for hours, drawing the attention of everyone from tourists, to street vendors, to wandering locals out for a night on the town.

The public face of social circus in Ecuador, especially in the capital city, Quito, is shaped by the shows performed by the various artists and aspiring artists that social circus attracts and cultivates. While the main focus of social circus is the transformation of social relations, self-conceptions, and ex- perience of embodiment that occurs through workshops (the *replicas*), it is with shows and presentations that the "process" emerges as a "product." In Ecuador, as around the world, there is frequently a tension between process and product. This tension highlights ongoing debate concerning the goals of the program and the nature of the transformation pro- moted (Snyder-Young 2013; Kester 2017).

As many have argued, the contribution of performance to social transformation is grounded in the form of sociality en- couraged and developed through arts-based practices (Flynn and Tinius 2015; Routledge 2012) The nature of performance in such an understanding, however, is not necessarily a publicly oriented show. Rather, the focus is on generating skills, honing sensibilities, and building solidarity through the act of creating as a collective; the act, that is, of creating collectivity itself. The role of performance within an arts-based community development approach is thus often contentious. In Ecuador, the official intention of the social circus programs at the outset was to help transform the mentality of citizens in line with the *Buen Vivir* philosophy. As we saw in chapter 3, at the macro-level this means offering programs and policies promoting holistic wellbeing across social classes, and honouring different cultural interpretations. At the micro-level, culture and wellbeing, in keeping with *Buen Vivir*, would presumably be approached as a community-based endeavour, radically reshaping the relationship between the social, the cultural, and the corporeal.

Around the world, nearly all art and development initiatives grapple with the power of capital to influence social and creative processes via the various institutional structures that shape their delivery. Within the context of social circus, much of the tension rests on the ways in which creativity, precarity, and their conjunction are understood. In 2004, activist Alex Foti offered a definition of precarity that included "the condition of being unable to predict one's fate or having some degree of predictability on which to build affection" (Oudenampsen and Sullivan 2004, 45). Performance theorist Nyong'o (2013) writes, "the keywords surrounding precarity – affective and cognitive labour; contingent and flexible employment; amateurism and virtuosity – have assuredly opened new thresholds in activism and theory." Far from academic buzzwords, these concepts, and the development of new approaches to the social arts that they inspire, are being re-generated in social circus, for better or worse.

In many ways, as the research shared throughout this book suggests, it is precisely this precarious condition that social circus seeks to alter. Debates concerning how to address precarity have been particularly intense in Latin America due to the history of colonialism and development schemas that have seen the continent as ripe for the extraction of surplus value for the benefit of Northern entrepreneurs. As discussed in chapter 3, this has led to much strain on communities and their youth. In recent years, with the spread of the "pink tide" and policies like *Buen Vivir*, however, previously informal economies and networks are (or at least, were) becoming formalized by the state-civil society nexus (Radcliffe 2012; Mezzadra and Gago 2017). Social circus networks and practices transformed under these changing conditions, deeply influencing the experiences and creative practices of those involved.

Social circus, as it evolved around the world since the 1990s, has increasingly had to become goal-oriented and build skills for surviving neoliberal system collapse, preparing participants to be "creative" and to forge their own paths, since jobs and socioeconomic support systems, as they have historically been conceived, are dwindling (Spiegel 2015c). In the case of Ecuador, and particularly in its capital city, Quito, navigation of these pressures took on a unique aura: the program evolved with state support as the country sought to distance itself from Western neoliberalism. On the one hand, programs reached out to youth to encourage personal growth via individual and collective creativity and embodiment. Trust, affection, discipline, and self-expression were all cultivated, while collectivity was further encouraged through a "giving back" to the community of what one has learned. On the other hand, the precarity that was actually experienced personally and collectively by participants posed an ongoing challenge. How socially engaged arts programs resolve such tensions has profound implications for the organization, recruitment, presentation style, and trajectories supported.

This chapter follows the evolution of program design in various cities in Ecuador and puts them into dialogue with social circus programs in the Canadian province of Quebec, where many consultants for Ecuador's program are based (Spiegel 2016c; Spiegel and Parent 2017). Drawing from interviews and participant observation conducted in 2013, 2014, and 2015 in both countries, the chapter asks the questions: What kind of social subjectivities and forms of collectivity are emerging from these programs? And what implications do they have for how we understand the relationships between art, politics, and social transformation?

A Changing Vision

We started in the street as jugglers. Afterwards we joined the circus
because we heard of a workshop about circus in the municipality
(Patronato) San Jose. After this we became part of the circus.

Long-term participant in social circus in Quito

The movement to support the development of youth often already creatively involved, or so inclined, underscores many social arts programs around the world and has been a guiding principle of social circus internationally. Indeed, as street performance and busking has increasingly become a way of life for homeless youth, social circus has expanded as a mode of outreach. While traditionally associated with "freaks" and alternative subcultures, the industry has grown, and recreational circus programs proliferate across the Americas, Europe, and beyond as leisure activity for the middle classes. This historical evolution, combined with the intrinsic pull between process and product entrenched in nearly all performance-oriented social initiatives, has placed immense pressure on social circus programs to redefine themselves.

In Ecuador, as was discussed in chapter 3, social circus training developed with the aid of practitioners from Montreal, a Canadian city renowned for its vibrant circus culture. Many of the artists, including the founders of *Cirque du Soleil*, began as street performers, and many of the institutions that started as social circus programs later were repurposed as centres for professional and recreational training (Spiegel 2016b). In Ecuador in the early years, before the government social circus program started, youth were recruited off the streets to participate in grassroots circus initiatives. There were no performances or TV ads to grab their attention. Word of mouth prevailed, and those approached were principally youth making a living busking at traffic lights. Indeed, before *Circo Social Ecuador* began, workshops that were offered free and primarily targeted street-involved youth were not formalized as "social circus."

According to a social worker with *Circo Social Quito* in its early years, at its onset the program was remarkably effective in reaching youth in high-risk situations and in supporting participants in taking control of their lives. However, she noted a change in focus and ethos:

> Most of the young people [recruited in the early years] were living in the streets, and did not want to study or improve their quality of life ... They consumed drugs, alcohol [and were] involved in that world. So that's what the initial project was about, trying to help them out of those high-risk situations ... The new kids, from what I have seen, come from a different background ... Some are high school students interested in circus art ... It's no longer because they are in a vulnerable situation ... I think that reflects the current vision of the program. I have a feeling they [municipal decision-makers] did not understand the objective of the project ... Now it is viewed as just another youth program, not keeping the 'mystique' it previously had ... Before it felt like a family, I am not sure what they [the participants] think now ... Maybe it's just like another program. (interview October 2015)

By November 2014, the goal of *Circo Social Quito* had shifted from primarily targeting youth in precarious situations to promoting social "mixity."

The coordinator described their participant base thus: "It is diverse. Many of them come because they don't have a place to go and then they stay because they like it; others like circus arts a lot and come to exercise and learn techniques. People are from different social classes [...] including street children who were [performing] at the traffic lights or kids in school who like arts and want to spend the evening, or kids who have decided to become circus artists and want to become professional" (interviewed February 2015).

For newer participants, the re-orientation of the program was appreciated for the way in which it promotes inclusion and social engagement. One said, "Social circus is a space where people from all ages converge. It is awesome to share different things, and it is exciting to do it in groups. In social circus, we achieve our dreams while we help the most vulnerable kids." Another participant explained: "We have seen everything from people who went to jail, have been in hospitals, have lived in very dangerous places – all the way to people who have money and go to private schools, adults to small kids. The circus is very inclusive. Everyone is welcome – whether you are skilled or not."

However, one long-term Quito social circus participant lamented the changing nature of the program:

> There was a new administration as well as new instructors. It also changed the way circus art was taught. It stopped being the welcoming circus; they stopped recruiting kids who had no ability to learn circus art. They started to focus on kids who already had the skills, the physical ability in their bodies, to be part of the circus. Someone already aligned with this career. When we started, we knew nothing, absolutely nothing. That started to change, you could see that other people clearly had more advanced skills, the feeling was different, a less welcoming and warm feeling. We had a sense that we were no longer equal ... The feeling was completely different – there was no passion. We did not fit in the group, the atmosphere felt 'dense'...
> We came back because we needed a space to improve our technique. We also practice in parks or at stop signs, but this eventually hurts your body, it's too hard. It's good to have a large space to practice and have the proper equipment ... since it's a social circus, I can take advantage of it.

The shift in ethos could have been due to multiple factors such as the initial recuperation of a small grassroots project into a large-scale government initiative, the growth of the state-sponsored program itself, and especially the municipal government having changed to one that no longer supported the *Buen Vivir* vision. While the extent to which different municipalities embraced *Buen Vivir* varied, at the onset of the program, *Buen Vivir* was very much at the heart of Quito's vision as publicized by (progressive) Mayor Barrera (Burgos-Vigna 2016a). This came to an end in 2014 when a new (right-wing) mayor was elected. With the change in municipal government, *Circo Social Quito* was maintained, but different elements began to be stressed, including the principles of social mixity and performance. The previous focus on marginalized and disenfranchised youth was de-emphasized, with the result that more youth from higher socio-economic brackets began to be attracted to social circus. Who was being reached, how they were invited to interact, and the entire socio-cultural tenor of the program began to shift.

The make-up and size of the team had also shifted from a program run by a single circus artist to one that paired circus instructors and social workers. By early 2017, the Quito team consisted of a coordinator with a social work background, three instructors, and a fluctuating number of volunteers and contracted instructors who provide occasional technical workshops. The structure that developed was complex. At the main site, *Circo Social Quito* was generally open to anyone who wanted to attend sporadically (level 1); level 2 was for people who had reached a higher level of training and attended on a regular basis; level 3 participants had a deeper interest in circus practices as well as the pedagogy of *Circo Social*; and level 4 accommodated small groups working together for a common interest collectively defined. As noted in chapter 3, the workshops are called *replicas* as the intent was whatever instructors and volunteers learned in their training would be "replicated" in other milieus. In 2013, *Circo Social Quito* was offering *replicas* in seven different organizations serving approximately 430 participants (see description of organizations hosting *replicas* in chapter 6). In addition to serving the *replicas*, *Circo Social Quito* at that time was providing 70 youths with regular training at their municipal facility (see photo 5.5).

By 2014, there were five active *replica* sites serving 135 participants, and 65 youths in training. (For annual fluctuations and comparisons with other *Circo Social* programs see table 3.1, and Spiegel et al. 2018.) This model of development – seeking to promote social inclusion through weaving institutional ties across cultural, social, health, and education sectors as well as multiple levels of government – was, in many ways, unique. The site of social and cultural transformation here remained corporeal. The chal-

Photo 7.1 Group of former volunteers from *Circo Social Cuenca* perform an exercise of trust and teamwork in 2013. José Sinche (base, below) supports Mauricio Illescas (above) who will fall back to be caught by the group, including Cristina Bustos (former instructor, right), Roberto Mayorga (left), and others, who are forming a net with linked arms.

lenges faced offer a case study in the vulnerabilities of corporeal arts within post-neoliberal governmentality.

Development and the Politics of Corporeality

Social circus, like most community arts, is inherently a social activity. Grounded in collective embodied creation, impacts on well-being are linked to how individuals engage with larger social and collective activities and conditions.

Around the world, the generation of social cohesion and inclusion have been key goals and claims for social circus programs, focusing on the roles of teamwork, trust, and controlled risk-taking inherent in the activity (see photo 7.1; Spiegel 2013, 2016c; Bessone 2017). Such goals are, however, ambivalent with respect to challenging neoliberal values. They contest the individualism associated with neoliberal success, while providing stop-gaps to avoid both disintegration of the social fabric as well as broad-based dissent by unruly youth (Bishop 2012; Haiven 2017). As an art form, circus has always straddled a liminal space of socially sanctioned spectacle through the display of exceptional – if not "freakish" – bodies, as well as the formation of nomadic and often precarious troupes and "families" made up of those whose identities or way of life has been marginalized (Thomson 1996; Stoddart 2000; Sussman 2013).

Engaging in artistic practice will have very different implications for those who have always worked in practical and manual labour than for those who have been engaged in abstract intellectual pursuits. Far from being universalizable, gender, culture. and class all affect how transformation occurs. Bringing together those from different walks of life through creative interaction, it becomes possible to launch a "molecular revolution" wherein social transformation is seeded by the kinds of interactions and horizons of possibility that small groups spark (Guattari and Rolnick 2007).

The site of transformation in social circus is, first and foremost, corporeal, being itself an embodied art form. As one participant put it, "I fell in love with circus because I came to ... know that we could do and learn so many things with our bodies. We discover our bodies using different materials like trapezes to discover oneself." The artistic pedagogy as well as the policies and structures surrounding performance are engaged in a form of biopolitical governmentality whose results are inherently uncertain, coming into contact, as they do, with embodied cultural histories that are diverse, complex, and multiple, incapable of being constrained in holding patterns of ethnicity, gender identity, or class. As Bessone argues, social circus becomes a site of organized cultural encounter in which "new bodily experiences and interactions, emotions and 'affective energies' (Lobo 2014) ... have the potential to unsettle existing social structures and relations of power" (Bessone 2017, 658).

While there are multiple, if not infinite, ways in which the corporeal encounters staged by social circus potentiate transformation, two dominant trends emerged within *Circo Social Ecuador*. Each of these trends gestured toward – at least provisionally – divergent approaches to social transformation within the context of neoliberal and postcolonial conditions of precarity. One pertained to developing the expressive nature of the body and the relationship this bears to empathy and community. As a participant from *Circo Social Quito* explained: "Since I have been in social circus, I have been able to perceive body language in a different way. I can understand other things. I can understand a situation without words." Some participants felt that their engagement in social circus helped them navigate the world with greater sensitivity through a heightening of social perception (see photo 5.27 in chapter 5, for example). In a related vein, many appreciated how the expressive qualities of social circus allowed them to share their own ways of perceiving the world with a broader community. As one participant, who had been recruited from the streets of Quito as the program was forming, said, "I don't even want to remember what it was like before. It was very bad. I had no future; [I was an] enemy of my own family and myself ... It [social circus] made me love myself and my family. It was a time to re-evaluate. I became a better human being, more sensible. Because we are circus artists, we can express our feelings when we perform. This enables us to communicate our deepest emotions, sadness, happiness, crying ... All the things that have happened to you as a child and throughout our lives, I really like that. It's almost like falling into an unconscious state, and in that state you are able to let go of those deep feelings, no matter what those are."

The plethora of circus techniques, as well as the ability of circus to absorb multiple aesthetic traditions, gestures toward a carnivalesque notion of corporeality supporting the flourishing of street cultures and the expression of "baser impulses" and "lower" classes (Bakhtin 1984). As such, it provides a public culture site for collective catharsis, where artists and audiences can come together to experience emotions, re-evaluate shared understandings, and create a space for joy and play.

The second trend was firmly anchored in discipline and self-control, gesturing toward a notion of corporeal expression approaching an ideal form. This is reminiscent of the role gymnastics plays in Plato's *Republic* in exalting human potential and encouraging high-level performance, thus elevating the collective. In this way, technique and self-control become signifiers of moral worth. One *Circo Social Quito* participant said, "I learned the technique; one must learn to control one's body and become better, not to compete with others but to make oneself a better person." "It made me a more patient and tolerant person; somehow it helped me a lot to know myself and to have control over myself," stated another.

These two ways of approaching corporeal expression point to a rift between the "social" and the "technical" aspects of social circus that prevail everywhere. The tension was particularly marked in Ecuador, due to the contentious politics of harmonious "good living" versus the extraction of surplus value through performance that pervaded policy debates. Combined, however, these trends point to cultural legacies of simultaneously absorbing and contesting hegemonic modes of being. The promotion of self-control through technique is resonant with the governmental goal of encouraging "excellence." In contrast to the Platonic vision of *maintaining* a social order, however, it is designed to *transform* the order. Corporeal technique becomes a form of "cultural capital" in the Bourdieusian sense, where the acquiring of this capital – notably, through learning artistic skills as well as how to engage in and be valued within the culture industry – aids social inclusion and personal self-worth. The body in this schema becomes the core site of engagement and inclusion within a broader social fabric; technique becomes the medium through which to integrate. As one participant put it, "Before I knew about the circus I did nothing, I lived in the streets. My body was not functioning. Once I learned about the circus, everything changed in me: my intellect, my heart. Now that everything has changed in me, things have also changed around me, and I have been able to adapt to it. Now it's a lot easier than before. When I knew nothing, I felt like the scum of the earth. Now I feel accepted."

Much cultural theorizing has focused on the disciplining of the body and the senses through colonial and postcolonial encounters. Bhaba (2012) famously demonstrated how modes of embodiment have been used to en-train colonial ways of seeing and knowing while anchoring a hierarchical system whereby the colonized is always a lesser mimic. However, he also showed how such mimesis could function as a site of subversion. In a similar vein, Taussig (1993) traced how, within the Latin American context, colonial representational technologies created notions of the "savage," but were also used by the Kuna peoples to subvert economies of representation and the ways in which a drive toward authenticity function. With the spread of circus arts as social intervention, the ambivalent globalization of creative technologies undergoes a new chapter. The body, or rather collective *bodies*, become carriers and conductors of what Taylor (2003) refers to as "transculturation." This, according to Taylor, is a three-step process: First, contact is made with a "foreign" culture (though in this case only partially foreign). Second, one's own culture is displaced (potentially the more "radical" street theatre that proliferates – but equally, for those alienated and living in the streets, the culture of precarious survival in a country ravaged by neoliberal imperialism). And then, finally, a "new" culture is created. Transformation in cultures of embodiment propelled by artistic modes of engagement is reflected in discourses of collective health. From the point of view of collective good living (*buen vivir*), there is an iterative relationship between community values and a sense of wellbeing in how one inhabits one's body. Breilh and colleagues (2010) showed that not only do socially-determined patterns of work, leisure, and consumption determine health and wellbeing, but so, too, do the culturally driven perceptions about the human body and its physical condition.

The two threads identified within the social circus program, each embodying a distinct way of perceiving the body and its physical and social potential, find their theoretical correlate in competing notions of the relationship between "physicality" and "literacy." On the one hand, there is the notion, common to dance studies, that physical literacy is closely linked to metaphor and emotional literacy is expressed in an embodied manner. On the other hand, there is a notion more closely linked to sports culture, in which physical literacy is linked to the ability of the individual to excel in the execution of technical tasks. While a commitment to performance as a corporeal process may connect the two ways of thinking about physical literacy (Whitehead 2010), how it plays out is far from politically neutral. As Martin has pointed out, in relation to hip hop, "technique does more than tool the body to what is dominant in the social order. Bodies can also be trained – or learn – in a manner that is inconsistent with dominance as such, which assumes investment in the logic and sensibility of exclusion and subordination. The key to subverting dominance lies in the anatomies of the participation necessary to be mastered by technique" (Martin 1998, 20).

Mastering and celebrating the techniques of circus so often seen in terms of virtuosity – physical feats accomplishable by only the most highly skilled – would seem to repeat a social aesthetic of hierarchy, even if it alters the dynamics of *who* is at the top of this hierarchy (for instance, street youth). However, the debate in the context of the processes of social circus suggests a more nuanced understanding of the embodiment of social values and social transformation. As discussed in chapter 4, the techniques learned are as social as they are aesthetic, and the process of learning orients how this plays out, underlining the importance of social circus pedagogy to model horizontal relations. Here, Latin American "pedagogies of the oppressed" (Boal [1985] 2008; Freire 1972), depoliticized by *Cirque du Monde* from their original "rehearsal for revolution" ambitions (born within the context of resistance to dictatorship in Brazil) have been hybridized with global circus culture, and again with Latin American traditions of street theatre. The politics of aesthetics transmutes the dramatization of structural oppression experienced by the artists-as-community-members germane to Boal's *Theatre of the Oppressed*. De-emphasizing narrative techniques for exploring dialectical struggle, social circus focuses on techniques for re-training bodily interactions to intercede viscerally in these structures.

A host of cultural, social, and economic considerations orient how bodily movement is approached by whom, as well as the range of motivations and other complicating factors that nuance how a practice is taken up by participants (Hylton 2013). As we saw in chapter 6, technique, corporeality, and sociality are all experienced differently depending on the social dynamic not only of the program, but also one's previous embodied experiences. Moreover, aspirations themselves are shaped by exposure and often conditioned by gender, ethnicity, and class. By engaging in new embodied practices, the kinds of aspiration that seemed possible changed. While some were attracted to circus to perform, others were simply drawn to it as a site of sociality and expanded horizons. Those who came for one reason often stayed for another. As one participant put it, "I can't say that my goals changed, because I didn't have any before." Now, however, her goals included touring to communities, learning their values and ways of life, and sharing her own skills. A form of collective subjectivity was forming that informed social circus with both a "technology of the self" (Foucault 1988) and a technology of togetherness through which modes of accomplishing objectives could take shape.

Collective Cultures, Collective Transformation

Collective embodiment as the creation of a cultural ethos, a national identity, or a collective image, are all frequently cited amongst the social roles of the arts. In Ecuador, the *Buen Vivir* policy sought to move beyond hegemonic notions of culture by explicitly naming pluri-nationalism amongst its social and cultural aims. This tied the country's vision of development more broadly to Indigenous concepts of good living that stress harmonious commitment to community. It also sought to move beyond an extractivist economy by developing the cultural sector.

This notion of collective wellbeing and collective culture within the context of a publicly funded program, built on supporting street-involved youth through the arts, dovetailed with a growing culture of street arts across Latin America. The transformation of public space in Latin America was a function of liberalization that occurred especially in Argentina, Brazil, and Mexico in the 1970s and 1980s – a period which saw much political upheaval (Avritzer 2009). The growth and transformation in social arts, and the kinds of social transformation embodied, are an integral part of this history. Youth, with shrinking employment options but growing artistic freedom, embraced circus as a way of life in the multiple senses of self-expression, community engagement, and employment (Infantino 2015). Across Latin America, the growth of street arts and circus became part of a new cultural formation. Its latest iteration in *Circo Social Ecuador* built on this culture, especially in Quito, where participants were frequently nomadic youth from not only elsewhere in the country but from across the continent.

However, with a pedagogy firmly anchored in the *Cirque du Monde* tradition, in the context of a (nominally "revolutionary") government-sponsored program, there was considerable variability concerning the cultural politics embodied in and through the performances. Avritzer has argued that "social actors in Latin America during liberalization developed a new form of collective identity ... social actors resisted the notion that they belonged to a homogenous, undifferentiated popular sector and started to understand themselves as belonging to a pluralistic social space ... This led to a different form of politicizing the social, one in which issues that had been contained at the private were brought into public" (Avritzer 2009, 83). The social arts emerged as part of this transforming of social and political subjectivity as a collective force for re-creating and re-performing identity. Coming-together to create a show, as well as community engagement of sharing skills and the magic of performance are all part and parcel of what makes social circus what it is.

While there is controversy over who the appropriate audience should be (peers, family members, those in one's larger network, or the community of fellow town or city-dwellers more broadly), the creation of a performance and the sharing of one's accomplishments with one's community provides a focus for the collective process. Shows further allow the program to extend its reach and draw in the larger community. The contested notion of who is to perform, for whom, when, speaks to pedagogical concerns delineated in chapter 4. However, this question of appropriate audience further points to a broader notion, implicit in the pedagogical concern, of safe community spaces for development as opposed to spaces for spectacle. As Schechner suggests, this "efficacy-entertainment braid" retains a level of fluidity (Schechner 1993). Its navigation lies at the heart of the transformation of culture for a "post-neoliberal" and "post-colonial" vision of development, particularly one grounded in the "social."

At *Circo Social Quito*, the official focus remains on process and its implications for those involved as well as those touched. Nonetheless, there

Photo 7.2 Photo after a social circus demonstration by volunteers from *Circo Social Quito*, 2015, at one of the centres where *replicas* are conducted, after *replica* participants had completed their own demonstrations for friends and family members.

are two distinct types of shows: recitals (or *muestras*) for peers, friends, and family, and shows (or *spectaculos*) for a broader public, performed in schools, public squares (photo 7.2), and municipal events amongst other venues.

These performances each tend toward a different aesthetic in keeping with their audiences and their purpose, negotiating various visions of corporeal expression as a site of transformation. The collective aesthetic generated by social circus builds on, and navigates, a turbulent history of circus ethics and aesthetics. As I noted elsewhere (Spiegel 2016b, 268–9):

In the eighteenth and nineteenth centuries, at the height of trad-itional circus in the era of late-colonial industrialism, an ethic of the triumphant individual had exalted the ingenuity and capacities of the worldly human body, extolling the exceptional nature of the individual performer and individual performances (Stoddart 2000). The aesthetics of the *nouveau* or contemporary circus, however, formed in the later decades of the twentieth century, point not only to individual possibilities and capacities but also to the power and potential of the collective. In this era of change, circus performers began to be presented not as oddities, but as inspiring individuals whom spectators may wish to emulate. Even as the forms of contemporary circus, seen through the work of Cirque du Soleil and the contemporary practices it has inspired, hinge to a large extent on the exceptional body (Graver 2005; Hurley 2008; Leroux 2012), the singular, expressive, and awe-inspiring bodies of the performers gesture toward a collective imaginary (Gagnon 2005; Hurley 2008). These new acts, which feature clowns, other-worldly aerialists, and even 'ordinary' naive and childlike characters who wander into the world of dreams suggested by these circus productions, work to bring their audiences along to be transported and transformed by the possibilities opened on the on-stage world (Hurley 2008).

Inspired in part by the contemporary circus tradition imported by *Cirque du Soleil, Circo Social Ecuador* is reshaping multiple aesthetics under a cultural policy that highlights harmony with nature and the collective. One would expect a complete reversal of the nineteenth-century circus aesthetic that turned nature and "the native" into a touring spectacle (Stoddart 2000; Davis 2002), and a re-anchoring of Indigenous processes within their social and cultural ecologies.

Within Latin America, such hybridization is not unprecedented. In Argentina, for instance, as early as the turn of the twentieth century, travelling circus troupes popularized what has become known as the Creole dramas. This led to the creation of the Creole circus, which was popular well into the twentieth and even twenty-first century (Acree 2016). This tradition took up such politicized subjects as migration, social stratification, and economic modernization. The Latin American *paseo* is known for engaging in folk traditions with social, cultural, and political sensibilities often associated with the carnivalesque: corporeal humour as a basis for questioning power. *Paseo*, like many other clowning traditions, is known for generating "irreverent and subversive transgression of rules and boundaries," thereby altering the conditions of possibility for both the performer and the audience (King 2013).

The vision of development in Ecuador was such that its cultural aesthetic developed rather differently than that of NGO-funded programs, particularly those in Northern cities like Montreal where a professionalized circus industry was already well-established. Whereas in Montreal "social circus" was only developed after – and indeed "by" – a thriving circus industry bolstered by government spending in the wake of Quebec's "Quiet Revolution" (Leslie and Rantisi 2010), Ecuador's social circus was designed to bring about a post-neoliberal, post-extractivist development model. This meant that while the aesthetic generated by social circus in Montreal is often consciously "alternative," in Ecuador, social circus has been a site for developing multiple aesthetics simultaneously, and on a much larger scale (Rivard 2007; Spiegel et al. 2015; Spiegel 2016b; Spiegel and Parent 2017).

The developing aesthetic of *Circo Social Quito* draws from a global contemporary circus scene and a rich tradition of Latin American street performance but attempts to make space for the cultural expression of those present, centring their creative impulses. Thus, in some of the *muestras* (the presentations given for small closed groups), participants present their new tricks with text in Spanish and in Kichwa concerning their own experiences and aspirations. Public presentations in the squares and schools, however, tend to be less personal, and dovetail more with expected street and circus culture. The social circus roots in such shows are less evident to the spectator. In public, the hybridization of cultural influences brings together global circus traditions with other Latin American public art forms such as carnival and the *murga*.

While carnivals and carnivalesque performance, in Latin America as elsewhere, have historically been sites of cultural transgression, the extent to which these are community artistic experiences for their own sake or sites of political identity-building, has varied considerably. In his *Barrio Democracy in Latin America: Participatory Decentralized Community Activism in Montevideo*, Canel (2010) discusses how *murgas* were embraced by trade unionists, blending a popular aesthetic with political sensibilities, offering a boost to community organizing and activism. While the social circus *murgas* in the tourist district of Quito leveraged this aesthetic, tapping into the jubilant Latin American tradition, its cultural politic was confined to integrating youth of various walks of life into the show. The performance drew in a wide range of spectators from wealthy tourists to impoverished children selling chewing gum for coins. Act after act dazzled the audience with seemingly impossible feats of acrobatics and juggling. One man even performed an acrobatic routine with his young daughter, expanding the horizon of what the youth of the community could do. As such, the show could be seen to bolster municipal and national goals of "social cohesion."

As with most of the public performances, nothing was particularly transgressive, at least not beyond the culturally ambivalent aesthetic of marginalized bodies capturing the attention of and delighting the public. In private recitals, however, cultural norms and their social implications were explored further. Thus, for instance, in a recital in the early years of the program, youth recruited largely off the streets explored how, through circus, they began to overcome their fear of heights. They began to see this fear as a metaphor, offering a verbal narration in a combination of Spanish and Kichwa, and redeveloped a language of the body through which to reorient themselves to social and cultural life. An aerial drop – a tumbling down on a silk – became a metaphor for facing an unraveling future without fear. A recital in a youth detention centre was far less literal, but blending breakdancing with circus explored how these interests could be combined to generate a unique cultural expression. By the time their performance met the public years later, such lessons were embodied in the shared aesthetic. The expectations of performance, however, meant that much of the social process had disappeared from what had become a more apolitical circus aesthetic.

In Quebec, the challenging of gender presentation in social circus performance is often explicit. For example, productions have featured a feminine wig passed from one performer to another regardless of the gender of the performer, as well as the performance of burlesque showgirl routines by male bodies (Spiegel 2016c; photo 7.3). In Ecuador, the re-performance of gender norms is more subtle. The aesthetic of femininity offered to the public is "sexy," with frequent tropes of allure and flirtation repeated in performance, but also one of extreme strength, as is required to perform acrobatics (photo 7.4).

While colonization imposed a gender binary in many instances unknown to Indigenous cultures (Lugones 2007), it would be difficult to argue that social circus is offering a means to reclaim Indigenous gender identities. Nevertheless, gender is being reworked as part of the resistance to border-based thinking (Schutte 2011). By offering an opening to nomadic youth in ways that reject colonial borders, identities – including gender identity – are being re-performed, subverting dominant tropes. Women in circus have always walked a line between offering highly sexualized images

Photo 7.3 A carnivalesque performance in a 2015 production by Montreal's *Cirque Hors Piste*.

Photo 7.4 *Circo Social Quito* instructor Soledad Contreras performing aerial acrobatics at an open circus in Quito, 2015.

Photo 7.5 Performance by Montreal's *Cirque Hors Piste*'s intensive workshop group at a "Youth for Human Rights" event in March 2015, depicting the prejudice lived by street youth. In this scene, a confrontation with the police is satirized.

for a dominant gaze, and performing acts requiring extreme physical strength, rising to power through an ability to leverage the "glamour" of circus (Tait 2005; Holmes 2017).

Navigation of the requirements of performance and the nature of the cultural aesthetic encouraged is necessarily grounded institutionally, oriented by pedagogies and funder expectations. Increased support from the state for programs in Northern neoliberal economies has meant increased prospects, but also greater state involvement. One social circus performance brought to our attention during the arts-based workshops (chapter 5) exemplifies the aspirations and tensions of the project, with concern in particular for youth living in precarious situations. The piece, directed by a former-participant-turned-instructor who had come to social circus from a life of street art in Chile, was co-created with current participants. The story was about a child living in poverty who shines shoes to survive until he encounters a magical world of the arts through which his dreams take shape. The aesthetic bridged contemporary circus, street theatre, and the whimsical escapism frequent in participant-generated performances (Liang 2014; Spiegel 2016c). Unfortunately, last-minute venue challenges due to a lack of municipal support meant that the target audiences of young people were never reached.

The exploration of politically charged topics via social circus is not uncommon around the world. In Montreal, participants often explore themes explicitly challenging the capitalist order. In one show, human pyramids were framed as a metaphor for capitalism itself, satirizing police culture and criticizing the police brutality experienced by those living in the streets (Spiegel 2016c; see photo 7.5).

The audiences intended for such performances are typically the family and friends of performers and, for those performances that take place in public space, ad hoc passersby. The aesthetic generated by social circus has gone largely unrecognized, despite the role of those trained within the programs in seeding further cultural initiatives (Spiegel 2016b, 2016c). This lack of recognition in most places is both a cause and a symptom of the reification of culture. Those "of the streets" are confined to performing for each other as a social intervention, in some cases developing an "alternative" arts scene, while the professional cultural industry remains the purview of companies led by those trained at elite institutions and thus, by implication, from more economically privileged backgrounds. This dynamic has implications for the kind of art being made.

New Visions for Social Engagement and the Re-structuring of Cultural Development

Social circus in Ecuador was intended as part of broader *Buen Vivir* policy initiatives. As such, it sought to address the dissolution of the social fabric that was the legacy of neoliberalism as an extension of colonization itself. While the pedagogical vision was always very much infused with Latin American collectivism, the developmental vision sought opportunities for individual advancement and the development of enterprises that would allow greater independence from the state. The program signaled the desire to bring about an unfinished project of socio-cultural transformation, one which shifted with changes in government and administration as well as with the efforts and visions of instructors and participants themselves.

Curiously, the shift away from youth living in precarious conditions was accompanied by a shift toward greater gender parity. Whereas in its early years social circus was largely male, possibly due to its association with street youth and the tendency of young men to wander further from their parents than young women, by 2017 the gender inclusion was relatively symmetrical. Women taught, trained, rigged, and performed alongside men. Stephan Mier, head of youth programs in Quito's *Patronato Muni-*

cipal San José, told us in an October 2015 interview that *Circo Social Quito* had achieved a gender balance of 50-50 that year. He attributed this to the implementation of aerial acrobatics – a circus art that was attractive to women and girls.

Mier also mentioned that there were more couples participating, and that women tended to use the space for socializing more than men, suggesting that although gender parity was being reached, the program continued to be experienced in a gendered manner. These implications have not yet been fully appreciated. How was instruction and outreach adapting to intersectional concerns, for instance, of low-income mothers wishing to explore artistically? As one participant pointed out, the imperative to train daily and take on increasing responsibilities means that without organized childcare, many women face obstacles not shared by their male counterparts. Nevertheless, their growing presence in social circus signals a kind of cultural emancipation for Latin American women, historically subjected to a "double colonization" (Richards 2004) by the patriarchal forces that Spanish colonialism, followed by global neoliberal imperialism, imposed.

The question that remains is the extent to which this art form navigates competing local and global pressures across gender as well as social, cultural, and economic levels. In the context of *Circo Social Quito,* this has played out in the competing visions and experiences of participants. As Burgos-Vigna notes (2016a, 2016b), when Ecuador sought greater cultural recognition on the global scene, the historic legacies of Quito as a cultural centre and UNESCO heritage site confounded the ways in which *Buen Vivir* policies were put in place. Drawing on the work of anthropologist Lucía Durán (2014), Burgos-Vigna argues that Quito was living the tension between enacting cultural policies that established itself as a "place to see" versus "a place to live." While this tension is not unique to Quito, it is more extreme here than in most cities. Perhaps this is due to a very explicit duality in the two poles of its cultural policy – maintaining its character as a global tourist destination versus a democratizing, if not decolonizing, reconstruction of policies to facilitate the "right to the city" of its inhabitants. This duality reflects the need to develop economies that support new social and professional networks that, at least in principle, are inclusive across genders, classes, and ethnicities.

In Latin America, the current trend toward professionalizing and promoting cultural identities encourages youth to redefine their sense of identity as well as their roles within broader social and cultural milieus. In Brazil, this has notably been the case with professionalization of capeoira, generating much controversy within the community itself (Wesolowski 2012). The multifaceted redefining of culture, as well as the plethora of pressures from which such transformation issues, likewise is generating mixed reactions amongst youth in social circus. In Quito, a circus industry as such has not (yet) developed, although some see it rising out of social circus itself. Indeed, many participants are now calling for the establishment of an elite circus school – a proposal being considered by the Ecuadorean government. As Scheper Hughes and Dalla Déa note, "state appropriation of local and traditional artistic expression often undermines the rhetorical potency of art as political resistance and as an expression of particular ethnic or cultural identity" (Hughes and Déa 2012, 8). In the case of circus arts, this cultural identity is less ethnic than global, with large numbers of youth involved immersed in street or traveler culture.

Partly because it is the largest program in the country, tensions within the social circus program have played out most transparently in Quito. Because there is no professional circus school in Ecuador, some participants want to focus on skills for professionalization, whereas others are drawn to its vision of creating a space for creative exploration for those often left aside. The "productivist" orientation suggested by the push to professionalize is two-pronged. On the one hand, there is a desire on the part of youth to be taken seriously as aspiring artists capable of succeeding regardless of their socio-economic background. On the other hand is their desire to be able to make a living doing something fulfilling. As one participant at the Quito photovoice workshop (described in chapter 5) explained: "When we perform on a stage, we are artists and are well regarded, but when we perform in the street [by stop lights] we are seen as beggars and street people. People don't realize the effort it takes to live as an artist and to survive as an artist."

The need to address economic precarity and the disparity of opportunity led directly to a deep-seated tension in the program's very structure. Participants still try to generate income by performing on the streets and at traffic lights, yet *Circo Social Quito* also organizes collective performances but does not generally pay participants for their participation in these events. Moreover, in the Ecuadorean model, volunteers who work with children in the *replicas,* or who perform at events at the request of the municipality, are not provided with a financial stipend. A coordinator of the Quito program noted that the training provided was their main compensation, and also described the different ways social circus participants can generate income, including a mask-making business (photo 7.6), a

Photo 7.6 Mask business run from the municipal venue of *Circo Social Quito.* Photo taken during a visit by the research team, 2015.

coffee shop with baked goods, and a shop to build monocycles. Explaining that the municipality supported such endeavours by providing physical space, promotion, and some expertise, she noted: "Because these are business ventures, they require some level of commitment and additional effort. Throughout this process they learn to share their skills with others ... those who are studying different careers can actually use those skills at these new business ventures. For example, one of them is studying business development and management, the groups have an expectation that this person will become the future manager of the business venture ... We are planning a big event soon and ... masks were going to be very important. So, everyone made a commitment of creating two masks each to sell. So this is what we consider a *colectivo.*"

The vision of collectivism thus became rooted in a sense of productivism, whereby the well-being of the collective and of society became linked to the extent to which participants, often economically and otherwise vulnerable, were expected to perform for the "greater good." However, the schism in decision-making, and especially the sense that it was repeatedly those in higher administrative and governmental positions, unfamiliar with the lives and processes of those actually involved in social circus, deciding how the greater good was to be served, further entrenched the social differences that the program was seeking to address. In the case of social circus, however, participants are courted as volunteers and instructors giving them, at least in principle, direct entrée into shaping the culture of the programs in which they participate. The challenge thus lies in communicating these values beyond the internal social circus community to those making policy decisions.

The interplay of collectivism with autonomous creation became a source of strength and inspiration for many participants. Several former participants have since been accepted into the professional circus school in Brazil. Nevertheless, the challenge of carrying out this vision is highlighted by the difficulty of adequately honouring the needs of those involved in maintaining arts programs and spaces. In the case of *Circo Social Quito,* threats to the program's sustainability were coming from the municipal government, and program administrators and coordinators were constantly needing to liaise and advocate.

The instability of institutional support for the development of socially-oriented practices and aesthetics is far from unique to Ecuador. It is ubiquitous across the globe. Indeed, governmental support for social practice was stronger here than in most other countries, even those with much higher GDPs. For instance, Quebec sites are neither framed nor funded as major contributors to the cultural life or cultural economy of the province. The programs receive no national financial support and very little provincial or municipal funding and have relied, in very large part, on funding from *Cirque du Soleil*, which has also supported smaller professional circus companies. Moreover, in Canada, social circus programs have been unable to secure arts funding, even when the National Arts Council claimed to support community endeavours.

The reliance on corporate arts funding, while providing some artistic autonomy, also underscores a reification of cultural strata – a phenomenon that Ecuador's program may be in a position to avoid. Relying on corporate funding also has its own economic vulnerabilities: many social circus sites in Quebec closed when a shift of *Cirque du Soleil's* strategic funding approach to social circus coincided with the sale of the majority *Cirque du Soleil* shares to financial firms. Ecuador's post-neoliberal vision seeks to avoid such problems, but the extent to which it will avoid alienating those for whom the program was originally set up to serve remains to be seen.

Embodied Futures: Beyond Precarity?

The objective is to transform each individual and gradually change society.
Learn not to judge others for their condition, appearance, or way of
thinking. It's a journey ... I feel it [social circus] has helped me find other

alternatives, roads. I feel a need to communicate with society ... I would like to get more involved with society. Before I had no interest at all in dealing with society; I wanted to be left aside. Now I am very interested in children. ... When you recognize yourself as an individual, then you can be part of society and have some sort of impact. Change starts with oneself.

Participant, Circo Social Quito

Ecuador's bold economic strategy facilitated programs like social circus, but the ongoing social policy tensions continue to filter down to the lived experience of the "beneficiaries" of these programs. The lack of financial compensation was particularly problematic for several young social circus artists, who stated that they "felt exploited" when asked to perform publicly. This issue was not unique to Quito; in 2016, a former instructor in Loja explained that "Once the local government put money into the project, they had the feeling of ownership of the project and the kids. It was like they could 'rent' them and make them perform during the different events the city organized."

This ongoing tension is much larger than that encountered in the Ecuadorean situation, and speaks to the experience *Circo Social Ecuador* shares with other urban centres in Latin America. As Canclini (2013) writes, "A report produced two years ago by the Iberian American Youth Organization has already revealed that in Latin America 'young people are the sector most vulnerable to irregular jobs, with the worst salaries.' In Mexico, Colombia, Ecuador, Panama, and Peru, while 50.3% of adults have informal employment, among young people between 15 and 29 years old the percentage jumps to 82.4%." The economic precarity of youth is, of course, globally widespread; that such programs run into difficulty regarding how to address this precarity points to a cultural lacuna produced by the economic order. The arts sector – so well suited as a milieu in which many of these youth can thrive and develop, and into which these youth are intentionally or otherwise being integrated – is itself always already notoriously precarious. As such, to the extent that such programs nurture artistic sensibilities, they run the risk of trading off one kind of precarity (correlated with social ostracism) for another equally unstable form of precarity (correlated with the economic instability commonplace amongst artists).

In Quito, as we have seen, those in the program spoke of a transformation in ways of seeing, embodying, and engaging with the world, including a transformation in how the very act of transmitting values and culture is approached and appreciated. Such transformation in how culture is experienced in a holistic manner is perhaps the biggest success of the national government's attempt to impart a *Buen Vivir* ethos. It offered an avenue through which to explore artistic traditions as well as investigate embodied social dynamics. It also, for some, offered a discipline through which to engage with others.

Nevertheless, that collectivism could be entrenched in a small-scale entrepreneurial spirit suggests a curious development in the kinds of socio-cultural transformation being set in motion. In some ways, it seemed a heightened case of creating what sociologist Maurizio Lazzarato (2012) has called a form of neoliberal subjectivity. In a global era mired in individual and collective debt, there has been a worldwide rise of programs whose success is measured by the extent to which participants do the free labour of working on themselves to become productive citizens capable of rising out of debt. This situation is confounded by nations whose debt often prevents them from providing their citizens and residents with the services and other aid they may require, thus perpetuating a cycle that individual-izes collective struggle. The development strategy adopted by Ecuador re-jected such traps, rejecting IMF and World Bank policies that had formerly tied the country to cycles of debt. The transition toward the development of new networks of social and cultural development relied on a "state-civil society" (Radcliffe 2012) or "state-social movement" (Escobar 2010) nexus, built on the creation of new forms of collective autonomy (Mezzadra and Gago 2017). Highlighting the legacies of social and cultural development strategies such as the one implemented in Ecuador, Mezzadra and Gago explain: "an intertwining of subjectivity, of modes of life, and of material infrastructures has been forming around the point of conjunction between political dynamics of struggle and 'popular economies' that escapes the im-aginaries and the languages of established 'social movements' as well as the policies of 'development' or 'social inclusion' that have been deployed in recent years by new progressive governments" (Mezzadra and Gago 2017, 485).

This intertwining of popular economies and modes of subjectivity played out classically in the case of the *Circo Social* programs and their on-going development and legacies. Though extrinsic to the evolution of so-cial circus itself, the numerous relationships, circus companies, and circus-themed festivals, as well as independent socially oriented circus gather-ings, connected communities not only within individual cities but across the country and beyond. The nomadism of circus culture – tied both to the professional realities of moving for contracts as well as lifestyle choices that embrace travel – allows the flourishing of trans-communal transform-ation that engages traditional class-based concerns alongside a penchant for not only cultural encounters but also innovation. Circus is, after all, an art associated with travel, and social circus is an art closely associated with street life and the transience it implies. One long-time participant explained a desire to "travel" and "try with different audiences, demographics and cultures" to use the expressive art of circus as a tool to interact with other cultures "to see people how they really are, and to learn to respect that as well." Social circus, as a site for both disciplining but also deconstructing ways of seeing, thus provides an opportunity for transmuting cultural encounters, and in so doing, altering the trajectories of cultural expression and cultural politics more broadly. This nomadic mode of life, built on social and cultural encounters, is intrinsically tied up with a vision of the popular economy that would support such a way of life.

A large number of former participants have gone on to create their own small circus companies and to organize festivals, many of which retain the vision and draw on the community of *Circo Social*. These festivals, or *encuentros*, attract attendees from across Latin America, often travellers already passing through the country. They also provide family-friendly venues where the future of social circus is being actively reshaped. These *encuentros*, and the "alternative" circus cultures they represent, point to both a deepening and a relocalization of a global trend very much present in the formation of social circus in Ecuador itself. The early precursor circus initiative, *Circulo,* was founded by an Ecuadorean-Chilean who moved back to Ecuador after learning about social circus in Chile. Moreover, the formalization of *Circo Social* via the partnership with *Cirque du Soleil* was implemented in part through consultation with Quebec-based instructors, artists, and former participants whose own aspirations for a nomadic, socially oriented artistic way of life led them to Latin America (Spiegel 2016b).

The development of the network *Tejido de Circo Social* as an avenue through which social circus could develop became one important way in which participants have become increasingly engaged as organizers and ultimately policy-makers. While some of the *Tejido* members had joined *Circo Social* as well-trained staff members, many gained their skills as former participants, and have since risen through the ranks. This social circus network is currently searching out new funding opportunities, developing their own pedagogical vision, projects, and commitments, as well as seeking to fortify the existing *Circo Social* programs with their values and skills.

Arguably it is through such micro-level changes that the "multiplier effect" sought by the government (and discussed in chapter 3) was able to produce a culturally significant legacy of projects for the youth who, in turn, influence their communities. This success can be partially attributed to the "Citizen's Revolution," although it approaches a "cultural democracy" more in line with that developed by arms-length organizations that arose in the late 1970s in North America with remnants of "welfare state" funding. The vision, however, is neither one of North American entrepreneurialism nor of a classic top-down socialism. Rather what is emerging is a form of creative collectivity shaped by those involved in *Circo Social*. Passionate about this embodied art and its social potential, the youth practicing social circus are developing their own sense of what transformative art might become. The evolution of social circus as a mode of addressing youth precarity within a society explicitly in transition toward what was named at the national level as post-colonial, post-neoliberal ambitions, signals a revaluation of the role of culture in collective development. In Ecuador, the most such programs could hope to offer was a collection of tools to be repurposed.

This study suggests that for arts-based practices to address questions of precarity, a radical shift in social organization from what is dominant throughout much of the world (INCITE! Women of Color Against Violence 2007; Barry-Shaw et al. 2012) will be required – one that the Ecuadoran experiment sought to broach, with limited success. In particular, the hierarchies governing the ways in which communities targeted by programs are supported continue everywhere to condition the possibilities. Young artists are now juggling challenges, balancing on fine lines, and tumbling head first toward collective horizons which are yet but a faint glow.

Epilogue

JENNIFER BETH SPIEGEL AND
BENJAMIN ORTIZ CHOUKROUN

In the years since we began the research for this book, much has changed. The ongoing challenges posed by global neoliberal institutions and the growing wealth gaps are such that a renewed sense of urgency permeates projects of collective mobilization. The main question now is what form they take – sectarian, nationalist, inclusive, revolutionary ...?

Community arts have historically served a host of sociocultural and political goals. On the world scene, polarization has been exacerbated between those supporting culturally diverse initiatives as a means of community-building, and those who favour individual prowess and singular cultural narratives. In the United States and some parts of Europe, such divisions have become accompanied by the rise of the far right alongside left-wing anti-austerity movements. Meanwhile, in Latin America, the collectivist "pink tide" that swept much of the continent in the early years of the millennium is waning and the far right has gained momentum. Within this global context, our examination of Ecuador's national social circus initiative provides some insights into the political conditions orienting the art of collectivity.

Social circus, like any other social, political, or artistic initiative, is in constant flux. In Ecuador, as elsewhere, it has been evolving in concert with civil society organization but also with political changes in the private sphere. Social circus has been linked to a communitarian culture, to circus cultures more broadly, to countercultural movements, and to the use of creativity as a tool to express and grow, leveraging relationships between the artistic and the social. Social circus programs seek to achieve positive change in society, to invigorate culture in everyday life, to aid in the collective expression of communities, and to provide a medium for social conscience to take shape. These programs have needed to be adapted, both to take advantage of present possibilities and in order to serve communities under changing socio-economic and cultural conditions.

Over the past five years, we have kept in constant contact with the social circus projects in Ecuador and their instructors in order to capture their new experiences. These reflect changing organizational structures, new directives, and transformations in methodology, as well differences in staff, volunteer, and participant profiles, and in the material resources available. The long-term nature of this collaboration has helped us to observe the concordance of these changes with local and national political shifts as well their relationship to global conditions. Almost seven years after the government of Ecuador launched the social circus program, we cannot say that either the national project or local projects have adopted a single unifying working model, a fixed methodology, or a consistent vision. The projects remain unstable, and their sustainability is not guaranteed. Since the beginning of our study, one city's program has folded (Tena), one has officially broken away from the national vision (Guayaquil), while the two programs that served as the primary sites for our research (Quito and Loja) have each changed their names, signaling a reconfiguration of identity with possible implications for their goals and pedagogical visions.

Around the world, socially oriented arts have been vulnerable to the pressures of fluctuating mandates and mixed motivations. At times, such projects have served as much to bolster public images, generate amiable public spectacles, and smooth over the rough edges of development strategies as they have to spark veritable cultural transformation. Ecuador's ambitious social circus initiative has not been immune to these pressures. In 2017, Lenin Moreno, responsible for launching the state project of social circus while serving as the country's vice president, was elected president of the Republic. In the previous presidential period, both Moreno and the social circus program were strongly criticized by the press, in large part because of confusion over the goals of social circus combined with accusations of mis-spending. During the 2017 presidential campaign, Moreno offered to reinvigorate the program. However, given the public criticism, doubt as to the continuity of his involvement has emerged. Current policies and statements do not point to social growth, whatever the reason.

Photo 8.1 Photo taken during the formation of the Ecuadorean network *Tejido de Circo Social*, Cuenca, 2015. It symbolizes the decision to work together for a common vision.

Indeed, the cultural sector in Ecuador is increasingly subject to the austerity familiar to social and cultural workers around the globe: a reduction to the budgets of existing programs and a relative stagnation in new government initiatives.

In early 2015, *Cirque du Soleil*, having grown for three decades to be an icon of Canadian and Quebecois circus culture and a major player in the development of social circus around the world, was sold to equity investment firms from Texas and Shanghai. The implications of this sale are only beginning to emerge, although certain directions have already been signaled. For example, the number of staff has been greatly reduced. Moreover, the ways in which *Cirque* fosters social circus is changing. In Ecuador, *Cirque du Monde* no longer focuses on training instructors, helping to ensure a first level of uptake and expansion of social circus, but rather on promoting strategies to make social circus viable long-term. Specifically, it has been encouraging the emerging social circus network (*Tejido*), an Ecuadorean network that aspires to generate deep and lasting foundations for social circus in Ecuador.

Still in its early years, *El Tejido* has generated a training program, inspired in part by the methodology of *Cirque du Monde*, which seeks to complement this information with workshops that respond to national and regional realities. Additionally, *Tejido* seeks to foster and disseminate research that aligns with the needs of this growing network for a better understanding of its own cultural history and the impact of its models. The research activities associated with this book, and ongoing conversations between academics and practitioners, have been instrumental in shaping the direction of this latter initiative, highlighting the open loop that exists between research and practice globally.

While the social goals of *Tejido* are broad, reflecting the vast array of objectives present amongst projects in the country, inclusivity remains a unifying principle. Indeed, a backbone of the growing global social circus movement is the idea that race, gender, religion, socio-economic status, or geo-political positioning ought not to be factors determining access to engagement in cultural exploration – that everyone deserves to be supported in building skills for personal and collective transformation. How this happens, and how tensions and disagreements in vision are navigated, however, varies greatly. It is toward addressing these questions that much research and networking is now oriented.

The trends we have observed in social circus in Ecuador are in keeping with global cultural initiatives and the backing they receive. Around the world, there are projects with a "productivist" vision in tune with the demands of neoliberal society that seeks the welfare of participants through economic insertion in society. At the same time, other initiatives follow the purview of social activists and seek the construction of a new society rather than simply the fostering of individual careers.

Amongst its first actions of 2018, *Cirque du Monde* funded a regional meeting of social circus organized by *El Picadero* in Montevideo, Uruguay. During this gathering, various projects and networks, including Ecuador's *Tejido*, agreed to the creation of a South American social circus network.

Despite internal restructuring, *Cirque du Monde*'s vision at the time of publication is to seek the empowerment of community-oriented, socially inclusive projects in Latin America. Its involvement with social circus projects, and its social commitment in general, will no doubt become more evident in the coming years.

During the time it has taken to conduct the research for this book, much interest has grown in both the practice and study of social circus, despite the relative decline of support from the *Cirque du Soleil/Cirque du Monde* network as compared to its previous commitments. Conferences on social circus have begun to proliferate, while networks such as the American Youth Circus Organization and Caravan in Europe have highlighted research and support of social circus as a priority. Simultaneously, social circus is being increasingly adopted as part of broader social and health intervention programs worldwide.

The push toward institutionalizing social circus, as with much socially-oriented art, is leading to mixed results – allowing programs to reach larger numbers of people but sometimes sidelining those for whom such initiatives were originally intended. Among the findings of this research, we noted a correlation between the results obtained and the collective, corporeal, and "counterculture" nature of the practice, with activities such as capoeira or parkour obtaining results close to those of some social circus groups. This trend underscores the value of a possible avenue for not only supporting youth marginalized by dominant systems but, in particular, highlighting the roles that collectivity, corporeal expression, and historically denigrated forms of cultural expression can play in transforming the cultural dynamics of society. Particularly in contexts where colonial histories exacerbated by neoliberal institutions have cast aside embodied ways of knowing and exalted individual achievement, these results and the policies and pedagogical visions that encourage their flourishing, have far-reaching implications.

Whereas abstracted modes of production have been valued over corporeal praxis, and individual capital production above collective transformation, community-based projects such as social circus challenge cultural categorizations. Likewise, within the academy, creative community-based research is increasingly contributing to both fuller understandings of cultural phenomena and more equitable distributions of power amongst knowledge-holders. The art of collectivity, we have been arguing, is not merely a tool for intervening in "at-risk populations"; rather, in the current socio-political climate, we are all "at risk" of creating divisions that keep us from sharing knowledge and experience across space, time, and communities of learning.

The transdisciplinary and international nature of our research has not been without its challenges. However, we would not have been able to cultivate the rich relationships and in-depth understanding of the individual and collective stakes of creative collective projects had we not engaged in such an endeavour. Evolution in the art of collectivity brings opportunities for destabilizing long-entrenched hierarchies in ways of knowing, seeing, and meaning-making that continue to permeate both arts-supporting institutions, as well as scholarly pursuits. As we complete this book and finalize a forthcoming complementary resource in Spanish, we continue to liaise with the various communities with whom we undertook this project, in the hope that the knowledge and relationships generated can strengthen practice and research not only in the Northern academy, but also amongst practitioners and scholars in Latin America and beyond.

The stakes of strong community-based social and cultural research, and the need to reach polarized communities, particularly those feeling the brunt of neoliberal policies – now, in the age of cultural divisiveness, social alienation, and wide-spread disgruntlement with prevailing institutions – cannot be understated. Collective futures and the abilities of communities of practice and knowledge to survive and flourish may depend on it.

ILLUSTRATIONS

Figures

Tables

Photos

GLOSSARY

Programs, organizations, and terms used in arts facilitation or circus arts (alphabetical)

"¿A quién le gusta?" This exercise (literally translated as "Who likes this?") is a facilitation technique to draw out social circus lessons for participants and allow them to learn about each other's capabilities and preferences so that performance tasks can be distributed accordingly.

Acción Social Municipal This is a public municipal enterprise in charge of implementing Cuenca's social policies aimed at assisting vulnerable groups. The *Circo Social Cuenca* program is run by this organization.

American Youth Circus Organization This US-based nonprofit organization includes the American Circus Educators Association; circus educators, organizations and youth circus participants are connected and linked to resources and institutions that can help them pursue their chosen paths.

capoeira This Brazilian martial art combines music, dance, and sport. First developed by West Africans in the sixteenth century, it mainly uses the lower body to make quick kicks and spins. Like social circus, it aims to create the concept of "family" for those from the same school or group within the community.

CARAVAN (Caravan International Youth Circus and Education Network) This organization provides support and training through a network of youth and social circus organizations worldwide, contributing to research on social circus pedagogy and developing links between social circus training and formal university recognition. See http://www.caravancircusnetwork.eu.

Circo del Mundo Chile This organization, founded in Chile in 1995 and legally constituted as a non-governmental organization (NGO) in 2000, aims to develop human potential through social circus. See http://www.elcircodelmundo.com/.

Circo Social del Sur This organization has operated in Buenos Aires since 1996 and was constituted as an NGO in 2002. It aims to use social circus as a cultural tool to promote personal growth and involvement in the community. See https://www.circodelsur.org.ar/.

Circo Social Cuenca The first social circus program implemented by *Circo Social Ecuador*, it is administered by *Acción Social Municipal* – a public enterprise owned by the Municipality of Cuenca in the Andes.

Circo Social Ecuador This initiative, started by Vice-President Lenin Moreno in 2011 as part of the *Ecuador Alegre y Solidario* project, implements social circus programs in different cities in Ecuador, and is the main focus of this book.

Circo Social Guayaquil This program, operated by the Municipality of Guayaquil and the *Huancavilca* Foundation since 2012, was established as part of *Circo Social Ecuador* but has operated more independently than the other programs (see chapter 3).

Circo Social Loja This program, operated by the Municipality of Loja, has been operating since April 2013 as part of the *Circo Social Ecuador* initiative.

Circo Social Quito This program evolved from pre-existing socially oriented programs using circus arts in Quito and has been part of the *Circo Social Ecuador* initiative since 2012, operated through the Municipality of Quito and Patronato San José.

Circo Social Tena This program operated in Tena from 2012 until the end of 2014 as part of the *Circo Social Ecuador* initiative.

Circomunidad An initiative managed by *Foundation Círculo,* active in Ecuador from 2008–11, it operated *in Casas Metropolitanas de las Juventudes* (youth centres across metropolitan Quito) applying a methodology similar to that of social circus.

Cirque du Monde *Cirque du Monde* is a social circus program targeted to at-risk youth, created by *Cirque du Soleil* and *Jeunesse du Monde*. It combines circus techniques with educational interventions to help young people build self-confidence, realize their strengths, and discover their hidden talents. *Cirque du Monde* offers training to trainers, social workers, and volunteers of *Circo Social Ecuador* and around the world. See http://imaginationforpeople.org/en/project/cirque-du-monde-a-social-circus/.

Cirque du Soleil Currently the largest circus producer in the world, *Cirque du Soleil* was founded in Baie-Saint-Paul, Quebec, in 1984 by two former street performers, Guy Laliberté and Gilles Ste-Croix. Its headquarters are in

Montreal, Canada, in the inner-city area of Saint-Michel. In 2015, majority shares of the company were sold to the American private equity firm TPG Capital and to China's Fosun.

Cirque Hors Piste *Cirque Hors Piste* is a Montreal-based organization offering marginalized young people an alternative and inclusive space for creation. The organization promotes individual and collective learning through circus arts.

Círculo **Foundation** This is an NGO that promotes artistic, educational, and humanitarian initiatives in the performing arts – what we call "arts for social change." Led by Matias Belmar and Tanya Sánchez, who were trained at *Circo del Mundo* in Chile, *Circulo* was the organization originally responsible for implementing the social circus program in Ecuador.

Confederación de Nacionalidades Indígenas de Ecuador (**CONAIE**) Ecuador's largest indigenous organization, CONAIE was formed in 1986 to pursue social change on behalf of the region's significant indigenous population.

Ecuador Alegre y Solidario **project** This program, also dubbed *Sonrie Ecuador* (Smile Ecuador), was launched by then-Vice President Lenin Moreno (now President) as part of public policy seeking the social inclusion of vulnerable populations through cultural interventions. It was within this program that *Circo Social Ecuador* was launched in 2011.

Ecuasol This institution helps vulnerable children and youth access high-quality education and thereby improve their socio-economic status. Founded in 1988, with legal status as a foundation obtained in 2006, Ecuasol offers economic and psychological support to families while providing tutoring, cultural outings, and medical support to the children and adolescents it hosts. Recognized by the Ecuadorean government and supported by *La Guilde du Raid*, Ecuasol works exclusively through donations from sponsors.

Encomma This Ecuadorian private enterprise based in Quito specializes in managing non-conventional artistic projects for social development.

Honrar la vida This Quito-based NGO, founded in 1996, develops educational programs for children who have suffered abuse in marginalized urban areas.

Huancavilca **Foundation** This NGO, founded in February 1993 in Guayaquil, aims to promote economic and social development in extremely poor regions through active participation of communities. *Circo Social Guayaquil* is one of the programs this foundation supports.

Jeunesse du Monde This Canadian organization was founded in 1971 by Jacques Hébert to manage international development programs in partnership with different local organizations. *Jeunesse du Monde* promotes international volunteering of youth to involve them in community problem-solving and make them agents of change.

Kichwa The dialect of the Quechua language spoken by the people of Ecuador. It is estimated that some two million people – mostly indigenous people in Peru, Ecuador, Bolivia, Argentina, Chile, and Colombia – speak a Quechuan language.

La Tarumba This Peruvian circus program, founded in 1984, implements social circus methodologies to improve the development of the population through community participation.

La Voladora de Urcuquí This is the cultural centre of the Yachay Public Corporation project, from which social circus was launched. Although it is not part of *Circo Social Ecuador* (CSE), it depends on governmental entities and works with the programs within CSE.

local pedagogical director The head of teaching activities within a local social circus program, whose main responsibility was to conduct training of instructors and supervise *replicas*. Additionally, they were in charge of local pedagogic direction, and were supposed to have authority to make decisions related to program structure and the organization of the local team.

Machincuepa **social circus** This social circus initiative, operating since 1999 in Aguilas Tarango, Mexico, serves adolescents and youth at-risk in the Mexico City area using *Cirque du Monde* social circus methods. See http://www.machincuepacircosocial.org/.

Ministerio de Cultura y Patrimonio Ecuador's Ministry of Culture and Heritage; responsible for the *Ecuador Alegre y Solidario* project management after Vice President Moreno left office and the program was transferred out of the vice presidency.

murga Traditional musical theatre and circus, usually performed during carnivals or other festivities in Latin America and Spain.

national pedagogical director After the end of the contract with the *Círculo* Foundation to manage the launch of CSE, a social circus specialist was recruited to the vice presidency to provide pedagogical direction at the national level. From January to June 2013, this position (held by co-editor Benjamin Ortiz Choukroun) worked in collaboration with the local pedagogical directors, forming a team to make joint decisions on topics related to workshops and training spaces.

One Drop Foundation This international non-for-profit organization, founded by *Cirque du Soleil*, aims to raise awareness about water issues and create behavioural change through social arts, including circus. Website: https://www.onedrop.org/en/.

parkour Based on the French word *parcours,* which may be translated as "journey," this art form uses the body's motor capabilities to move rapidly and efficiently through complex urban environments.

Patronato Municipal San José This local government organization in Quito is in charge of implementing social programs for vulnerable population, including children, youth, the elderly, people with disabilities or health problems, and those suffering from the impacts of violence and/or poverty. Its mandate includes the social circus program, which, since the end of the formal period of this study, has been renamed "Circo de Luz" (Circus of Lights).

Plan Nacional Para el Buen Vivir The Ecuadorean government's strategic plan proposed in conjunction with a new constitution in 2008, aimed to "strive for good living for all its citizens not only by means of economic growth but by seeking a more equitable society, promoting solidary and sustainable growth that respects culture and nature." This book is largely about how the social circus program played out as part of the vision articulated in this post-neoliberal plan. The *Plan Nacional Para el Buen Vivir* 2009–13 included policies focusing on social and intercultural inclusion, aiming to eradicate violence against children and adolescents and ensure their access to education. The 2013–17 development plan also emphasized new conceptualizations that encourage citizens to constitute "a critical, entrepreneurial, creative and supportive society."

Primera Escuela de Circo del Ecuador (**PECE**) This project, managed by the *Círculo* foundation between 2009 and 2011, merged into *Circo Social Ecuador*. It was the first attempt to organize a professional social circus school.

"Puedo? Venga!" This facilitation activity (translated as "May I come?") is used during circus lessons to teach participants about the relevance of communication in performing arts. This activity reminds students to interact with their partners every time they are performing together to ensure that their partners are ready.

Red Argentina de Circo Social This network, based in Argentina, coordinates efforts between social circus programs across the country.

Red Chilena de Circo Social This network, based in Chile, links social circus programs across the country to maximize their impact on populations in terms of arts, pedagogy, emotions, psycho-social and physical environment. See http://www.redcircosocial.cl/.

Rede Circo do Mundo Brasil This social circus network, formed in 2000 from the collaboration of five circus organizations in Brazil and *Jeunesse du Monde*, aims to maximize youth development.

replicas This is the name given to *Circo Social Ecuador* workshops with children and youth, which incorporate social circus pedagogical values at its fullest. They are called *replicas* because they replicate what instructors and volunteers were taught in the morning lessons, but in a compressed format. Activities preformed in CSE that are not named *replicas* generally constitute technical training.

Secretaria Técnica de Discapacidades This government organization in Ecuador was created in 2013 to boost technical and scientific research and educational inclusion in *Escuelas del Milenio* (Millennium Schools), among other responsibilities. It hosted *Circo Social Ecuador* on an interim basis at the end of Mr Moreno's mandate as vice president, until it was relocated from the vice presidency to the Ministry of Culture and Heritage later that year.

Social Agenda for Children and Adolescents (ASNA) This refers to the Ecuadorean public policy that guides activities focused on achieving the goals in the National Decentralized System for Childhood and Adolescence Integral Protection (2007–10). ASNA public policies are designed to guarantee rights enshrined in the Code for Children and Adolescents.

Sonrie Ecuador See *Ecuador Alegre y Solidario* project.

SOS Children's Village The mandate of this international NGO is the social development of children without, or at risk of, losing parental care. The organization aims to provide "a family" for abandoned or orphaned children and contribute to "community development." https://www.sos-childrensvillages.org/.

tatami The soft spongy mats used in circus activities to protect participants from injury during exercises and demonstrations.

Tejido de Circo Social This is the name adopted by the Ecuadorean social circus network started in October 2015 and legally constituted in 2017 by private institutions, four social circus projects, and professionals from diverse social circus backgrounds or interested in this arts-based intervention for social change.

Virgilio Guerrero (Centro de Orientación Juvenil Virgilio Guerrero) This public institution is for adolescent males detained for breaking the law. The institution seeks to improve their quality of life through comprehensive educational interventions with the support of a professional team. Social circus was one of the activities offered.

Washington Consensus This is a set of economic policy statements recommended by the International Monetary Fund, the World Bank and various neoliberal economists as the basis of a "reform package" for low- and middle-income countries in financial crisis. Ecuador's *Plan Nacional para el Buen Vivir* poses a break with this ideology, instead proposing a "post-neoliberal" vision for development.

REFERENCES

A Forrester Consulting Thought Leadership Paper Commissioned by Adobe. 2014. *The Creative Dividend: How Creativity Impacts Business Results.*

Acosta, Alberto. 2011. "Extractivism and Neoextractism: Two Sides of the Same Curse." In *Más allá del desarrollo*, edited by Miriam Lang and Dunia Mokrani, 61–85. Quito: Abya Yala Ediciones.

Acree, William G. Jr. 2016. "The Creole Circus and Popular Entertainment in 19th Century Argentina and Uruguay." In *Oxford Research Encyclopedia of Latin American History*. http://latinamericanhistory.oxfordre.com/view/10.1093/acrefore/9780199366439.001.0001/acrefore-9780199366439-e-104.

Afghan Mobile Mini Children's Circus. 2017. Wikipedia. https://En.Wikipedia.Org/Wiki/Afghan_Mobile_Mini_Children%27s_Circus.

Agencia publicia de noticias del Ecuador y Suramerica (ANDES). 2013. "Ecuador Reduced Child Labor from 17% to 8.3% over the Past Six Years." http://www.andes.info.ec/en/sociedad/ecuador-reduced-child-labor-17-83-over-past-six-years.html.

Ahearne, Jeremy. 2006. "Public Intellectuals within a 'Multiple Streams' Model of the Cultural Policy Process." *International Journal of Cultural Policy* 12 (1): 1–13.

ALAMES. 2011. *Determinación social o determinantes sociales de la salud? Diferencias conceptuales e implicaciones praxiológicas.* Mexico: Universidad Autónoma Metropolitana.

ALAMES et al. 2011. El Debate y la acción sobre la determinación social de la salud: Posición sesde los movimientos sociales. Rio de Janeiro. http://www.alames.org/documentos/dsssoccivil.pdf.

Alavi, Hamid Reza. 2011. "The Role of Self-Esteem in Tendency towards Drugs, Theft and Prostitution." *Addiction and Health* 3 (3–4): 119.

Alberto, Acosta. 2016. "Aporte al debate. El Extractivsmo como categoría se saqueo y devastación." *FIAR* 9 (2): 24–33.

Alonso González, Pablo, and Alfredo Macías Vázquez. 2015. "An Ontological Turn in the Debate on *Buen Vivir-Sumak Kawsay* in Ecuador: Ideology, Knowledge, and the Common." *Latin American and Caribbean Ethnic Studies*, 1–20.

Alvarez, Natalie, and Catherine Graham. 2011. "Performance and Health." *Canadian Theatre Review* 146: 3–5.

American Dance Therapy Association. 2012. "About Dance / Movement Therapy." http://www.adta.org/Default.aspx?pageId=378213.

Andrews, David L., and Michael L. Silk. 2011. "Toward a Physical Cultural Studies." *Sociology of Sport Journal* 28 (1): 4–35.

Appelbaum, David. 1995. *The Stop*. Albany, NY: State University of New York Press.

Archambault, Kim. 2014. "Évaluation d'un programme movateur de réadaptation par les arts de la scène pour des jeunes présentant un trouble psychiatrique stabilisé: Le programme Espace de Transition." PhD diss., Université de Montréal.

Arendt, Hannah. 1958. *The Human Condition*. Chicago: University of Chicago Press.

– 1961. *Between Past and Future: Six Exercises in Political Thought*. New York: Viking.

Atkinson, Michael. 2009. "Parkour, Anarcho-Environmentalism, and Poiesis." *Journal of Sport and Social Issues* 33 (9): 169–94.

Austin, Peter. 2011. "An Introduction to Propensity Score Methods for Reducing the Effects of Confounding in Observational Studies." *Multivariate Behavioral Research* 46 (3): 399–424.

Ávalos, Stephanie. 2012. "The Indigenous Quest for Power Sharing in Post-Colonial Ecuador." *Intercultural Communication Studies* 21 (1): 140–53.

Avritzer, Leonardo. 2009. *Democracy and the Public Space in Latin America*. Princeton: Princeton University Press.

Bagley, Carl, and Mary Beth Cancienne. 2001. *Dancing the Data*. New York: Peter Lang.

Bailly, B. 2002. "Circus, an Intervention Tool Suitable for Young People in Difficulty." Paper presented at the First International Gathering on Circus and Social Work, La Seyne-sur-Mer, France.

Baker, D., and P.A. Witt. 1996. Evaluation of the Impact of Two After-School Programs. *Journal of Park and Recreation Administration* 14 (3): 6–81.

Baker, Natialie, Catherine Willinsky, and Katherine Boydell. 2015. "Just Say Know: Creatively Engaging Young People to Explore the Link between Cannabis Use and Psychosis in Order to Promote Informed Decision-Making about Substance Use." *World Cultural Psychiatry Research Review* 10 (3/4): 201–20.

Bakhtin, Mikhail. 1984. *Rabelais and His World* (Vol. 341). Translated by Hélène Iswolsky. Bloomington: Indiana University Press.

Barndt, Deborah. 2011. *¡Viva!: Community Arts and Popular Education in the Americas*. Albany, NY: SUNY Press.

Barnett, Michael L. 2007. "Stakeholder Influence Capacity and the Variability of Financial Returns to Corporate Social Responsibility." *Academy of Management Review* 32 (3): 794–816.

Barreto, Dimitri. 2007. "Causas principales de enfermedad y muerte. Violencia social." In *La equidad en la mira: la salud pública en Ecuador durante las últimas décadas,* 134–41. Quito: Organización Panamericana de la Salud (OPS/MSP/CONASA).

Barry-Shaw, Nikolas, and Dru Oja Jay. 2012. *Paved with Good Intentions: Canada's Development NGOs from Idealism to Imperialism.* Halifax: Fernwood Publishing.

Barton, Stuart. 2000. "Which Clinical Studies Provide the Best Evidence? The Best Rct Still Trumps the Best Observational Study." *BMJ* 321 (7256): 255–6.

Baumgold, Jessica. 2017. "Exploring the Experiences of Adults Participating in Community Circus Classes: The Synergistic Relationship between Circus and Occupational Therapy." Master of science thesis, Utica College, New York.

Be More. 2018. "About Be More." http://www.be-more.nl/.

Becker, Marc. 2011. "Correa, Indigenous Movements, and the Writing of a New Constitution in Ecuador." *Latin American Perspectives* 38 (1): 47–62.

– 2012. *¡Pachakutik! Indigenous Movements and Electoral Politics in Ecuador.* Lanham, MD: Rowman and Littlefield.

– 2013. "The Stormy Relations between Rafael Correa and Social Movements in Ecuador." *Latin American Perspectives* 40 (3): 43–62.

– 2014. "Rafael Correa and Social Movements in Ecuador." In *Latin America's Radical Left: Challenges and Complexities of Political Power,* edited by Steve Ellner, 127–48. Lanham, MD: Rowman and Littlefield.

Belfiore, Eleonora. 2002. "Art as a Means of Alleviating Social Exclusion: Does It Really Work? A Critique of Instrumental Cultural Policies and Social Impact Studies in the UK." *International Journal of Cultural Policy* 8 (1): 91–106.

Belfiore, Eleonora, and Oliver Bennett. 2010. "Beyond the 'Toolkit Approach': Arts Impact Evaluation Research and the Realities of Cultural Policy-Making." *Journal for Cultural Research* 14 (2): 121–42.

Belknap, Ruth Ann, Kristin Haglund, Holly Felzer, Jessica Pruszynski, and John Schneider. 2013. "A Theater Intervention to Prevent Teen Dating Violence for Mexican-American Middle School Students." *Journal of Adolescent Health* 53 (1): 62–7.

Belliveau, George, and Graham Lee. 2016. *Research-Based Theatre as Methodology: An Artistic Methodology.* Bristol, UK: Intellect.

Benard, Bonnie. 1991. "Fostering Resiliency in Kids: Protective Factors in the Family, School and Community." Washington, DC: Western Regional Center for Drug-Free Schools and Communities. https://files.eric.ed.gov/fulltext/ED335781.pdf.

Bennett, Kate. 2005. "Social Engagement as a Longitudinal Predictor of Objective and Subjective Health." *European Journal of Ageing* 2 (1): 48–55.

Benoit, Cecilia, Mikhael Jansson, Alison Millar, and Rachel Phillips. 2005. "Community-Academic Research on Hard-to-Reach Populations: Benefits and Challenges." *Qualitative Health Research* 15 (2): 263–82.

Bessone, Ilaria. 2013a. *Circo Verso: Outlooks in Social Circus for the Development of Active Citizenship.* http://www.bibliotheque.enc.qc.ca/Record.htm?idlist=0 &record=19130965124919581479.

- 2013b. "Circo Verso: Outlooks in Social Circus for the Development of Active Citizenship." *Juggling Magazine*. http://www.jugglingmagazine.it/new/fileadmin/ Image_Archive/04_CircoperBambinieRagazzi/CircoVerso/Circo_verso_ ING_150.pdf.

- 2017. "Social Circus as an Organised Cultural Encounter Embodied Knowledge, Trust and Creativity at Play." *Journal of Intercultural Studies* 38 (6): 651–64.

Betancourt, Z. 1992. "Aproximación inicial al conocimiento de la epidemiología se los accidentes y violencia en El Ecuador." In *Panorama epidemiológico del Ecuador*, 93–128. Quito: Ministerio de Salud Pública.

Bhabha, Homi K. 2012. *The Location of Culture*. London: Routledge.

Biddle, Stuart J.H. 2000. "Emotion, Mood and Physical Activity." In *Physical Activity and Psychological Well-Being*, edited by Stuart J.H. Biddle, Ken Fox, and Steve Boutcher, 63–86. London: Routledge.

Biehl, João, and Peter Locke. 2010. "Deleuze and the Anthropology of Becoming." *Current Anthropology* 51 (3): 317–51.

Birn, Anne-Emanuelle. 2009. "Making It Politic(Al): Closing the Gap in a Generation: Health Equity through Action on the Social Determinants of Health." *Social Medicine* 4 (3): 166–82.

Bishop, Claire. 2012. *Artificial Hells – Participatory Art and the Politics of Spectatorship*. New York: Verso Books.

Bland, J. Martin, and Douglas G. Altman. 1997. "Cronbach's Alpha." *BMJ* 314 (7080): 572.

Blum, Robert. 2005. "A Case for School Connectedness." *The Adolescent Learner* 62 (7): 16–20.

Boal, Augusto. (1985) 2008. *Theatre of the Oppressed*. Translated from the Spanish by Charles A. and Maria-Odilia Leal Mcbride. New York: Theatre Communications Group.

Bogdan, Robert. 1988. *Freak Show: Presenting Human Oddities for Amusement and Pleasure*. Chicago: University of Chicago Press.

Boles, Sharon M., and Karen Miotto. 2003. "Substance Abuse and Violence: A Review of the Literature." *Aggression and Violent Behavior* 8 (2): 155–74.

Bolton, Reginald. 2004. "Why Circus Works: How the Values and Structures of Circus Make It a Significant Developmental Experience for Young People." PhD diss., Murdoch University, Perth. www.regbolton.org/circus_library/ PHD-extract.pdf.

Booth, Sue. 1999. "Researching Health and Homelessness: Methodological Challenges for Researchers Working with a Vulnerable, Hard to Reach, Transient Population." *Australian Journal of Primary Care* 5 (3): 76–81.

Borradori, Giovanna. 2003. *Philosophy in a Time of Terror: Dialogues with Jurgen Habermas and Jacques Derrida*. Chicago: University of Chicago Press.

Boydell, Katherine M. 2011. "Making Sense of Collective Events: The Co-Creation of a Research-Based Dance." *Forum Qualitative Sozialforschung (Forum Qualitative Social Research)* 12 (1): Art. 5.

- 2013. "Using Visual Arts to Enhance Mental Health Literacy in Schools" In *Youth, Education and Marginality*, edited by Kate Tilleczek, 229–40. Kitchener, ON: Wilfred University Press.

Boydell, Katherine M., Brenda M. Gladstone, Tiziana Volpe, Brooke Allemang, and Elaine Stasiulis. 2012. "The Production and Dissemination of Knowledge: A Scoping Review of Arts-Based Health Research." *Forum Qualitative Sozialforchung/Forum: Qualitative Social Research* 13 (1): Art. 32.

Boydell, Katherine M., Michael Hodgins, Brenda M. Gladstone, Elaine Stasiulis, George Belliveau, Hoi Cheu, Pia Kontos, and Janet Parsons. 2016. "Arts-Based Health Research and Academic Legitimacy: Transcending Hegemonic Conventions." *Qualitative Research* 16 (6): 681–700.

Boydell, Katherine M., Siona Jackson, and John S. Strauss. 2012. "Help-Seeking Experiences of Youth with First Episode Psychosis: A Research-Based Dance Production." In *Hearing Voices: Qualitative Inquiry in Early Psychosis*, edited by Katherine M. Boydell and H. Bruce Ferguson, 25–44. Waterloo, ON: Wilfrid Laurier University Press.

Braveman, Paula, and Sofia Gruskin. 2003. "Poverty, Equity, Human Rights and Health." *Bulletin of the World Health Organization* 81 (7): 539–45.

Breilh, Jaime. 1979. *Epidemiología: Economía, Medicina y Política*. Quito, Ecuador: Universidad Central.

- 2007. "Nuevo modelo de acumulación y agroindustria: Las Implicaciones ecológicas y epidemiológicas de la floricultura en Ecuador." *Ciência & Saúde Coletiva* 12 (1): 91–104.

- 2011. "Una Perspectiva emancipadora de la investigación e incidencia basada en la determinación social de la salud." In *Determinación social o determinantes sociales de la salud?* Vol. 1, 1st edition, 45–70. México: ALAMES – Universidad Autónoma Metropolitana de Xochimilco.

- 2012. "La Determinación social de la salud como herramienta de transformación hacia una nueva salud pública." *Revista Facultad Nacional de Salud Pública* 31 (Suppl 1): 13–37.

- 2017. "Extractivismo petrolero, crisis múltiple de la vida y los desafíos de la investigación." Quito, Ecuador: UASB Digital. http://repositorio.uasb.edu.ec/bitstream/10644/5787/1/Breilh%2C%20J-CON-261-Extractivismo.pdf

Breilh, Jaime, Arturo Campaña, Orlando Felicita, et al. 2009. *Environmental and Health Impacts of Floriculture in Ecuador Research Report Project IDRC-CRDI (103697-001)*. Quito, Ecuador: CEAS.

Breilh, Jaime, Edgard Matiello Júnior, and Paulo Capela. 2010. "A Globalização e a Indústria do esporte: Saúde ou negócio?" In *Ensaios alternativos Latino-Americanos de Educação Física, Esportes e Saúde*, edited by Edgard Matiello Junior, Paulo Capela, and Jaime Breilh, 15–41. Florianópolis: Copiart. http://repositorio.uasb.edu.ec/bitstream/10644/3398/1/Breilh%2c%20J-CON-098-Ensaios.pdf

Breilh, Jaime, Nino Pagliccia, and Annalee Yassi. 2012. "Chronic Pesticide Poisoning from Persistent Low-Dose Exposures in Ecuadorean Floriculture Workers: Toward Validating a Low-Cost Test Battery." *International Journal of Occupational and Environmental Health* 18 (1): 7–21.

Breilh, Jaime, Jerry Spiegel, and Annalee Yassi. 2014. "Conceptualizing the Social Determination of Health: Insights from Collaborative Research in Latin America." Working Paper, Peter Wall Institute for Advanced Study International Reearch Colloquium.

Brook, Peter. 1968. *The Empty Space.* New York: Penguin.

Bryan, Julia. 2005. "Fostering Educational Resilience and Achievement in Urban Schools through School-Family-Community Partnerships." *Partnerships/Community* 8 (3): 219–27.

Brysk, Alison. 2000. *From Tribal Village to Global Village: Indian Rights and International Relations in Latin America.* Stanford, California: Stanford University Press.

Burgos-Vigna, Diana. 2016a. "Quito, patrimoine culturel de l'humanité ou ville du Buen Vivir?" *Cahier des Ameriques Latines* 83: 93–111.

– 2016b. "Villa El Salvador: From a Self-Management Project to Territorial Marketing." In *Learning from the Slums for the Development of Emerging Cities*, edited by Jean-Claude Bolay, Jérome Chenal, and Yves Pedrazzini, 59–69. Switzerland: Springer.

Buys, Laurie, and Evonne Miller. 2009. "Enhancing Social Capital in Children via Schoolbased Community Cultural Development Projects: A Pilot Study." *International Journal of Education and the Arts* 10 (3): 1–19.

Cadwell, Stephen, and Brendan Rooney. 2013. *Galway Community Circus – Community Impact Survey.* Galway, Ireland: Galway Community Circus. http://www.academia.edu/10219178/Galway_Community_Circus_Impact_Study.

Cameron, Marsaili, Nikki Crane, Richard Ings, and Karen Taylor. 2013. "Promoting Well-Being through Creativity: How Arts and Public Health Can Learn from Each Other." *Perspectives in Public Health* 133 (1): 52–9.

Campaña, A. 2014. "Tasas de suicidio y homicidio en adolescentes y jóvenes, calculadas en base a datos del Anuario de Estadísticas Vitales – nacimientos y defunciones 2014, del Instituto Nacional de Estadísticas y Censos (INEC) del Ecuador": Defunciones totales por tipo de certificación y grupos de edad, según provincia, sexo y causas de muerte. Lista corta de agrupamiento de las principales causas de muerte CIE – 10, 388–475.

Canadian Coalition for Global Health Research (CCGHR). 2017. "Partnership Assessment Tool (Pat)." http://www.ccghr.ca/resources/partnerships-and-networking/partnership-assessment-tool/.

Canclini, Néstor García. 2013. "Precarious Creativity: Youth in a Post-Industrial Culture." *Journal of Latin American Cultural Studies* 22 (4): 341–52.

Canel, Eduardo. 2010. *Barrio Democracy in Latin America: Participatory Decentralization and Community Activism in Montevideo*. University Park, PA: Penn State University Press.

Caravan – European Youth and Social Circus Network. 2011. "Framework for Competences for Social Circus Trainers." http://www.Caravancircusnetwork.Eu/.

– 2016. *Circus +: Research on Youth and Social Circus Pedagogy – Towards a Level 4 and 6 Training Programmes in Youth and Social Circus*. https://www.ecbru.be/assets/files/caravan/Caravan-Circus+.pdf.

– 2018. "Home Page." http://www.Caravancircusnetwork.Eu/.

Caria, Sara, and Rafael Dominguez. 2016. "Ecuador's Buen Vivir: A New Ideology for Development." *Latin American Perspectives* 43 (1): 18–33.

Carriel Mancilla, Jorge. 2012. "Public Expenditure in Health in Ecuador [Gasto Público en Salud en El Ecuador]." *Rev Med FCM-UCSG* 18 (1): 53–60.

Carrión Mena, Fernando. 1994. "De la Violencia urbana a la convivencia ciudadana." In *Seguridad ciudadana, ¿espejismo o realidad?* edited by Fernando Carrióncon auspicio de la Facultad Latinoamericana de Ciencias Sociales (FLACSO), 13–58. Quito: Sede Ecuador y la representación de la OPS/OMS en Ecuador.

Casadesus-Masanell, Ramon, and Maxime Aucoin. 2009. "Cirque Du Soleil: The High-Wire Act of Building Sustainable Partnerships." Harvard Business School Case 709–411. Boston: Harvard Business School.

Centro Brasileiro de Estudos de Saúde (CEBES). 2010. "Determinação social da saúde e reforma sanitária." Organizador: Roberto Passos Nogueira. Rio de Janeiro: CEBES.

Chaney, Paul. 2015. "Parties, Promises and Politics: Exploring Manifesto Discourse on Arts Policy in Westminster, Scottish, Welsh and Northern Irish Elections 1945–2011." *International Journal of Cultural Policy* 21 (5): 611–30.

Cherry, Katie E., Eric Jackson Walker, Jennifer Silva Brown, Julia Volaufova, Lynn R. LaMotte, David A. Welsh, L. Joseph Su, S. Michal Jazwinki, Rebecca Ellis, Robert H. Wood, and Madlyn I. Frisard. 2013. "Social Engagement and Health in Younger, Older, and Oldest-Old Adults in the Louisiana Healthy Aging Study." *Journal of Applied Gerontology* 32 (1): 51–75.

Christensen, Donna Hendrickson, and Carla M. Dahl. 1997. "Rethinking Research Dichotomies." *Family and Consumer Sciences Research Journal* 25 (3): 269–85.

Circesteem. 2017. http://Circesteem.org/.

CircusInfo Finland. 2017. "Social Circus – Circus in Finland." http://sirkusinfo.fi/en/circus-in-finland/education-and-training/social-circus/.

Cirque du Monde, Cirque du Soleil. 2013. "Social Circus Trainer's Guide – Basic Training." http://109.200.216.137/~peyceu/wp/wp-content/uploads/2016/02/Social-Circus-Trainer%E2%80%99s-Guide-Version-April-2013.pdf.

– 2014. "Participant Handbook Cirque Du Monde Training – Part 1." http://www.educircation.eu/documentation/item/download/155_5da0b54e21de67e186e15cb021054135.

Cirque du Soleil. 2016. "An Intervention Approach: Social Circus." https://www.cirquedusoleil.com/en/about/global-citizenship/social-circus.aspx.

"Cirque Du Soleil Arrives in Ecuador to Train Street Kids." 2011. *La Republica*. http://www.larepublica.ec/blog/politica/2011/05/24/el-cirque-du-soleil-desembarca-en-ecuador-para-entrenar-a-chicos-de-la-calle-2/.

Clift, Stephen. 2012. "Creative Arts as a Public Health Resource: Moving from Practice-Based Research to Evidence-Based Research." *Perspectives in Public Health* 132 (3): 120–7.

Clowns Without Borders. 2017. "About Clowns Without Borders." http://www.clownswithoutborders.org/.

Cohen-Cruz, Jan. 1998. *Radical Street Performance: An International Anthology*. London and New York: Routledge.

– 2010. *Engaging Performance: Theatre as Call and Response*. London and New York: Routledge.

– 2013. *Radical Street Performance: An International Anthology*. London and New York: Routledge.

– 2015. *Remapping Performance – Common Ground, Uncommon Partners*. London: Palgrave Macmillan.

Colborn-Roxworthy, Emily. 2004. "Role-Play Training at 'Violent Disneyland': The FBI Academy's Performance Paradigms." *TDR: The Drama Review* 48 (4): 81–108.

Colby, Sarah E., and Lauren Haldeman. 2007. "Peer-Led Theater as a Nutrition Education Strategy." *Journal of Nutrition Education and Behavior* 39 (1): 48–9.

CONAIE. 1990. *Las Nacionalidades Indígenas en el Ecuador*. Nuestro Proceso Organizativo. Quito.

Conrad, Diane, and Anita Sinner. 2015. *Creating Together: Participatory, Community-Based and Collaborative Arts Practices and Scholarship across Canada*. Waterloo, ON: Wilfred Laurier University Press.

Constitución de la República del Ecuador, Government of Ecuador. 2008. "Constitución de la República del Ecuador." Last edition 13 July 2011. http://www.oas.org/juridico/pdfs/mesicic4_ecu_const.PDF.

Coombs, Tim, Angela Nicholas, and Jane Pirkis. 2013. "A Review of Social Inclusion Measures." *Australian and New Zealand Journal of Psychiatry* 47 (2): 906–19.

Corbin, J. Hope, and Maurice B. Mittelmark. 2008. "Partnership Lessons from the Global Programme for Health Promotion Effectiveness: A Case Study." *Health Promotion International* 23 (4): 365–71.

Coryat, Diana. 2015. "Latin American Struggles| Extractive Politics, Media Power, and New Waves of Resistance against Oil Drilling in the Ecuadorian Amazon: The Case of Yasunidos." *International Journal of Communication* 9: 3741–60.

– 2017. "Extractivism and Resistance: Media, Protest and Power in Ecuador." PhD diss., University of Massachusetts – Amherst. http://scholarworks.umass.edu/cgi/viewcontent.cgi?article=2033&context=dissertations_2.

Cox, Susan M., and Katherine M. Boydell. 2016. "Ethical Issues in Arts-Based Health Research." In *Creative Arts, Health, and Wellbeing: International Perspectives on Practice, Policy, and Research*, edited by Stephen Clift and Paul M. Camic, 83–94. New York: Oxford University Press.

Cox, Susan M., Darquise Lafrenière, Pamela Brett-Maclean, Kate Collie, Nancy Cooley, Janet Dunbrack, and Gerri Frager. 2010. "Tipping the Iceberg? The State of Arts and Health in Canada." *Arts and Health: An International Journal for Research, Policy and Practice* 2 (2): 109–24.

Cruz-Ferreira, Ana, José Marmeleira, Alexandra Formigo, Dulce Gomes, and Jorge Fernandes. 2015. "Creative Dance Improves Physical Fitness and Life Satisfaction in Older Women." *Research on Aging* 37 (8): 837–55.

Cueva, Agustin. 1979. *El desarrollo del capitalismo en América Latina*. México, EDICOL.

Da Silva Rodrigues Avrillon, Helizete. 2011. "Le Cirque social du rire aux larmes: Espace de médiation et de reconfiguration identitaires et artistiques aux Etats-Unis et au Brésil." PhD diss., Université de Lyon. http://theses.univ-lyon2.fr/documents/lyon2/2011/da_silva_rodrigues_h#p=0a=top.

Daskalaki, Maria, and Oli Mould. 2013. "Beyond Urban Subcultures: Urban Subversions as Rhizomatic Social Formations." *International Journal of Urban and Regional Research* 37 (1): 1–18.

Dávalos, Pablo. 2014. *Alianza pais o la reinvención del poder: Siete ensayos sobre el Posneoliberalismo en el Ecuador*. Bogotá: Ediciones Desde Abajo.

Davis, A. Brent, Dennis J. Sumara, and Thomas E. Kieran. 1996. "Cognition, Co-Emergence, Curriculum." *Journal of Curriculum Studies* 28 (2): 151–69.

Davis, Janet N. 2002. *The Circus Age: Culture and Society under the American Big Top*. Chapel Hill, NC: University of North Carolina Press.

de Freitas, Elizabeth. 2012. "The Classroom as Rhizome: New Strategies for Diagramming Knotted Interactions." *Qualitative Inquiry* 187 (7): 557–70.

Deletemyaccount17. 2013. "Cultural Appropriation under the Big Top, or, Why I Had an Uncomfortable Evening." *Groupthink – Kinja*. https://groupthink.kinja.com/cultural-appropriation-under-the-big-top-or-why-i-ha-1483568141.

Deleuze, Gilles, and Felix Guattari. 1987. *A Thousand Plateaus: Capitalism and Schizophrenia*. Translated by Brian Massumi. Minneapolis: University of Minnesota Press.

De Martini Ugolotti, Nicola, and Eileen Moyer. 2016. "'If I Climb a Wall of Ten Meters': Capoeira, Parkour and the Politics of Public Space among (Post) Migrant Youth in Turin, Italy." *Patterns of Prejudice* 50 (2): 188–206.

DeVellis, Robert F. 2012. *Scale Development: Theory and Applications*. Los Angeles: Sage.

Dewey, J. (1938) 1997. *Experience and Education*. New York: Touchstone, Simon and Schuster.

Diamond, Elin. 1992. "The Violence of 'We': Politicizing Identification." In *Critical Theory and Performance*, edited by Janelle G. Reinelt and Joseph R. Roach, 390–8. Ann Arbor, MI: University of Michigan Press.

DuBois, David L., Bruce E. Holloway, Jeffrey C. Valentine, and Harris Cooper. 2002. "Effectiveness of Mentoring Programs for Youth: A Meta-Analytic Review." *American Journal of Community Psychology* 30 (2): 157–97.

Duffy, Bernadette. 2006. *Supporting Creativity and Imagination in the Early Years*, 2nd Edition. Berkshire, GB: Open University Press.

Duncombe, Stephen. 2007. "(From) Cultural Resistance to Community Development." *Community Development Journal* 42 (4): 490–500.

Durán, Lucia. 2014. "Entre el espectáculo, el estgma y lo cotidiano: Es posible habitar el patrimonio?" In *Habitar el patrimonio: Nuevos aportes al debate desde América Latina*, edited by Lucia Durán, Eduardo Kingman Garcés, and Mónica Lacarrieu, 66–85. Quito: Instituto Metropolitano de Patrimonio.

Dutch Creative World Foundation. 2017. "About Dutch Creative World Foundation." http://www.creatievewereld.nl.

Eccles, Jacqueline S., and Janice Templeton. 2002. "Extracurricular and Other After-School Activities for Youth." *Review of Research in Education* 26 (1): 113–80.

Ekeland, Eilin, F. Heian, and K.B. Hagen. 2005. "Can Exercise Improve Self Esteem in Children and Young People? A Systematic Review of Randomised Controlled Trials." *British Journal of Sports Medicine* 39 (11): 792–8.

Ermine, Willie, Raven Sinclair, and Bonnie Jeffery. 2004. "The Ethics of Research Involving Indigenous Peoples: Report of the Indigenous Peoples Research Centre to the Interagency Advisory Panel." Saskatoon: Indigenous Peoples Health Research Centre. http://iphrc.ca/assets/Documents/ethics_review_iphrc.pdf.

Escobar, Arturo. 2005. "El 'Postdesarrollo' como concepto y práctica social." In *Políticas de economía, ambiente y sociedad en tiempos de globalización*, edited by Daniel Mato and Sarah L. Babb, 17–32. Caracas: Universidad Central de Venezuela.

– 2010. "Latin America at a Crossroads." *Cultural Studies* 24 (1): 1–65.

Falconí, Fander. 2013. "Crisis civilizatoria y alternativas de la humanidad." http://Issuu.Com/Falconifander/Docs/Ecosocialismo__11_06_2013.

Farah, Ivonne, and Luciano Vasapollo. 2011. "Vivir Bien: ¿Pardigma co capitalista?" La Paz: CIDES.

Fels, Lynn. 1998. "In the Wind, Clothes Dance on a Line." *JCT: Journal of Curriculum Theorizing* 14 (1): 27–36.

– 2009. "When Royalty Steps Forth – Role Drama as an Embodied Learning System." *Complicity: An International Journal of Complexity and Education* 6 (12): 124–42.

– 2012. "Collecting Data through Performative Inquiry: A Tug on the Sleeve." *Youth Theatre Journal* 26 (1): 50–60.

Fels, Lynn, and George Belliveau. 2008. *Exploring Curriculum: Performative Inquiry, Role Drama and Learning*. Vancouver, BC: Pacific Education Press.

Fels, Lynn, Karen Myer, and R. Martin. 2011. "Angel Words inside Prison Gates: Participatory Action Research as an Action of Restorative Justice." In *International Perspectives on Restorative Justice in Education*, edited by John Charlton, Sandra Pavelka, and Philip Verrecchia, 69–88. Kanata, ON: J. Charlton Publishing.

Filewood, Alan. 2011. *Committing Theatre: Theatre Radicalism and Political Intervention in Canada*: Toronto: Between the Lines.

Flynn, Alex, and Jonas Tinius. 2015. *Anthropology, Theatre, and Development. The Transformative Potential of Performance*. London: Palgrave Macmillan UK.

Fornssler, Barbara, Holly A. McKenzie, Colleen Anne Dell, Larry Laliberte, and Carol Hopkins. 2014. "'I Got to Know Them in a New Way': Rela(y/t)ing Rhizomes and Community-Based Knowledge (Brokers') Transformation of Western and Indigenous Knowledge." *Cultural Studies – Critical Methodologies* 14 (2): 179–93.

Foucault, Michel. 1975. *The Birth of the Clinic: An Archaeology of Medical Perception*. Translated by Alan Sheridan Smith. New York: Vintage Books.

– 1988. *Technologies of the Self: A Seminar with Michel Foucault*. Edited by Luther H. Martin, Huck Gutman, and Patrick H. Hutton. Amherst: University of Massachusetts Press.

Foucault, Michel, Arnold Davidson, and Graham Burchell. 2008. *The Birth of Biopolitics: Lectures at the Collège de France, 1978–1979*. Translated by Graham Burchell. New York: Palgrave Macmillan.

Fournier, Cynthia, Mélodie-Anne Drouin, Jérémie Marcoux, Patricia Garel, Emmanuel Bochud, Julie Théberge, Patrice Aubertin, Gil Favreau, and Richard Fleet. 2014. "Cirque Du Monde as a Health Intervention: Perceptions of Medical Students and Social Circus Experts." *Canadian Family Physician* 60 (11): e548–53.

Freeman, Kelsey J. 2016. "The Rising Tide of Indigenous Mobilization: Identity and the Politics of Refusal in Mexico and Ecuador." Honors project, Bowdoin College. https://digitalcommons.bowdoin.edu/cgi/viewcontent.cgi?referer=https://scholar.google.ca/&httpsredir=1&article=1058&context=honorsprojects.

Freidenberg, Flavia, and Manuel Alcántara Sáez. 2001. "Movimiento unidad plurinacional Pachakutik – Nuevo Pais." *Partidos Políticos De América Latina*. Salamanca: Ediciones Universidad de Salamanca. http://www.flacsoandes.edu.ec/biblio/catalog/resGet.php?resId=23022.

Freire, Paulo. 1972. *Pedagogy of the Oppressed*. Translated by Myra Bergman Ramos. Harmondsworth, Middlesex: Penguin.

French, John D., and Alexandre Fortes. 2005. "Another World *Is* Possible: The Rise of the Brazilian Workers' Party and the Prospects for Lula's Government." *Labor: Studies in Working-Class History of the Americas* 2 (3): 13–31.

Fricker, Karen. 2016. "'Somewhere between Science and Legend': Images of Indigeneity in Robert Lepage and Cirque Du Soleil's Totem." In *Cirque Global – Quebec's Expanding Circus Boundaries*, edited by Louis Patrick Leroux and Charles R. Batson, 140–60. Montreal: McGill-Queen's University Press.

Frohlich, Katherine L., and Louise Potvin. 2008. "Transcending the Known in Public Health Practice." *American Journal of Public Health* 98 (2): 216–21.

Frohlich, Katherine L., Ellen Corin, and Louise Potvin. 2001. "A Theoretical Proposal for the Relationship between Context and Disease." *Sociology of Health and Illness* 23 (6): 776–97.

Fuggle, Sophie. 2008. "Discourses of Subversion: The Ethics and Aesthetics of Capoeira and Parkour." *Dance Research* 26 (2): 204–22.

Funk, Alison. 2017. "Circus Education in Québec: Balancing Academic and Kinaesthetic Learning Objectives through an Artistic Lens." Master's thesis, Concordia University.

Gagnon, Lysianc. 2005. "Las Vegas du Nord." *La Presse*, October 15.

Gago, Verónica. 2017. *Neoliberalism from Below: Popular Pragmatics and Baroque Economies*. Durham, NC: Duke University Press.

Galeano, Eduardo. 1973. *Open Veins of Latin America: Five Centuries of the Pillage of a Continent [Las venas abiertas de América Latina]*. Translated by Cedric Belfrage. New York: Monthly Review Press.

Gallagher, Kathleen. 2014. *Why Theatre Matters: Urban Youth, Engagement, and a Pedagogy of the Real*. Toronto: University of Toronto Press.

Galloway, Susan. 2009. "Theory-Based Evaluation and the Social Impact of the Arts." *Cultural Trends* 18 (2): 125–48.

Gardner, Sally May, Paul Komesaroff, and Rachel Fensham. 2008. "Dancing beyond Exercise: Young People's Experiences in Dance Classes." *Journal of Youth Studies* 11 (6): 701–9.

Gattinger, Monica, and Diane Saint-Pierre. 2010. "The 'Neoliberal Turn' in Provincial Cultural Policy and Administration in Québec and Ontario: The Emergence of 'Quasi-Neoliberal' Approaches." *Canadian Journal of Communication* 35 (2): 279–302.

Gilchrist, Paul, and Belinda Wheaton. 2011. "Lifestyle Sport, Public Policy and Youth Engagement: Examining the Emergence of Parkour." *International Journal of Sport Policy and Politics* 3 (1): 109–31.

Giroux, Henry A., and David E. Purpel. 1983. *The Hidden Curriculum and Moral Education: Deception or Discovery?* Berkeley, CA: McCutcheon.

Godoy, Horatio H. 1968. "Latin American Culture and Its Transformation." In *Cultural Factors in Inter-American Relations*, edited by Samual Shapiro, 165–85. Notre Dame: University of Notre Dame Press.

Goldbard, Arlene. 2006. *New Creative Community: The Art of Cultural Development*. New York: New Village Press.

Goldbard, Arlene, and Don Adams. 2001. *Creative Community: The Art of Cultural Development*. New York: Rockefeller Foundation.

Goldenberg, Maya J. 2006. "On Evidence and Evidence-Based Medicine: Lessons from the Philosophy of Science." *Social Science and Medicine* 62 (11): 2621–32.

Goldstein, E. Bruce. 2010. *Encyclopedia of Perception*. Thousand Oaks, CA: SAGE Publications.

Gonçalves, Susana, and Suzanne Majhanovich. 2016. *Art and Intercultural Dialogue*. Netherlands: Sense.

González-Andrade, Fabricio, Ramiro López-Pulles, Santiago Gascón, and Javier García Campayo, S. 2011. "Epidemiological Issues Regarding Suicides in Ecuador: An 8-Year Report." *Journal of Public Health* 19 (2): 161–9.

Gordon, Mordechai. 2001. "Hannah Arendt on Authority: Conservatism in Education Reconsidered." In *Hannah Arendt and Education: Renewing Our Common World*, edited by Mordechai Gordon, 11–36. Boulder, CO: Westview.

Government of Ecuador. 2008. "Republic of Ecuador – Constitution of 2008." http://pdba.georgetown.edu/Constitutions/Ecuador/english08.html.

Gramsci, Antonio. 1971. *Selections from the Prison Notebooks*. Translated by Quentin Hoare and Geoffrey Nowell Smith. London: Lawrence and Wishart.

Graver, David. 2005. "The Actor's Bodies." In *Performance: Critical Concepts in Literacy and Cultural Studies*, edited by Philip Auslander, 157–74. New York: Routledge.

Gray, Clive. 2007. "Commodification and Instrumentality in Cultural Policy." *International Journal of Cultural Policy* 13 (2): 203–15.

Greene, Maxine. 1978. *Landscapes of Learning*. New York: Teachers College Press.

Grinspun, Ricardo, and Jennifer Mills. 2015. "Canada, Extractivism, and Hemispheric Relations." In *Beyond Free Trade*, edited by Kate Ervine and Gavin Fridell, 133–51. London: Palgrave Macmillan.

Grossman, Jason, and Fiona J. Mackenzie. 2005. "The Randomized Controlled Trial: Gold Standard, or Merely Standard?" *Perspectives in Biology and Medicine* 48 (4): 516–34.

Grumet, Madeleine R. 1988. *Bitter Milk: Women and Teaching*. Boston, MA: University of Massachusetts Press.

Grunstein, Rose, and Don Nutbeam. 2007. "The Impact of Participation in the Rock Eisteddfod Challenge on Adolescent Resiliency and Health Behaviours." *Health Education* 107 (3): 261–75.

Guattari, Félix. 1995. *Chaosmosis: An Ethico-Aesthetic Paradigm*. Sydney: Power Publications.

Guattari, Félix, and Suely Rolnick. 2007. *Molecular Revolution in Brazil*. Cambridge, MA: The MIT Press.

Gudynas, Eduardo. 2009. "Diez tesis urgentes sobre el nuevo extractivismo: Contextosy demandas bajo el progresismo Sudamericano actual." In *Extractivismo, Política y Sociedad*, edited by Jürgen Schuldt, Alberto Acosta, Alberto Barandiarán, Anthony Bebbington, Mauricio Folchi, Alejandra Alayza, and Eduardo Gudynas, 187–225. Quito: CAAP/CLAES.

– 2014. "Buen Vivir." In *Degrowth: A Vocabulary for a New Era*, edited by Giacomo D'Alisa, Federico Demaria, and Giorgos Kallis, 201–4. New York: Routledge.

Gudynas, Eduardo, and Alberto Acosta. 2011. "El Buen Vivir más allá del desarrollo." *Revista Qué Hacer* 181: 70–81.

Guerra Vilaboy, Sergio. 2006. *Breve historia de América Latina*. Playa, La Habana: Intituto Cubano Del Libro.

Guetzko, Joshua. 2002. "How the Arts Impact Communities: An Introduction to the Literature on Arts Impact Studies." Working paper, Taking the Measure of Culture Conference. Princeton: Princeton University.

Guillemin, Marilys. 2004. "Understanding Illness: Using Drawing as a Research Method." *Qualitative Health Research* 14 (2): 272–89.

Guzmán, Rafael González. 2009. "Latin American Social Medicine and the Report of the WHO Commission on Social Determinants of Health." *Social Medicine* 4 (2): 113–20.

Gwyther, Gabrielle, and Alphia Possamai-Inesedy. 2009. "Methodologies à la Carte: An Examination of Emerging Qualitative Methodologies." *International Journal of Social Research Methods* 12 (2): 99–115.

Haiven, Max. 2017. "Participatory Art within, against and beyond Financialization: Benign Pessimism, Tactical Parasitics and the Encrypted Common." *Cultural Studies* 32 (4): 530–59.

Hammond, John L. 2003. "Another World Is Possible." *Latin American Perspectives* 30 (3): 3–11.

Hamon, K. 2011. "The Practical Rhizome: Heterogeneity." Blog post, *Communications & Society*, 30 November.

Hampshire, Katherine Rebecca, and Mathilde Matthijsse. 2010. "Can Arts Projects Improve Young People's Wellbeing? A Social Capital Approach." *Social Science and Medicine* 71 (4): 708–16.

Hancock, Trevor. 1983. "The Evolution, Impact and Significance of the Healthy Cities/Communities Movement." *Journal of Public Health Policy* 14: 5–18.

Hancock, Trevor, and Leonard Duhl. 1986. "Healthy Cities: Promoting Health in the Urban Context." WHO Healthy Cities Paper No. 1. Copenhagen: FADL Publications.

Hanna, Judith Lynne. 2006. *Dancing for Health: Conquering and Preventing Stress*. Lanham, MD: Rowman Altamira.

Hardt, Michael, and Antonio Negri. 2004. *Multitude: War and Democracy in the Age of Empire*. New York: Penguin Books.

Hawe, Penelope, and Louise Potvin. 2009. "What Is Population Health Intervention Research?" *Canadian Journal of Public Health* 100 (1): 8–14.

Heath, Shirley Brice, and Adelma Aurora Roach. 1998. "The Arts in the Nonschool Hours." Briefing materials for President's Committee on the Arts and the Humanities. Menlo Park, CA: Stanford University. Available at http://www.shirleybriceheath.net/pdfs/SBHBriefingMaterialsArtsInNonschool Hours02MarchMeeting.pdf

Helguera, Pablo. 2011. *Education for Socially Engaged Art: A Materials and Techniques Handbook*. New York: Jorge Pinto Books.

Henriksen, Ann-Karin, and Jody Miller. 2012. "Dramatic Lives and Relevant Becomings: Toward a Deleuze and Guattari-Inspired Cartography of Young Women's Violent Conflicts." *Theoretical Criminology* 16 (4): 435–61.

Hesmondhalgh, David, Melinda Nisbett, Kate Oakley, and David Lee. 2015. "Were New Labour's Cultural Policies Neo-Liberal?" *International Journal of Cultural Policy* 21 (1): 97–114.

Hewison, Robert. 2014. *Cultural Capital: The Rise and Fall of Creative Britain.* London and Brooklyn: Verso.

Higueras-Fresnillo, Sara, Irene Esteban Cornejo, Ana González-Galo, Gonzalo Bellvis-Guerra, and David Martínez-Gómez. 2015. "The Association of Dance Participation with Body Fat and Physical Fitness among Youth Girls." *Nutrición Hospitalaria* 32 (3): 1396–7.

Ho, Daniel E., Kosuke Imai, Gary King, and Elizabeth Stuart. 2007. "Matching as Nonparametric Preprocessing for Reducing Model Dependence in Parametric Causal Inference." *Political Analysis* 15 (3): 199–236.

Hock, Michael F., Kim A. Pulvers, Donald D. Deshler, and Jean B. Schumaker. 2001. "The Effects of an After-School Tutoring Program on the Academic Performance of at-Risk Students and Students with LD." *Remedial and Special Education* 22 (3): 172–86.

Holmes, Kate. 2017. "Aspirational Circus Glamour: Rethinking the Circus Grotesque through Female Aerialists of the Inter-War Period." *Early Popular Visual Culture* 15 (3): 299–314.

Howard, George S. 1980. "Response-Shift Bias a Problem in Evaluating Interventions with Pre/Post Self-Reports." *Evaluation Review* 4 (1): 93–106.

Hughes, Jennifer Scheper, and Ariane Dalla Déa. 2012. "Authenticity and Resistance: Latin American Art, Activism, and Performance in the New Global Context." *Latin American Perspectives* 39 (2): 5–10.

Hunter, Dale. (1994) 2007. *The Art of Facilitation.* San Francisco: Jossey-Bass.

Hurley, Erin. 2008. "Les Corps multiples du Cirque du Soleil." Translated by Isabelle Léger. *Globe: revue internationale d'études québécoises* 11 (2): 135–57.

Hurtubise, Roch, Shirley Roy, and Céline Bellot. 2003. "Youth Homelessness: The Street and Work: From Exclusion to Integration." In *Youth and Work in the Post-Industrial City of North America and Europe*, edited by Laurence Roulleau-Berger, 395–407. Boston: Brill Leiden.

Huxley, Peter, S. Evans, S. Madge, M. Webber, T. Burchardt, David McDaid, and Martin Knapp. 2012. "Development of a Social Inclusion Index to Capture Subjective and Objective Life Domains (Phase II): Psychometric Development Study." *Health Technology Assessment* 16 (1): 1–248.

Hylton, Kevin. 2013. *Sports Development: Policy, Process and Practice.* Third Edition. London: Routledge.

INCITE! Women of Color Against Violence. 2007. *The Revolution Will Not Be Funded: Beyond the Non-Profit Industrial Complex.* North Carolina: South End Press.

Infantino, Julieta. 2015. "A Contemporary History of Circus Arts in Buenos Aires, Argentina: The Post-Dictatorial Resurgence and Revaluation of Circus as a Popular Art." *Popular Entertainment Studies* 6 (1): 42–61.

Instituto de Investigaciones Económicas UCE. 1975. *Ecuador: Pasado y presente*. Quito, Ecuador: Universidad Central, Editorial Universitaria.

Instituto Nacional de Estadística y Censos (INEC). 2001. "Unidad de información y análisis-siise de la Secretaría Técnica del Frente Social del Gobierno del Ecuador con la colaboración del Instituto Nacional de Estadística y Censos (Inec), Pobreza por necesidades insatisfechas." http://www.siise.gob.ec/siiseweb/ PageWebs/pubsii/pubsii_0040.pdf.

Instituto Nacional de Estadísticas y Censos (INEC). 2012. Primera Encuesta Nacional de Trabajo Infantil (Enti).

Inter-American Drug Abuse Control Commission. 2015. "Report on Drug Use in the Americas, 2015." http://www.cicad.oas.org/oid/pubs/DrugUseAmericas_ ENG_web.pdf.

Ives, Peter. 2004. *Language and Hegemony in Gramsci*. London: Pluto Press London.

Jackson, Shannon. 2011. *Social Works: Performing Art, Supporting Publics*. Abingdon, UK: Routledge.

Jancovich, Leila. 2011. "Great Art for Everyone? Engagement and Participation Policy in the Arts." *Cultural Trends* 20 (3–4): 271–9.

Jeannotte, M. Sharon. 2010. "Going with the Flow: Neoliberalism and Cultural Policy in Manitoba and Saskatchewan." *Canadian Journal of Communication* 35 (2): 303–24.

Jeffrey, Bob, and Anna Craft. 2004. "Teaching Creatively and Teaching for Creativity: Distinctions and Relationships." *Journal of Educational Studies* 30 (1): 77–87.

Jermyn, Helen. 2001. "The Arts and Social Exclusion: A Review Prepared for the Arts Council of England." London: Arts Council of England.

Johar, Matura, Rosita Abdul Latif, Haizan Mohd Taha, and Mardian Shah Omar. 2016. "Effect of Senamseri™ Dance Therapy Intervention on Psychological Well-Being among Sedentary Adults." In *Proceedings of the 2nd International Colloquium on Sports Science, Exercise, Engineering and Technology 2015*, edited by Shariman Ismadi Ismail, Norasrudin Sulaiman, and Rahmat Adnan, 237–46. Singapore: Springer.

Kawachi, Ichiro, and Lisa F. Berkman. 2001. "Social Ties and Mental Health." *Journal of Urban Health* 78(3): 458–67.

Keeshin, Brooks R., and Kristine Campbell. 2011. "Screening Homeless Youth for Histories of Abuse: Prevalence, Enduring Effects, and Interest in Treatment." *Child Abuse and Neglect* 35 (6): 401–7.

Kelaher, Margaret, and David Dunt. 2009. "Evaluation of the Community Arts Development Scheme." Final Report. https://www.vichealth.vic.gov.au/~/media/ .../arts/cads/cads_final_for_web.pdf?la=en: VicHealth.

Kester, Grant H. 2011. *The One and the Many: Contemporary Collaborative Art in a Global Context*. Durham: Duke University Press.

– 2017. "The Limitations of the Exculpatory Critique: A Response to Mikkel Bolt Rasmussen." *FIELD: A Journal of Socially Engaged Art Criticism* (6). http://field-journal.com/issue-6/mikkel-bolt-rasmussen.

Khan, Rimi. 2013. "Re-Thinking Cultural Capital and Community-Based Arts." *Journal of Sociology* 49 (2–3): 357–72.

Kidd, Sean A. 2009. "'A Lot of Us Look at Life Differently': Homeless Youths and Art on the Outside." *Cultural Studies – Critical Methodologies* 9 (2): 345–67.

Kiez, Tia K.M. 2015. The Impact of Circus Arts Instruction on the Physical Literacy of Children in Grades 4 and 5. Master of Science thesis, University of Manitoba.

Kilpatrick, Dean G., Ron Acierno, Benjamin Saunders, Heidi S. Resnick, Connie L. Best, and Paula P. Schnurr. 2000. "Risk Factors for Adolescent Substance Abuse and Dependence: Data from a National Sample." *Journal of Consulting and Clinical Psychology* 68 (1): 19–30.

Kindon, Sara, Rachel Pain, and Mike Kesby. 2008. "Participatory Action Research." In *International Encyclopedia of Human Geography*, edited by Rob Kitchin and Nigel Thrift, 90–5. London: Elsevier.

King, Barnaby. 2013. "Carnivalesque Economies: Clowning and the Neoliberal Impasse." *Kritika Kultura* 21/22: 472–89. https://repository.edgehill.ac.uk/6086/1/21_King_Carnivalesque_Economies.pdf.

Kinnunen, Riitta, Jukka Lidman, Sofia-Charlotta Kakko, and Katri Kekäläinen. 2013. *"They're Smiling from Ear to Ear": Wellbeing Effects from Social Circus*. Tampere, Finland: University of Tampere.

Kiwan, Nadia. 2007. "A Critical Perspective on Socially Embedded Cultural Policy in France." *International Journal of Cultural Policy* 13 (2): 153–67.

Knowles, J. Gary, and Ardra L. Cole. 2008. *Handbook of the Arts in Qualitative Research: Perspectives, Methodologies, Examples, and Issues.* Thousand Oaks, CA: Sage Publishing.

Krieger, Nancy. 2005. "Embodiment: A Conceptual Glossary for Epidemiology." *Journal of Epidemiology and Community Health* 59 (5): 350–5.

Krieger, Nancy, Margarita Alegría, Naomar Almeida-Filho, Jarbas Barbosa da Silva, Maurício L. Barreto, Jason Beckfield, Lisa Berkman, et al. 2010. "Who, and What, Causes Health Inequities? Reflections on Emerging Debates from an Exploratory Latin American/North American Workshop." *Journal of Epidemiology and Community Health* 64 (9): 747–9.

Kriellaars, Dean. 2013. "Physical Literacy and the Circus." Paper presented to the Working Group on Circus Research, National Circus School, 1 November.

Kumar, Arun. 2013. "Serv(Ic)Ing the Country." In *Youth: Responding to Lives*, edited by Andrew Azzopardi, 27–43. Switzerland: Springer.

Lane, Jill. 2003. "Digital Zapatistas." *TDR/The Drama Review* 47 (2): 129–44.

Lange, Elizabeth A. 2004. "Transformative and Restorative Learning: A Vital Dialectic for Sustainable Societies." *Adult Education Quarterly* 54 (2): 121–39.

Latorre, Sara, Katharine N. Farrell, and Joan Martínez-Alier. 2015. "The Commodification of Nature and Socio-Environmental Resistance in Ecuador: An Inventory of Accumulation by Dispossession Cases, 1980–2013." *Ecological Economics* 116: 58–69.

Lavers, Katie, and Jon Burtt. 2015. "Social Circus in the Arctic: Cultivating Resilience." *Journal of Arts and Communities* 7 (3): 125–39.

Lazzarato, Maurizio. 2012. *The Making of an Indebted Man*. Translated by Joshua David Jordan. Los Angeles: Semiotext(e).

Lee, Valerie E., and David T. Burkam. 2002. *Inequality at the Starting Gate: Social Background Differences in Achievement as Children Begin School*. Washington, DC: Economic Policy Institute.

Leroux, Louis Patrick. 2012. "Cirque in Space! The Ethos, Ethics, and Aesthetics of Staging and Branding the Individual of Exception." Paper presented at the Centre for Canadian Studies, Duke University, Durham North Carolina.

– 2016. "Reinventing Tradition, Building a Field: Quebec Circus and Its Scholarship." In *Cirque Global – Quebec's Expanding Circus Boundaries*, edited by Louis Patrick Leroux and Charles R. Batson, 3–20. Montreal: McGill-Queen's University Press.

Leroux, Louis Patrick, and Charles R. Batson. 2016. *Cirque Global: Quebec's Expanding Circus Boundaries*. Montreal: McGill-Queen's University Press.

Leslie, Deborah, and Norma M. Rantisi. 2010. "Creativity and Place in the Evolution of a Cultural Industry: The Case of the Cirque Du Soleil." *Urban Studies* 48 (9): 1771–87.

Levison, Natasha. 2001. The Paradox of Natality: Teaching in the Midst of Belatedness. In *Hannah Arendt and Education: Renewing Our Common World*, edited by Mordechai Gordon, 11–36. Boulder, CO: Westview.

Liang, Shen. 2014. "Performing Dream or Reality: The Dilemma of Chinese Community-Based Theatre." *TDR: The Drama Review* 58 (1): 16–23.

Lobo, Michele. 2014. "Affective Energies: Sensory Bodies on the Beach in Darwin, Australia." *Emotion, Space and Society* 12: 101–9.

Loiselle, Frederic. 2015. "Retombées du Cirque Social (Cirque Du Soleil) en contexte de réadaptation sur la participation sociale de jeunes adultes avec déficiences physiques en transition vers la vie active – Étude qualitative." Master's Thesis, Faculté de médecine, Université de Montréal.

Lowe, Seana S. 2000. "Creating Community: Art for Community Development." *Journal of Contemporary Ethnography* 29 (3): 357–86.

Lugones, María. 2007. "Heterosexualism and the Colonial/Modern Gender System." *Hypatia* 22(1): 186–09.

Macas, Luis. 2010. "Sumak Kawsay: La Vida en plenitud." *América Latina en Movimiento* 452: 14–16.

Macías Vázquez, Alfredo, and Pablo Alonso Gonzalez. 2016. "Between 'Neodevelopmentalism' and 'Postdevelopmentalism': Towards a Theory of a Dispersed Knowledge Economy in Ecuador." *Canadian Journal of Development Studies/ Revue canadienne d'études du développement* 37 (1) : 47–65.

Maclean, Kate. 2012. "Gender, Risk and Micro-Financial Subjectivities." *Antipode* 45 (2): 455–73.

Marcuse, Judith. 2015. "Keynote Presentation." Paper presented at the Creative Catalyst Conference, Ryerson University, Toronto.

Marmot, Michael, Susan Friel, Ruth Bell, Tanja A.J. Houweling, and Sebastian Taylor, on behalf of the Commission on Social Determinants of Health. 2008. "Closing the Gap in a Generation: Health Equity through Action on the Social Determinants of Health." *The Lancet* 372 (9650): 1661–9.

Marontate, Jan, and Catherine Murray. 2010. "Neoliberalism in Provincial Cultural Policy Narratives: Perspectives from Two Coasts." *Canadian Journal of Communication* 35 (2): 325–43.

Martin, Randy. 1998. *Critical Moves: Dance Studies in Theory and Politics.* Durham, NC: Duke University Press.

– 2004. "Dance and Its Others: Theory, State, Nation, and Socialism." In *Of the Presence of the Body: Essays on Dance and Performance Theory*, edited by André Lepecki, 47–63. Middletown, CT: Wesleyan University Press.

– 2012. "A Precarious Dance, a Derivative Sociality." *TDR: The Drama Review* 56 (4): 62–77.

Masny, Diana. 2013. "Rhizoanalytic Pathways in Qualitative Research." *Qualitative Inquiry* 19 (5): 339–48.

– 2016. "Problematizing Qualitative Research: Reading a Data Assemblage with Rhizoanalysis." *Qualitative Inquiry* 22 (8): 666–75.

Matarasso, François. 1997. *Use or Ornament: The Social Impact of Participation in the Arts.* Stroud: Comedia.

– 2003. "Smoke and Mirrors: A Response to Paola Merli's 'Evaluating the Social Impact of Participation in Arts Activities.'" *International Journal of Cultural Policy* 9 (3): 337–46.

– 2013. "'All in This Together': The Depoliticisation of Community Art in Britain, 1970–2011." https://parliamentofdreams.files.wordpress.com/2013/08/2013-all-in-this-together-matarasso.pdf.

– 2015. "Making 'Arts Engagement' a Reality." https://parliamentofdreams.com/2015/07/16/making-arts-engagement-a-reality/.

Mauthner, Natasha S., and Andrea Doucet. 2003. "Reflexive Accounts and Accounts of Reflexivity in Qualitative Data Analysis." *Sociology* 37 (3): 413–31.

McAllister, Janet. 2014. "'Lazy' Cultural Stereotypes in Totem." *Newspaper Rock*, August 31. http://newspaperrock.bluecorncomics.com/2014/08/lazy-cultural-stereotypes-in-totem.html.

McCaffery, Nick. 2011. "Streetwise Community Circus, Knockavoe School Evaluation: An Evaluation of the Impact of Teaching Circus Skills to People with Learning Disabilities." Strabane, UK: Streetwise Disability Circus Project at Knockavoe.

McCauley, James. 2011. "The Circus She Calls Me: Youth at Risk in a Social Circus." Master's thesis, International Development MSc, University of Amsterdam. http://dare.uva.nl/cgi/arno/show.cgi?fid=207817.

McCutcheon, Sharon. 2003. "Negotiating Identity through Risk: A Community Circus Model for Evoking Change and Empowering Youth." Thesis, Charles Sturt University, Bathurst, Australia. http://bibliotheque.enc.qc.ca/Record.htm? idlist=1&record=19139637124919578199.

McKenzie, Michelle, Jacqueline Peterson Tulsky, Heather L. Long, Margaret Chesney, and Andrew Moss. 1999. "Tracking and Follow-up of Marginalized Populations: A Review." *Journal of Health Care for the Poor and Underserved* 10 (4): 409–29.

Meyerhoff, Eli, and Elsa Noterman. 2017. "Revolutionary Scholarship by Any Speed Necessary: Slow or Fast but for the End of This World." *ACME: An International Journal for Critical Geographies*, December. https://www.acme-journal.org/ index.php/acme/article/view/1429.

Mezzadra, Sandro, and Verónica Gago. 2017. "In the Wake of the Plebeian Revolt: Social Movements, 'Progressive' Governments, and the Politics of Autonomy in Latin America." *Anthropological Theory* 17 (4): 474–96.

Miller, John P., and Wayne Seller. 1985. *Curriculum: Perspectives and Practice*. White Plains, NY: Longman.

Milz, Sabine. 2010. "Introduction: Neoliberalism and Provincial Cultural Policy and Administration." *Canadian Journal of Communication* 35 (2): 275–78.

Ministerio de Desarrollo Urbano y Vivienda. 2016. "National Social Housing Program." http://www.habitatyvivienda.gob.cc/wp-content/uploads/downloads/ 2015/04/PROYECTO-PROGRAMA-NACIONAL-DE-VIVIENDA-SOCIAL- 9nov-1.pdf.

Moody, Douglas J. 2002. "Undergoing a Process and Achieving a Product: A Contradiction in Educational Drama?" In *Body and Language: Intercultural Learning through Drama*, edited by G. Bråuer, 135–60. Westport, CT: Ablex.

Moreno, Claudia. 2013. "The MIF, Cirque Du Soleil and Three Latin American Social Circus Schools Join Forces to Promote Youth Employability." Press Release, Multilateral Investment Fund (MIF). http://www.Fomin.Org/En-Us/ Home/News/Pressreleases/Artmid/3819/Articleid/995.Aspx.

Moyer, Eileen. 2005. "Street Corner Justice in the Name of Jah: Imperatives for Peace among Dar Es Salaam Street Youth." *Africa Today* 51(3): 31–58.

Munck, Ronaldo. 2003. "Neoliberalism, Necessitarianism and Alternatives in Latin America: There Is No Alternative (Tina)?" *Third World Quarterly* 24 (3): 495–511.

Mzaku, Thamsanqa. 2014. "Professional Development through Community Arts Projects: A Study of the Influence of Thesele Creative Society on the Career Paths of Five People." Master of arts thesis, University of the Witwatersrand, Johannesburg. http://wiredspace.wits.ac.za/xmlui/bitstream/handle/10539/13576/ PROFESSIONAL%20DEVELOPMENT%20THROUGH%20COMMUNITY %20ARTS%20PROJECTS_T%20Mzaku.pdf?sequence=4&isAllowed=y.

Navarro, Vicente. 2009. "What We Mean by Social Determinants of Health." *International Journal of Health Services* 16 (1): 5–16.

Newman, Tony, Katherine Curtis, and Jo Stephens. 2003. "Do Community-Based Arts Projects Result in Social Gains? A Review of the Literature." *Community Development Journal* 38 (4): 310–22.

Norris, Joe. 2010. *Playbuilding as Qualitative Research: A Participatory Arts-Based Approach.* Walnut Creek, CA: Left Coast.

Nyong'o, Tavia. 2013. "Situating Precarity between the Body and the Commons." *Women and Performance* 23 (2): 157–61.

Oudenampsen, Merijn, and Gavin Sullivan. 2004. "Precarity and N/European Identity: An Interview with Alex Foti (ChainWorkers)" *Mute* 2. http://www.metamute.org/editorial/articles/precarity-and-neuropean-identity-interview-alex-foti-chainworkers.

One World Experience. 2017. "About One World Experience."

O'Sullivan, Simon D. 2002. "Cultural Studies as Rhizome-Rhizomes in Cultural Studies." *Critical Studies* 20 (1): 81–93.

O'Toole, John. (1992) 2005. *The Process of Drama: Negotiating Art and Meaning.* New York: Routledge.

Out of Area. 2017. "More Information About Out of Area." http://www.outofarea.nl/default.aspx.

Palomeque Vallejo, Édison. 2000. *Diagnóstico Sobre Seguridad Ciudadana En El Ecuador.* Quito: FLACSO.

Pan-American Health Organization. 2009. "Lima Declaration on Arts as a Bridge to Health and Social Development." Paho/WHO – Signed by the Latin American Network of Arts for Social Transformation and the Pan-American Health Organization. http://www.bvsde.paho.org/texcom/CD045364/Declaracionde Lima19agostoVF3Set.pdf.

Parker, Jennifer S., and Mark J. Benson. 2004. "Parent-Adolescent Relations and Adolescent Functioning: Self-Esteem, Substance Abuse, and Delinquency." *Adolescence* 39 (155): 519.

Parkinson, Clive, and Mike White. 2013. "Inequalities, the Arts and Public Health: Towards an International Conversation." *Arts and Health: An International Journal for Research, Policy and Practice* 5 (3): 177–89.

Peñafiel Anchundia, Doleres Daniela. 2017. "Traditional Food Consumption and Its Nutritional Contribution in Guasaganda, Central Ecuador." PhD diss., Biodiversity collaboration project between Escuela Superior Politécnica del Litoral and Ghent University, Guayaquil, Ecuador.

Perlmutter, Jane C., and Louise Burell. 1995. "Learning through 'Play' as Well as 'Work' in the Primary Grades." *Young Children* 50 (5): 14–21.

Peters, Michael A. 2009. "Education, Creativity and the Economy of Passions: New Forms of Educational Capitalism." *Thesis Eleven* 96 (1): 40–63.

Plastow, Jane. 2014. "Domestication or Transformation? The Ideology of Theatre for Development in Africa." *Applied Theatre Research* 2 (2): 107–18.

– 2015. "Embodiment, Intellect, and Emotion: Thinking about Possible Impacts of Theatre for Development in Three Projects in Africa." In *Anthropology, Theatre and Development: The Transformative Potential of Performance*, edited by Alex Flynn and Jonas Tinius, 107–26. New York: Palgrave MacMillan.

Poland, Blake, Katherine L. Frohlich, and Margaret Cargo. 2008. "Context as a Fundamental Dimension of Health Promotion Program Evaluation." In *Health Promotion Evaluation Practices in the Americas*, edited by Louise Potvin and David McQueen, 299–317. New York: Springer.

Posner, Jill K., and Deborah Love Vandell. 1994. "Low-Income Children's After-School Care: Are There Beneficial Effects of After-School Programs?" *Child Development* 65 (2): 440–56.

Prendergast, Monica, Carl Leggo, and Pauline Sameshima. 2009. *Poetic Inquiry*. Rotterdam: Sense Publishers.

Price, Jonathan. 2015. "Contesting Agendas of Participation in the Arts." *Journal of Arts and Communities* 7 (1–2): 17–31.

Prickett, Stacey. 2016. "Constrained Bodies: Dance, Social Justice, and Choreographic Agency." *Dance Research Journal* 48 (3): 45–57.

Programa Circo Social Ecuador. 2012. "Mision y objectivos." Quito. http://www.vicepresidencia.gob.ec/programas/sonrieecuador/circo-social-yartistico.

Purcell, Roderick. 2009. "Images for Change: Community Development, Community Arts and Photography." *Community Development Journal* 44 (1): 111–22.

Purovaara, Tomi, and Sari Lakso. 2015. "Cascas – Experiment Diversity with the Street Arts and Circus: An Overview of Circus and Street Arts in Finland." CASCAS. http://sideshow-circusmagazine.com/research/downloads/overview-circus-and-street-arts-finland-cascas.

Putland, Christine. 2008. "Lost in Translation: The Question of Evidence-Linking Community-Based Arts and Health Promotion." *Journal of Health Psychology* 13 (2): 265–76.

Radcliffe, Sarah A. 2012. "Development for a Postneoliberal Era? *Sumak Kawsay*, Living Well and the Limits to Decolonisation in Ecuador." *Geoforum* 43 (2): 240–9.

Rancière, Jacques. 2004. *The Politics of Aesthetics: The Distribution of the Sensible*. Translated by Gabriel Rockhill. London: Continuum.

Randolph, Justus J., Kristina Falbe, Austin Kureethara Manuel, and Joseph L. Balloun. 2014. "A Step-by-Step Guide to Propensity Score Matching in R." *Practical Assessment, Research and Evaluation* 19 (18): 1–6.

Rankin, Katherine N. 2002. "Social Capital, Microfinance, and the Politics of Development." *Feminist Economics* 8 (1): 1–24.

Read, Jason. 2009. "A Genealogy of Homo-Economicus: Neoliberalism and the Production of Subjectivity." *Foucault Studies* 6: 25–36.

Reddy, Ranjini, Jean E. Rhodes, and Peter Mulhall. 2003. "The Influence of Teacher Support on Student Adjustment in the Middle School Years: A Latent Growth Curve Study." *Development and Psychopathology* 15 (1): 119–38.

Rednose Foundation. 2017. "Rednose Foundation – Hidung Merag – Helping Children Build Dreams." http://www.rednosefoundation.org/.

Rice, Pranee Liamputtong, and Douglas Ezzy. 1999. *Qualitative Research Methods: A Health Focus*. Melbourne: Oxford University Press.

Richards, Patricia. 2004. *Pobladoras, Indígenas, and the State: Conflicts over Women's Rights in Chile*. Piscataway, NJ: Rutgers University Press.

Richardson, Laurel. 2000. "Getting Personal: Writing Stories." *Qualitative Studies in Education* 14 (1): 33–8.

Richman, Charles L., M.L. Clark, and Kathryn P. Brown. 1985. "General and Specific Self-Esteem in Late Adolescent Students: Race × Gender × SES Effects." *Adolescence* 20 (79): 555–66.

Ricken, Olivia. 2001. "ZirkuspäDagogik in Der Kinder- Und Jugendarbeit." Master's thesis, Universität Bielefeld.

Rivard, Jacinthe. 2007. "Le Mouvement paradigmatique autour du phénomène des jeunes qui vivent des difficultés: L'exemple du programme Cirque Du Monde" [The New Paradigm for Youth Who Live with Difficulties: The Example of the Cirque Du Monde Program]. PhD thesis, Montreal, Université de Montréal.

Rivard, Jacinthe, Guy Bourgeault, and Céline Mercier. 2010. "Cirque Du Monde in Mexico City: Breathing New Life into Action for Young People in Difficult Situations." *International Social Science Journal* 61 (199): 181–94.

Robinson, William I. 2008. *Latin America and Global Capitalism: A Critical Globalization Perspective*. Baltimore: John's Hopkins University Press.

Robitschek, Christine. 1998. "Personal Growth Initiative: The Construct and Its Measure." *Measurement and Evaluation in Counseling and Development* 30 (4): 183–98.

Rockwell, S. Kay, and Harriet Kohn. 1989. "Post-Then-Pre Evaluation: Measuring Behavior Change More Accurately." *Journal of Extension* 27 (2).

Rodríguez, José I., Marc D. Rich, Rachel Hastings, and Jennifer L. Page. 2006. "Assessing the Impact of Augusto Boal's 'Proactive Performance': An Embodied Approach for Cultivating Prosocial Responses to Sexual Assault." *Text and Performance Quarterly* 26 (3): 229–52.

Rose, Nikolas. 1999. *Powers of Freedom: Reframing Political Thought*. Cambridge: Cambridge University Press.

Routledge, Paul. 2012. "Sensuous Solidarities: Emotion, Politics and Performance in the Clandestine Insurgent Rebel Clown Army." *Antipode* 44 (2): 428–52.

Ryan, Richard, and Edward L. Deci. 2000. "Self-Determination Theory and the Facilitation of Intrinsic Motivation, Social Development, and Well-Being." *American Psychologist* 55 (1): 68–78.

Sacco, Leonardo. 2017. "Cultural Identity, Religion, and Globalization in Latin America: Our Lady of Guadalupe and Saint Martín De Porres as Clear Examples of Interculturalism and Instruments of Mediation among Different Weltanschauungen." *International Journal of Latin American Religions* 1 (1): 1–22.

Sader, Emir. 2008. "The Weakest Link? Neoliberalism in Latin America." *New Left Review* 52: 5–31.

Salverson, Julie. 2011. *Community Engaged Theatre and Performance*. Toronto: Playwrights Canada.

Sankey, Kyla. 2016. "What Happened to the Pink Tide?" *Jacobin*, July 27. https://www.jacobinmag.com/2016/07/pink-tide-latin-america-chavez-morales-capitalism-socialism/.

Santos, Boaventura Sousa. 2014. *Epistemologies of the South: Justice against Epistemicide*. New York: Routledge.

Savolainen, Aleksei, and Sara Suoniemi. 2015. "Empowering and Grouping Effects of Social Circus among Namibian Kids." Bachelor of health care thesis. Kymenlaakso University of Applied Sciences, Finland.

Schechner, Richard. 1993. *Performance Theory*. London: Routledge.

Schutte, Ofelia. 2011. "Engaging Latin American Feminisms Today: Methods, Theory, Practice." *Hypatia* 26 (4): 783–803.

Schwan, Kaitlin Jessica, and Ernie Lightman. 2013. "Fostering Resistance, Cultivating Decolonization: The Intersection of Canadian Colonial History and Contemporary Arts Programming with Inuit Youth." *Cultural Studies Critical Methodologies* 15 (1): 15–29.

Secretaria Nacional de Planificación y Desarrollo. 2009. "Plan nacional para el Buen Vivir 2009–2013: Construyendo un estado plurinacional e intercultural." Quito: SENPLADES.

– 2013. "Plan nacional para el Buen Vivir 2013–2017." Quito: SENPLADES.

Sermijn, Jasmina, Patrick Devlieger, and Gerrit Loots. 2008. "The Narrative Construction of the Self: Selfhood as a Rhizomatic Story." *Qualitative Inquiry* 14 (4): 632–50.

Seymour, Kirsty. 2012. "How Circus Training Can Enhance the Well-Being of Autistic Children and Their Families." BA Creative Arts, Griffith University.

Shediac-Rizkallah, Mona C., and Lee R. Bone. 1998. "Planning for the Sustainability of Community-Based Health Programs: Conceptual Frameworks and Future Directions for Research, Practice and Policy." *Health Education Research: Theory and Practice* 13 (1): 87–108.

SIISE. 2000. "Sistema integrado de indicadores sociales (Integrated System of Social Indicators." Versión 2.0.

Simpson, Audra. 2014. *Mohawk Interruptus: Political Life across the Borders of Settler States*. Durham, NC: Duke University Press.

Simpson, Leanne Betasamosake. 2011. *Dancing on Our Turtle's Back: Stories of Nishnaabeg Re-Creation, Resurgence, and a New Emergence*. Winnipeg: Arbeiter Ring Publishers.

Slutzky, Carly B., and Sandra D. Simpkins. 2009. "The Link between Children's Sport Participation and Self-Esteem: Exploring the Mediating Role of Sport Self-Concept." *Psychology of Sport and Exercise* 10 (3): 381–9.

Smith, Linda J. 2008. "How Ethical Is Ethical Research? Recruiting Marginalized, Vulnerable Groups into Health Services Research." *Journal of Advanced Nursing* 62 (2): 248–57.

Snowber, Celeste. 2012. "Dancing a Curriculum of Hope." *JCT: Journal of Curriculum Theorizing* 28 (2): 118–25.

– 2016. *Embodied Inquiry: Writing, Living, and Being through the Body*. Rotterdam, The Netherlands: Sense.

Snyder-Young, Dani. 2013. *Theatre of Good Intentions – Challenges and Hopes for Theatre and Social Change*. London: Palgrave Macmillan UK.

Spiegel, Jennifer Beth. 2014a. "Critique from the Margins: Cirque Hors Piste and the Dialectics of Inclusion." Paper presented at the International Conference of Social Theory, Politics and the Arts (STPandA), Ottawa, ON.

– 2014b. "Social Circus as an Art for Social Change: Promoting Social Inclusion, Social Engagement and Cultural Democracy." In *Studying Social Circus: Openings and Perspectives*, edited by Katri Kekäläinen, 70–5. Tampere: University of Tampere.

– 2015a. "Masked Protest in the Age of Austerity: State Violence, Anonymous Bodies, and Resistance 'In the Red.'" *Critical Inquiry* 41 (4): 786–810.

– 2015b. "*Rêve Général Illimité?* The Role of Creative Protest in Transforming the Dynamics of Space and Time during the 2012 Quebec Student Strike." *Antipode* 47 (3): 770–91.

– 2015c. "The Value of Social Circus: Creative Process, Embodied Critique, and the Limits of 'Capital.'" Paper presented at the Canadian Association for Theatre Research, Montreal.

– 2016a. "Performing 'in the Red': Transformations and Tensions in Repertoires of Contention during the 2012 Quebec Student Strike." *Social Movement Studies* 15 (5): 531–8.

– 2016b. "Singular Bodies, Collective Dreams: Socially Engaged Circus Arts and the 'Quebec Spring.'" In *Cirque Global – Quebec's Expanding Circus Boundaries*, edited by Louis Patrick Leroux and Charles R. Batson, 266–83. Montreal: McGill-Queen's University Press.

– 2016c. "Social Circus: The Cultural Politics of Embodying 'Social Transformation.'" *TDR: The Drama Review* 60 (4): 50–67.

Spiegel, Jennifer Beth, Maria-Christina Breilh, Arturo Campana, Judith Marcuse, and Annalee Yassi. 2015. "Social Circus and Health Equity: Results of a Feasibility Study to Explore the National Social Circus Program in Ecuador." *Arts and Health: An International Journal for Research, Policy and Practice* 7 (1): 65–74.

Spiegel, Jennifer Beth, Benjamin Ortiz Choukroun, Arturo Campana, Jaime Breilh, and Annalee Yassi. 2018. "Social Transformation, Collective Health and Community-Based Arts: 'Buen Vivir' and Ecuador's Social Circus Program." *Global Public Health*. https://doi.org/10.1080/17441692.2018.1504102.

Spiegel, Jennifer Beth, Benjamin Ortiz Choukroun, Arturo Campaña, Lynn Fels and Annalee Yassi. (Forthcoming). *Circo Social y Salud Colectiva: Un estudio inter-*

nacional interdisciplinario de Circo Social Ecuador [*Social Circus and Collective Well-Being: An international interdisciplinary study of Circo Social Ecuador*]. Quito, Ecuador.

Spiegel, Jennifer Beth, and Stéphanie N. Parent. 2016. "Rapport des résultats de L'étude de recherche sur le cirque social au Québec." Vancouver. http://med-fom-ghrp-spph.sites.olt.ubc.ca/files/2017/02/rapport.pdf.

– 2017. "Re-Approaching Community Development through the Arts: A 'Critical Mixed Methods' Study of Social Circus in Quebec." *Community Development Journal.* https://doi.org/10.1093/cdj/bsx015.

Spiegel, Jennifer Beth, Stephanie N. Parent, Shira Taylor, and Annalee Yassi. 2014. "Report on the Questionnaire Survey Conducted among Social Circus Participants at the 'Rassemblement' Event, Quebec, May, 2014: An Art for Social Change Project." Vancouver: University of British Columbia. http://med-fom-ghrp-spph.sites.olt.ubc.ca/files/2015/01/Rassemblement-report_FINAL.pdf.

Spiegel, Jennifer Beth, and Annalee Yassi. 2007. "Theatre of Alliances? Role-Play, Representation and Ecohealth in Ecuador." *Theatre Topics* 17 (2): 129–40.

Spiegel, Jerry M., Jaime Breilh, and Annalee Yassi. 2015. "Why Language Matters: Insights on the Social Determination of Health through North-South Collaborative Research." *Globalization and Health* 11: 9–26.

Springgay, Stephanie, Rita L. Irwin, and Sylvia Wilson Kind. 2005. "A/R/Tography as Living Inquiry through Art and Text." *Qualitative Inquiry* 11 (6): 897–912.

Stathopoulou, Georgia, Mark B. Powers, Angela C. Berry, Jasper A.J. Smits, and Michael W. Otto. 2006. "Exercise Interventions for Mental Health: A Quantitative and Qualitative Review." *Clinical Psychology: Science and Practice* 13 (2): 179–93.

Stein, Catherine H., and David A. Faigin. 2015. "Community-Based Arts Initiatives: Exploring the Science of the Arts." *American Journal of Community Psychology* 55 (1–2): 70–3.

Stephens, Lindsay Katyana. 2015. "The Economic Lives of Circus 'Artists': Canadian Circus Performers and the New Economy." *Canadian Journal of Communication* 40 (2): 243.

Stoddart, Helen. 2000. *Rings of Desire: Circus History and Representation.* Manchester: Manchester University Press.

Stuckey, Heather L., and Jeremy Nobel. 2010. "The Connection between Art, Healing, and Public Health: A Review of Current Literature." *American Journal of Public Health* 100 (2): 254–63.

Sugarman, Robert. 2001. *Circus for Everyone: Circus Learning around the World.* Shaftsbury, Vermont: Mountainside Press.

Sullivan, Gail M., and Anthony R. Artino Jr. 2013. "Analyzing and Interpreting Data from Likert-Type Scales." *J Grad Med Educ* 5 (4): 541–2.

Sumara, Dennis J., and Brent Davis. 1997. "Enlarging the Space of the Possible: Complexity, Complicity, and Action Research Practices." *Action Research as a Living Practice* 67: 299–312.

Sussman, Mark. 2013. "A Queer Circus: Amok in New York." In *Radical Street Performance: An International Anthology*, edited by Jan Cohen-Cruz, 262–70. Abingdon, Oxon: Routledge.

Tait, Peta. 2005. *Circus Bodies: Cultural Identity in Aerial Performance*. Abingdon, Oxon: Routledge.

Taussig, Michael T. 1993. *Mimesis and Alterity: A Particular History of the Senses*. New York: Routledge.

Taylor, Diana. 2003. *The Archive and the Repertoire: Performing Cultural Memory in the Americas*. Durham, London: Duke University Press.

Thomson, Rosemarie Garland. 1996. *Freakery: Cultural Spectacles of the Extraordinary Body*. New York: NYU Press.

Tilleczek, Kate, and Janet Loebach. 2015. "Research Goes to the Cinema: The Veracity of Videography with, for and by Youth." *Journal of Research in Comparative and International Education* 10 (3): 354–66.

Tillmanns, Tanja, Charlotte Holland, Francesca Lorenzi, and Pierre McDonagh. 2014. "Interplay of Rhizome and Education for Sustainable Development." *Journal of Teacher Education for Sustainability* 16 (2): 5–17.

Trotman, Rachael. 2012. "Building Character and Community – Community Circus: A Literature Review." http://www.simplycircus.com/node/631.

Twenge, Jean M., and W. Keith Campbell. 2002. "Self-Esteem and Socioeconomic Status: A Meta-Analytic Review." *Personality and Social Psychology Review* 6 (1): 59–71.

Unger, Jennifer B., Michele D. Kipke, Thomas R. Simon, Susan B. Montgomery, and Christine J. Johnson. 1997. "Homeless Youths and Young Adults in Los Angeles: Prevalence of Mental Health Problems and the Relationship between Mental Health and Substance Abuse Disorders." *American Journal of Community Psychology* 25 (3),: 371–94.

United Nations Population Fund. 2008. "Ecuador: La migración internacional en cifras." Quito: UNFPA/FLACSO.

Varela, Francisco. 1987. "Laying Down a Path in Walking." In *Gaia, A Way of Knowing*, edited by William Irwin Thompson, 48–64. Hudson, NY: Lindisfarne.

Velasco, Fernando. 1981. *Ecuador: Subdesarrollo y dependencia*. Quito: Foro de Emancipación e Identidad de América Latina.

Velásquez, Teresa A. 2011. "The Science of Corporate Social Responsibility (CSR): Contamination and Conflict in a Mining Project in the Southern Ecuadorian Andes." *Resources Policy* 37 (2): 233–40.

Vice-President, Ecuador. 2011. "Vicepresente con creatividad, Circos Sociales, rescartaran a mies de jovenes en riesgo." Report to the Nation, National Assembly, August 10.

Vigh, Henrik. 2009. "Motion Squared: A Second Look on the Concept of Social Navigation." *Anthropological Theory* 9 (4): 419–38.

Virno, Paolo. 2004. *A Grammar of the Multitude: For an Analysis of Contemporary Forms of Life*. Cambridge, MA: MIT Press.

Vision 360. 2016. "Luces, Cámaras, Derroche? Parte 2 | Programa 16 – Bloque 2 | Visión 360 Iii Temporada." https://www.youtube.com/watch?v=CvMsaEk-cqk.

Walsh, Catherine. 2009. *Interculturalidad, Estado, Sociedad: Luchas (de) coloniales de nuestra época*. Quito: Universidad Andina Simón Bolívar.

– 2010. "Development as *Buen Vivir*: Institutional Arrangements and (De)Colonial Entanglement." *Development* 53 (1): 15–21.

Wang, Caroline C., Jennifer L. Cash, and Lisa S. Powers. 2000. "Who Knows the Streets as Well as the Homeless? Promoting Personal and Community Action through Photovoice." *Health Promotion Practice* 1 (1): 81–9.

Weisbrot, Mark, Jake Johnston, and Lara Merling. 2017. "Decade of Reform: Ecuador's Macroeconomic Policies, Institutional Changes, and Results." Washington: Centre for Economic and Policy Research. http://cepr.net/publications/reports/decade-of-reform-ecuador-s-macroeconomic-policies-institutional-changes-and-results.

Wesolowski, Katya. 2012. "Professionalizing Capoeira: The Politics of Play in Twenty-First-Century Brazil." *Latin American Perspectives* 39 (2): 82–92.

Wheaton, Belinda. 2007. "After Sport Culture: Rethinking Sport and Post-Subcultural Theory." *Journal of Sport and Social Issues* 31 (3): 283–307.

Whitehead, Margaret. 2010. *Physical Literacy: Throughout the Lifecourse*. Abingdon, Oxon: Routledge.

Whyte, William Foote. 1991. *Participatory Action Research*. Thousand Oaks, CA: Sage Publications.

Wilson, Japhy, and Manuel Bayón. 2017. "The Nature of Post-Neoliberalism: Building Bio-Socialism in the Ecuadorian Amazon." *Geoforum* 81: 55–65.

Wilson, Nance, Meredith Minkler, Stefan Dasho, Nina Wallerstein, and Anna C. Martin. 2008. "Getting to Social Action: The Youth Empowerment Strategies (Yes!) Project." *Health Promotion Practice* 9 (4): 395–403.

Women's Circus. 2016. "More Information about Women's Circus." http://womenscircus.org.au/.

World Health Organization. 2008. "Closing the Gap in a Generation: Health Equity through Action on the Social Determinants of Health." Geneva: WHO.

Yarber, Laura, Carol A. Brownson, Rebekah R. Jacob, Elizabeth A. Baker, Ellen Jones, Carsten Baumann, Anjali D. Deshpande, et al. 2015. "Evaluating a Train-the-Trainer Approach for Improving Capacity for Evidence-Based Decision Making in Public Health." *BMC Health Services Research* 15: 547.

Yassi, Annalee, Jaime Breilh, Shafik Dharamsi, Karen Lockhart, and Jerry M. Spiegel. 2013. "The Ethics of Ethics Reviews in Global Health Research: Case Studies Applying a New Paradigm." *Journal of Academic Ethics* 11 (2): 83–101.

Yassi, Annalee, Karen Lockhart, Pat Gray, and Trevor Hancock. 2017. "Is Public Health Training in Canada Meeting Current Needs? Defrosting the Paradigm Freeze to Respond to the Post-Truth Era." *Critical Public Health*. https://doi.org/10.1080/09581596.2017.1384796.

Yassi, Annalee, Jennifer Beth Spiegel, Karen Lockhart, Lynn Fels, Katherine Boy-dell, and Judith Marcuse. 2016. "Ethics in Community-University-Artist Part-nered Research: Tensions, Contradictions and Gaps Identified in an 'Arts for Social Change' Project." *Journal of Academic Ethics* 14: 199–220.

Yassi, Annalee, Muzimkhulu Zungu, Jerry M. Spiegel, Barry Kistnasamy, Karen Lockhart, David Jones, Lyndsay M. O'Hara, et al. 2016. "Protecting Health Work-ers from Infectious Disease Transmission: An Exploration of a Canadian-South African Partnership of Partnerships." *Globalization and Health* 12: 10.

Yates, Julian S., and Karen Bakker. 2013. "Debating the 'Post-Neoliberal Turn' in Latin America." *Progress in Human Geography* 38 (1): 62–90.

Yudice, George. 2003. *The Expediency of Culture.* Durham: Duke University Press.

Zhang, Tracy Y. 2016. "The Chinese Connection: The Transnational Origins of Québécois Circus Arts." In *Cirque Global – Quebec's Expanding Circus Bound-aries*, edited by Louis Patrick Leroux and Charles R. Batson, 202–22. Montreal: McGill-Queen's University Press.

– 2016. "From China to the Big Top: Chinese Acrobats and the Politics of Aesthetic Labor, 1950–2010." *International Labor and Working Class History* 89: 40–63.

ZipZap Circus School. 2016. "More Information about Zipzap Circus School." http://www.zip-zap.co.za/.

Zorba, Myrsini. 2009. "Conceptualizing Greek Cultural Policy: The Non-Democratization of Public Culture." *International Journal of Cultural Policy* 15 (3): 245–59.

CONTRIBUTORS

KATHERINE BOYDELL is a professor of mental health, Black Dog Institute, University of New South Wales, Australia, having recently re-located from University of Toronto, Canada. Dr Boydell's research is both methodological and substantive; substantively, it focuses on understanding the complex pathways to care for young people experiencing a first episode of psychosis, the use of new technologies in child and youth mental health, and the science of knowledge translation. Methodologically, it focuses on advancing qualitative inquiry in arts-based health research.

ARTURO CAMPAÑA hold an MD and PhD from the Central University of Ecuador and obtained his specialist training in psychiatry and mental health from the B.M. Bekhterev Institute in Leningrad. He was a professor of medical psychology and postgraduate research and administration in Health of the Faculty of Medical Sciences before becoming a co-founder and former director of the Center for Studies and Social Assistance in Quito. He is also a co-founder and former director of the National Directorate of Mental Health of the Ministry of Public Health in Ecuador. He is the author of the book *Mental Health: Consciousness vs. Seduction by Madness* and is co-author of several books and essays in the field of collective health.

LYNN FELS is an associate professor in the Faculty of Education, Simon Fraser University. Her research interests and field of expertise are in theatre/drama education, performative inquiry, performative writing, pedagogy, curriculum, instruction, and evaluation. Dr Fels's current research focuses on exploring leadership through the arts, arts and technology, arts for social change, and participatory action research.

JUDITH MARCUSE, adjunct professor, Faculty of Education, Simon Fraser University; founder and co-director, International Centre of Art for Social Change, is an artist (dancer, choreographer, director, producer) whose creative projects drew her to the field of art for social change. Early choreographic work often explored social issues (e.g., women and feminism, social roles, consumerism). Later projects more explicitly explored similar issues: teen suicide; and environmental issues. Dr Marcuse is the principal investigator of a five-year (2013–18), Social Sciences and Humanities Research Council-funded national research partnership on Arts for Social Change, involving twenty-five researchers, six universities, and fifteen community partners.

BENJAMIN ORTIZ CHOUKROUN served as the Ecuadorean coordinator for the interdisciplinary study on which this book is largely based. He is is a director, playwright, and artist specializing in circus arts (particularly clowning) as well as theatre and street art. As an expert in the pedagogy of social circus, he trained instructors in *Circo Social Tena* (one of the municipal programs of *Circo Social Ecuador* [CSE]) in 2012, was the pedagogical director of CSE for five months in 2013, and later became the national circus specialist in Ecuador's Ministry of Culture and Heritage. He works as a trainer for *Cirque du Monde* and is currently director of the *Tejido,* a national network of social circus practitioners in Ecuador.

JENNIFER BETH SPIEGEL holds a PhD in cultural studies from Goldsmiths (University of London) in the United Kingdom and is a research fellow in the Faculty of Education at Simon Fraser University, British Columbia. As a Montreal-based artist, scholar, activist, and community worker, she teaches performance studies, critical theory, and communications at Concordia University and McGill. Since 2013, Dr Spiegel has been researching creativity in social movements and critical theories of art for social change, as well as the impacts of and tensions in social circus. Her work has been published in *Theatre and Drama Review (TDR), Community Development Journal, Antipode, Critical Inquiry, Social Movement Studies, Theatre Topics,* and the *International Journal of Art and Health,* among others.

ANNALEE YASSI, professor, Tier 1 Canada Research Chair in Global Health and Capacity Building, is a specialist in public health and preventive medicine. Her research focuses on issues and methods in community-based health research, transdisciplinarity, and North-South partnerships. Dr Yassi is interested in ethics in global health research, the link between clinical care and the social and environmental determinants of health, an ecosystem approach to health, and the use of arts-based methods in health intervention research.

INDEX

Abya Yala, 57, 61, 88

addiction, 106, 177, 197

aesthetics: in circus, 238–9; in arts-based inquiry, 127; ethico-aesthetic paradigm, 33–4; global, 71–2; social, 235; street, 79; in the traditions of social circus, 233, 240–4, 248

age group: and alcohol, 63, 89, 176–7, 195, 197, 219, 228; analysis of, 177, 180–1, 183, 187, 190; and depression, 63; gender comparability, 183; personal growth, 200; and *replicas*, 75; and social circus participation, 75, 200; and social class/income, 184; and social support, 209

Alianza Pais, 57, 77, 82–3, 85, 88

American Youth Circus Organization, 257, 265

Arendt, Hannah, 34, 70, 98, 109, 123–4

arts facilitation, 31, 265. *See also* facilitation

arts-based inquiry, 35, 43, 123, 127–48

austerity, 3, 7, 9, 253, 255

Barndt, Deborah, viii, 24–6

Becker, Mark, 5, 58, 60–1

Belmar, Matias, 68, 75, 89, 109, 267

Bhabha, Homi, 8, 234

binaries/binary, 35, 44, 241

Boal, Augusto, 22–3, 41, 70–1, 98, 103, 127, 131, 235

Bochud, Emmanuel, viii, 17, 94, 96, 98–100, 102, 104, 106, 109, 122, 281

body: disciplining of the, 234; language of, 116, 232

Bolton, Reginald, 11, 94–5

Brazil: early social circus in, 11–12; and Mexico, 70, 103, 235–6; participation with other circus performers, 16, 92. *See also* Boal, Augusto; capoeira; Freire, Paolo

Breilh, Jaime, 41, 49, 175–6, 235

Buen Vivir: and collectivity, 5–9, 26, 226–7, 252–3, 257–8; ethical focus of, 57; and income, 28, 62; lifestyle in Ecuador, 63–4, 173; post-neoliberal vision of, 4–5, 7, 27–8; partnerships in, 69, 79; pedagogy of, 126; and pink tide, 9; and social circus, 17; wellbeing, 5, 28–30, 45, 62, 67, 86, 95, 173, 247

Bueno, Julio, 73–4